BOTTOMS UP

A HISTORY
OF
ALCOHOL

IN NEWFOUNDLAND AND LABRADOR

SHEILAH ROBERTS LUKINS

Breakwater Books
P.O. Box 2188, St. John's, NL, Canada, A1C 6E6
www.breakwaterbooks.com

A CIP catalogue record for this book is available from Library and Archives Canada.
ISBN 978-1-55081-801-7 (softcover)

We acknowledge the support of the Canada Council for the Arts. *Nous remercions le Conseil des arts du Canada de son soutien.* We acknowledge the financial support of the Government of Canada and the Government of Newfoundland and Labrador through the Department of Tourism, Culture, Industry and Innovation for our publishing activities.

Printed and bound in Canada.

Breakwater Books is committed to choosing papers and materials for our books that help to protect our environment. To this end, this book is printed on a recycled paper and other sources that are certified by the Forest Stewardship Council®.

Canada Council   Conseil des Arts
for the Arts   du Canada

Canada

Newfoundland Labrador

Cheers!
Best Regards,
Sheilah Roberts Lukins

CONTENTS

ACKNOWLEDGEMENTS

I would like to thank Michael Power, who provided invaluable research assistance and information on his family's involvement in the tavern industry. Also, many thanks to Jean Pierre Andrieux, James Casey, John Bull Cook, Thomas J. Dunne, Ed Fitzgerald, Justin Fong, Barbara Harris, Frank Kelly, Janet Kelly, Don Maher, H. H. Mason, Liam McKenna, Janet Michael, Steve Mills, Ana Morida, Larry O'Keefe, Katie Parnham, Helen Porter, Ron Pumphrey, Trapper John, Wm. Clarence Tucker, Raymond Walsh, and Jim Weist. Thanks to Dr. Maudie Whalen and Azzo Rezori for help and advice. Many thanks to the staff of the A.C. Hunter Library, Memorial University's Centre for Newfoundland Studies, Queen Elizabeth II Library, and the Memorial University of Newfoundland Folklore and Language Archive. I would also like to thank the staff at the Provincial Archives of Newfoundland and Labrador, the City of St. John's Archives, my publisher, Rebecca Rose, publicist Samantha Fitzpatrick, designers Rhonda Molloy and John van der Woude, and my editors James Langer and Jocelyne Thomas, along with all the rest of the staff at Breakwater Books. I would like to gratefully acknowledge support in the form of a grant from the City of St. John's.

PREFACE

When I was growing up on the west coast, my father drank and would sometimes playfully offer me a sip of his beer or a taste of his scotch as my mother looked on disapprovingly. When I got older, most of my social life revolved around alcohol, from my first beer at Al Kawaja's bar in Corner Brook at the age of fifteen to university beer bashes and bar-hopping in my twenties. My extended family was riddled with staunch teetotallers on one end of the spectrum and heavy drinkers on the other. So why is alcohol such a strong part of our culture? How did it become entrenched in our daily lives? And why do some people enjoy it with abandon while others abstain as if avoiding a plague? These were the questions that inspired my research into the subject, and what follows is a record of my curiosity.

From the seventeenth to the twenty-first century, Newfoundlanders and Labradorians have guzzled beer, rum, wine, brandy, and more. *Bottoms Up* is the story of alcohol in Newfoundland and Labrador: what people drank, why they drank, where they drank, and especially of the cultural evolution of drinking.

The book itself is laid out somewhat chronologically, but there is overlap as I've divided my study of the history of alcohol into seven *ages*. First, there is the age of necessity, then trade, excess, and control. Then the age of the teetotaller and the temperance movement in Newfoundland. Lastly, we move through the prohibition period and into our current age.

The book then takes a tour through our historically well-known taverns and bars, and local breweries. The appendices give a glimpse into local news and historical data. To be sure, the book is heavily weighted towards St. John's, where most of the activity was recorded, but the province's watering holes outside the capital are also well represented. It was interesting to note how many women ran taverns years ago. In many cases, they simply assumed control after their husbands passed on. This acted as a form of social security for the women, who perhaps would have been destitute without it.

The primary and secondary sources used include academic papers, books, newspapers, archival records, and personal interviews. As with anything, no source is infallible and may contain errors; newspapers often make mistakes, people's memories fade and become confused. Any other errors are solely my own. In the shifting sands of history, certain terms changed throughout the years. Beer and ale, for example, up until the 1500s, were different drinks, but they eventually became lumped under the term *beer*, and early texts often used them interchangeably.

One very important aspect of the book involves the amounts of alcohol imported and consumed by Newfoundlanders and Labradorians. Unfortunately, old measurements were not standardized, and there may be variations in the conversion amounts. As a result, these should be taken as approximates. In addition, old spellings have been retained in the quotations found throughout the book, in most cases without the use of the term *sic*.

With regard to the tavern and pub locations provided, addresses that are close together may be one and the same building. Sometimes it was obvious, especially when two individuals were part of the same family. In other cases, if there was doubt, separate entries were used to record the taverns and owners. Alternative name spellings appeared everywhere, but most have been included in brackets beside the original spellings. Whenever possible, home addresses are also given and, in some cases, former occupations.

I would like to especially thank several people for their invaluable help and encouragement in the writing of this book. First and foremost, my (ever-patient, long-suffering) editor James Langer. I would also like to thank Michael Power for sharing his family history and for his invaluable research help. Stephen Mills gave me permission to use his research into alcohol and generally fed me all sorts of wonderful historical tidbits. Retired CBC journalist Azzo Rezori helped by putting me on the right organizational path, and of course, I have to thank my wonderfully patient husband, who has watched, waited, read, commented, and encouraged my writing for the past seventeen years.

Hopefully this book will serve as a cultural mirror into which we can glance and perhaps shed some light on our own family histories and ancestral behaviours.

CHAPTER ONE

NECESSITY
Benevolent Booze

"Ye mariners all, as ye pass by,
Come in and drink when you are dry.
Come spend, my lads, your money brisk,
And pop your nose in a jug of this

Oh when I'm in my grave and dead,
And all my sorrows are past and fled,
Transform me then into a fish,
And let me swim in a jug of this
—Excerpt from the Dorset sea shanty "Ye Mariners All"[1]

WHETHER DESCRIBED AS "CORK HIGH AND BOTTLE DEEP," "incandescent," or "three sheets to the wind," we often associate alcohol consumption and its desired effects with leisure, pleasure, and the relief of stress. And it seems to have always been this way. During the early-modern period—roughly from the Elizabethan age until the end of the French Revolution—the paintings and etchings of the time depict rosy-cheeked, jovial drinkers sitting or standing with pewter mugs held high in a toast. They slap their companions on the backs and seem to bellow with laughter while others around them smoke thin clay pipes and play cards. Drinking has always been associated with a good time. But the early moderns had other reasons to drink besides pleasure.

It all started innocently enough. When people gathered in crowded, dirty, urban centres with no sanitation facilities, many of the waterways inevitably ran foul, polluted with human waste, and not fit to drink. When people drank tainted water, they often fell ill with diseases like dysentery, typhoid, and cholera. If they drank fermented or distilled liquids, purified in the brewing/distilling process, they felt fine—often a bit better than fine. As a result, alcohol replaced water as the preferred thirst quencher. Seventeenth-century ladies and gents knew nothing of bacteria and viruses or of alcohol's ability to neutralize these organisms; they just knew by experience that alcohol seemed a safer choice in the way of a beverage. With the price of ale in the Tudor era at just one penny or less per gallon, it couldn't have been too difficult to substitute alcohol for water. Easy enough to do if you were on land, just run out to the local merchant and grab a cask, but if you were on the high seas, you'd better have lots of supplies laid in. The dawn of the great sea voyages brought with it the discovery of a wealth of fish off the coasts of Newfoundland,

A necessity but also a recreational pastime, alcohol filled up the long winter evenings as the new settlers ate, drank, and smoked pipes of tobacco. *Image in public domain.* CC-BY-SA-3.0.

and visiting ships from many nations crossed the Atlantic to harvest this plentiful resource. The long journey over from Europe to the New World required enough supplies to last not only for the voyage, but also for the many months the crews would be away from home engaged in the fishery. Easy enough to pack the food supplies, but what to drink?

Any water taken on board these long journeys, if they did manage to find a pure source, spoiled very quickly, and not enough rainwater could be captured to service the needs of a thirsty crew. Even several centuries later, on a voyage to Greece, one unhappy traveller described the drinking water on board his ship as "putrid thick and stinking that often I have held my nose with my hand while I drank it strained through my pocket handkerchief."[2] And such was the case for water during the long sea voyages to Newfoundland. Beer, on the other hand, did not spoil as quickly, worked just as well as a thirst quencher, and had the added advantage of keeping the men happy and hard-working. Therefore, English fishermen who came to Newfoundland considered beer and ale staples along with their bread, cheese, biscuit, and butter. Large quantities of beer washed down their daily meals and satisfied their thirst.

An early reference for a Newfoundland voyage in 1613, entitled "A noate for the provision of 20 men," suggested they needed fifty hogsheads of beer for the journey.[3] Although measurements were not standard, one hogshead was equal to about 52.5 ale gallons,[4] so fifty hogsheads would translate to approximately 2,625 gallons or 9,937 litres. That's a lot of beer for a voyage to Newfoundland! But one has to remember that these were very hard-working men, and their supplies had to last for the entire voyage and possibly well into the fishing season before more supplies arrived. By 1702, your average mariner guzzled about seven gallons of beer a week,[5] the equivalent of eight pints a day.

And so, the great fishery continued with many nations mooring their boats in the harbours of Newfoundland. They all brought alcohol of differing sorts to sustain them until they arrived back in their home ports. Up until the seventeenth century, there had been no interest in encouraging people to stay year-round on the island of Newfoundland. Eventually, with so many nationalities fishing off the coast, certain merchant adventurers in England believed that sponsored colonization might be the best way to monopolize the island's rich sea resources, so settlers came and put down roots in small colonies. Two such colonies were established at Cuper's Cove (now Cupids), in 1610, and at the Colony of Avalon (now Ferryland), in 1621.

The settlers who migrated to this new land still had little faith in the purity of the water, as shown by a note from February 1613, which stated that apprentice Edward Garton of Cupids died from "much drinking of water in the winter." There was evidence to the contrary, however. Captain Edward Wynne, in a letter from Ferryland on August 17, 1622, wrote, "The water [here] is both clear and wholesome."[6] And Nicholas Hoskins reported that he went on a trip with a companion deep into the woods where they came upon a "sweet brook of running water," which quenched their thirst "as well as any Beere, and much refresh us both, and never offended our stomackes at all."[7] These testimonies did little to change the settlers' drinking habits though, and beer remained the 'safer' beverage. These were people of faith, not rationalism, and they did not yet question what they believed about the world around them. They had little concept of health care beyond what tradition and anecdotal evidence dictated, and so alcohol, considered a health necessity, was a common entry on the supply lists for the colonies.

In August 1611, fourteen pipes of beer were included in the inventory of provisions left at Cupids. Because of beer's tendency to turn a bit sour on the long Atlantic crossings, the colonists ordered that malt be sent over so they could make their own beer and ale locally. The colonies wasted no time in establishing their brewhouses. In Cupids, the brewhouse was one of the first buildings erected in 1613. The settlers at Ferryland didn't drag their heels either. After arriving in 1621, a report from 1622 stated they had "broken much ground for a brewhouse room and other tenements." With everyone nicely established, it was down to the business of fishing: a full-time job and then some. Finding the time to bake and brew became a problem, so they soon wrote home requesting "strong maids that (besides other work) can both brew and bake."[8] With the men out fishing, someone had to brew the beer. The 'maids' soon came, and the beer poured freely.

With shipments of brewing supplies few and far between, the brewers would probably have 'stretched' the malt and used it to brew the weaker 'small ale.' With their distrust of the local fresh water, and coffee and tea not in common use yet, almost everyone drank small ale or beer with their meals, even the children. Regular ale had more alcohol and was aged, but housewives brewed the weaker small ale, weekly or biweekly, for everyday use. Small ale came from the second fermentation of the wort that had already produced the stronger brew.[9]

By the 1700s, alcohol and beer brewing supplies occupied top spots in the supply lists. For example, on March 26, 1710, Benjamin Marston, a merchant in Salem, Massachusetts, brought supplies to Ferryland, which included purchases by a Dr. Amass [Amiss] of Ferryland: a cider pale, a large runlet (a cask of varying capacity for liquor), a small cask, two barrels of malt, and kegs of hops.[10] When it came to sending alcohol to Newfoundland from England to slake the thirsts of the early colonists, in addition to malt, they continued to send beer and cider, but they also imported other forms of alcohol such as aqua vitae and wine. Aqua vitae was an early form of distilled alcohol, much like brandy or whisky. It gained more popularity as time went on and settlers increased their demand for it.

OUT ON THE HIGH SEAS, FROM 1588 TO 1650, DAILY RATIONS IN the British navy included eight pints of beer per seaman per day,[11] but by the mid-1600s, one-half a pint of brandy (aqua vitae) often replaced the beer ration. Serving up spirits such as brandy became more practical due to the economics of both money and space. Distilled spirits also had the advantage of lasting much longer than any wine or beer.

As distilled alcohol usage increased, changes in world politics, major conflicts, and expanding trade among the colonies allowed a new player to enter the fray and strut its stuff: rum.

The British Navy discovered rum on a voyage to the West Indies in 1655. Vice Admiral William Penn captured Jamaica and took on rum from the islands to refresh his spent supplies of beer and brandy, and thus began the unofficial use of the rum ration. This unofficial use of rum carried on for some time until, in 1687, a Jamaican planter offered to supply the West Indies fleet on a regular basis with local rum. James II, no doubt delighted at the prospect of breaking the English dependency on French brandy, showed interest in the use of rum, but wanted to test it first to see what effects it would have on his sailors health and well-being. Unfortunately, the king's constant conflicts with parliament sparked the English Revolution of 1688, and he lost his throne before the results of his little experiment were known. When war with France erupted in 1688, resulting in the loss of imported French brandy, the matter was clinched. Rum ruled.

Drinking straight alcohol and trying to run a ship, however, brought many problems. One captain reported of his crew that "one third of the ship's company was more or less intoxicated or at least muddified and half stupefied."[12] As you might imagine, it is not easy to work pie-eyed. So on August 4, 1740, Vice Admiral Lord Edward Vernon decided that the straight alcohol "impaired health, ruined morals, and generally led to crime." He then began the practice of watering the rum down, much to the chagrin of his men—one quart of water to a half pint of rum, administered in two daily doses, one at 11 a.m. and another at 5 p.m. At first only adopted on the ships under Admiral Vernon's watch, in 1756 the navy officially began using this version of the daily ration. The unhappy seamen nicknamed the concoction *grog* after the material of Admiral Vernon's cloak, grosgrain, a mixture of silk (or a silk, worsted, and mohair mix)

Sailors belowdecks passing the time drinking, singing, and storytelling. *Image in public domain. CC-BY-SA-3.0.*

often stiffened with gum. It wasn't until 1815 that metal water tanks were introduced on ships for better and safer water storage, so the alcohol in the grog, no doubt, purified the questionable water used to dilute it and masked any unpleasant odours or tastes. The daily grog ration remained at sea for a very long time. Old habits die hard.

Meanwhile, back in Newfoundland, although the pirate Peter Easton may have transported the first barrels of Caribbean rum to his fort in Harbour Grace as early as 1610,[13] rum did not arrive in any great quantity until the latter part of the seventeenth century. This cheap, strong, plentiful beverage became very popular and quickly took over the role of quenching the local thirst. It became so important to the Newfoundland fishermen that by 1812 the "Merchants and House Keepers" of St. John's complained about the duties placed on spirits imported to the island, and requested the exemption from duties for all articles used directly or indirectly in the fishery. This included the kegs of rum the planters ordered with their winter supplies.[14] Some historians believe that the North American colonist's diet of heavy, oily, salty foods increased their desire for highly concentrated distilled spirits.[15]

Not only used as a thirst quencher and drinking-water substitute, alcohol took on an important health role here in Newfoundland. The settler population eventually scattered over a large area of coastline, and with few doctors, if someone got ill, they pretty well had to heal themselves. As we have faith in our antibiotics and vaccines today, our ancestors saw alcohol as a medical panacea. With no miracle drugs to cure them, and being completely ignorant of modern science, drinking alcohol was viewed as a means to prevent disease as well as a cure-all if you did get sick. These beliefs dated back to antiquity.

HEALTH CARE IN THE SEVENTEENTH CENTURY REVOLVED AROUND a system based on the ancient Greek humours. The Greeks believed everyone had a dominant humour, and for good health one's humours had to balance. The humour system, developed by the Greek physician Galen, consisted of blood, phlegm, yellow bile/choler, and black bile/

melancholy. These, in turn, were based on the four natural elements of earth, air, fire, water and the complementary elements of cold, dry, hot, and wet. Different foods contained the elements of these four humours, so you could influence your health by what you ate or drank. Your environment affected you as well. And Newfoundland's sometimes unforgiving

If you did get sick, the treatments could be extreme or you might take a draught of Cock-Ale: "To make Cock-Ale. Take eight gallons of Ale, take a Cock and boil him well; then take four pounds of Raisins of the Sun well stoned, two or three Nutmegs, three or four flakes of Mace, half a pound of Dates; beat these all in a Mortar, and put to them two quarts of the best Sack: and when the Ale hath done working, put these in, and stop it close six or seven days, and then bottle it, and a month after you may drink it." (Kenelme Digbie, the Closet of the Eminently Learned Sir Kenelme Dibgie (London: 1669). I bet patients went back for seconds on this one. *Image in public domain.* CC-BY-SA-3.0.

climate seemed nothing less than a prescription for alcohol. The hot dry properties of alcohol and tobacco were thought to counteract the cold, wet weather typical on the island's coastline. Red wine and distilled spirits were considered warm, while beer, ale, and white wine were considered cold. The health professionals of the day recommended aqua vitae in particular for balancing the humours in cold, damp climates. The new Newfoundland settlers soon discovered the climate to be very cold and damp and even though they were culturally predisposed to beer drinking, in the long tradition of self-medicating, they soon started asking that more aqua vitae be sent over.

The medical uses for alcohol were myriad. Throughout the seventeenth century, the principal forms of alcohol used for medicinal purposes were beer, wine, and aqua vitae. From the eighteenth century onward, rum became the elixir of choice for curing an early Newfoundlander's woes.

Distilled alcohol played an important role as a painkiller and anaesthetic for many centuries. Peter Brennan, the famous bonesetter in nineteenth-century St. John's, used a block and tackle apparatus and strong dark rum.

Sometimes extra ingredients helped the alcohol effect the cure. With no acetaminophen, ibuprofen, or other fever-reducing medicines, if the early settlers and visitors to Newfoundland suffered a fever, they may have drunk alcohol with bread or toast floating in their drink. The liquids replaced fluids lost through fever, and the starch in the bread helped to give the sufferer more energy, replenishing carbohydrates. Any time our ancestors felt a little under the weather, they drank a 'toast.' After a few toasts of hot spiced ale or wine, no doubt they felt quite salubrious. It probably wasn't long before they started throwing the toast to the dog and drinking their beverage straight up, toasting the return of their health and that of their good friends. From this comes our modern term "to drink a toast." In the 1800s, the belief still persisted that alcohol prevented fevers and infectious diseases. Doctors prescribed it as a stimulant, as a cure for pneumonia, for lowering temperatures, and also as a sleep enabler. The patent medicines popular in the nineteenth and early twentieth centuries included alcohol as one of their principal ingredients. Some of these tonics had a higher alcohol content than straight whisky. When prohibition arrived in the twentieth century, people began to self-medicate with a vengeance. Throughout the centuries, alcohol as a medicine took many forms.

Women in Newfoundland often drank what they referred to as punch, a drink made up of hot water, a shot of rum, and a spoonful of sugar stirred together. They used this to relieve the pain of menstrual cramps.[16] Other local cures included rum mixed with molasses, butter, vinegar, or pepper to alleviate anything from sore throats and earaches to bronchitis, constipation, and indigestion. It was used for purifying the blood, or just for cuts. With little access to professional medical assistance, the afflicted sometimes took rum and molasses in an attempt to cure tuberculosis. Newfoundlanders rubbed straight booze onto painful muscles, and used it to ease rheumatism, and 'fibrositis.' Doctors believed alcohol brought down swelling and worked as a rubefacient, reddening and warming the skin around the afflicted area and thereby reducing pain. A cure for the 'throttles' (diphtheria) called for the patient to smoke a clay pipe loaded with oakum, which was first soaked in brimstone, after which the victim then had to swallow a pint of black rum drawn straight from the keg.[17] Was it the oakum or rum that effected the supposed cure?

Alcohol could be used as a resuscitator as well. If you walked up Carter's Hill in the nineteenth century, you may have come across the house of Nancy Coyle, a woman the government employed to see to the needs of the dead. She attended many of the unidentified bodies that showed up in the harbour. Once, she brought a Dutch sailor 'back to life' by administering several doses of strong rum just before he was to be nailed into a coffin. Saved from being buried alive, he was soon back to his old self again.[18]

And then there was that other necessity—work. Although they had to be careful not to indulge in too much alcohol (as that really put the kibosh on things), spirits—along with beer, ale, and wine—served as an important source of nutrients and calories for the settlers. With the fishing work so hard and the diet so poor, alcohol helped 'feed' them. From the time of early settlement and well into the twentieth century, alcohol gave workers stamina for hard labour. A good example of this is the story of porter, the dark rich beer so popular in England and Newfoundland in the eighteenth and nineteenth centuries. Porter came into existence circa 1750. At that time in England, the working class drank three types of malt liquors: ale, beer, and something called twopenny, a Scottish pale ale sold at two pence per pint. Many people drank a mixture of two sorts called half-and-half—half beer and half twopenny—or sometimes a third each of ale, beer, and twopenny. Eventually, a clever brewer made one beer consisting of a mix of these three. This hearty drink nourished people like London porters who, run ragged, had little time to eat or drink. They could grab a quick nourishing, calorie-rich 'porter' and be on their merry way.[19] Newfoundlanders probably used alcohol for much the same purpose.

For those making a living on the ocean, alcohol eased seasickness—very handy if you encountered rough seas in the North Atlantic. William Vaughan, the Welsh poet and adventurer who sent settlers out to his colony in the Renews area of Newfoundland, had a remedy for the nausea and queasiness: "Worme-wood wine or salt of worme-wood in Beere or wine." Later on, rum took over as a preventative measure to ward off the seasickness.

When it came to scurvy, that other dreaded affliction of those living on the briny seas, spruce beer came to the rescue. With no fresh fruit available and scurvy rampant among the seagoing population, spruce beer provided the excellent source of vitamin C needed to combat this disease. This mild beer had a humble start, with the original brew probably being little more than tea. In the winter of 1534-35, the Iroquois on the mainland taught Jacques Cartier and his French sailors how to brew this tea. They used white cedar, but because this tree did not grow in Newfoundland, black spruce (*picea mariana*), also high in vitamin C, became the tree of choice for the brew. When sugar or molasses and native air-borne yeast combined with this essence of spruce, it fermented into an alcoholic version of the scurvy tea.

Naturalist Joseph Banks came to Newfoundland in the mid-1700s. His 1766 recipe for spruce beer instructed you to:

Take copper that Contains 12 Gallons fill it as full of the Boughs of Black spruce as it will hold Pressing them down pretty tight Fill it up with water

Boil it till the Rind will strip off the Spruce Boughs which will waste it about one third take them out & add to the water one Gallon of Melasses Let the whole Boil till the Melasses are disolvd take a half hogshead & Put in Nineteen Gallons of water & fill it up with the Essence. work it with Barm or Beer grounds & in Less than a week it is fit to Drink from this Liquor in itself Very Weak, are made three Kinds of Flip Cald here Callibogus, Egg Calli & King Calli, the first.[20]

And if you overindulge in these interestingly named drinks, the cure was available for that as well.

In 1794, seaman Aaron Thomas recommended spruce beer as a hangover cure, and claimed it was the best 'antiscorbutic' in existence.[21] Sailors would stop into a little inlet called Brewing Cove near Caplin Bay, now known as Calvert on the Southern Shore, and brew their spruce beer on the beach. "When brew'd, is laid on the ground in Casks to work. The ship's Boats then take it on board for use."[22]

The British navy thought so highly of the curative properties of spruce beer that when they built what was possibly Newfoundland's first hospital in 1725 on the south side of the harbour of St. John's, they equipped it with a brewhouse for brewing spruce beer to treat scurvy in their crews.

Perhaps other types of alcohol found a useful place in this hospital. Historically, even without our modern understanding of bacteria, the Greeks discovered alcohol could be used to dress and disinfect wounds. In addition to this, distilled alcohol acted as a wonderful preservative, a base liquid for healing potions, an antiseptic, and an anaesthetic. Brandy was thought to be a cure for the Black Death, and of course a cure for the never-ending stomach ailments that plagued many early moderns.[23]

One of the odder medicinal uses for alcohol included getting rid of worms. Our ancestors believed taking a couple of shots of rum or whisky made the worms drunk. They then staggered, if one can stagger with no legs, out.

One very early recipe even recommended beer as a mouthwash for dental hygiene:

And whosoever shall use to drink milk, because it is hurtfull to the Gummes and Teeth; for the one it maketh flacide, and the other subject to putrefaction; must have speciall regard to wash his mouth presently after the drinking of it, with Wine or Strong Beer and also rub the Teeth and gummes with a dry cloth, for the clensing away the fliminese of the Milk, and for strengthening the gummes and Teeth.[24]

Self-care was as important for health then as it is today. If you fell ill beyond the scope of self-medication, there were no hospitals and few medical professionals to assist you. Your only hope for help would have been the local residents.

After settlements were established on the island, large crews of seasonal fishermen still came over from England for the fishing season, and they often depended on the support of overwintering planters. If they fell sick, the planters' wives took them in and cared for them. Almost every home had a dual function as a tippling house where fishermen could get a ready supply of small luxuries such as tobacco and alcohol. So not only were they nursed back to health in a homey environment, but they had the added bonus of living in a tavern. In a report written by Captain Poole for the Committee for Trade and Plantations in the 1700s, he pointed out that, when the fishermen came over early in the season, they had to deal with the miserable Newfoundland spring: "What would become of such poore men at such a cold season, if they were not releeved by the planters?"[25]

Even into the twentieth century, Newfoundlanders considered alcohol a health necessity. One of the few exemptions to the prohibition regulations included the use of alcohol for medicinal reasons and people could procure alcohol with a prescription from a doctor.

Today, Newfoundlanders and Labradorians still take hot toddies to ward off a cold or flu.

My uncle, an old navy man, loved his rum and took his daily tot religiously. After he passed away, my aunt, more of the teetotalling persuasion, rarely touched a drop. The only exception was when she felt a sniffle or a sneeze coming on. She would then stand tiptoed in the kitchen reaching into the back of the top cupboard to pull down the bottle and pour a goodly amount in a glass, mixing it with hot water, brown sugar, and perhaps a splash of lemon. To complete the cure, she wrapped herself with plenty of blankets in order to 'sweat' out the fever. Apparently, it nipped the brewing malady directly in the bud.

For physical ailments, alcohol certainly played an important role, but perhaps more vital in this land of cold, rain, and fog, were the psychological effects it had on the settlers.

In spring, at the beginning of the fishing season, ships' captains hurriedly launched their small boats and raced ashore to claim the best part of the beach for drying the summer's catch. The woeful cry of gulls echoing off steep rocky cliffs and the wet clouds of fog drifting over the pebbled beaches must have made the landscape look strange and dangerous to new arrivals. For these fishermen, there was no escape from the damp and cold that settled into their very core.

In letters from the colonies home to England, early Newfoundlanders quite often requested the ever-popular aqua vitae to be sent out. The increased alcohol content of this spirit gave a pleasant burn and the perception of warmth to frigid settlers. Alcohol and tobacco acted as welcome balms for soothing their discomforts, and they took great pleasure in doing so.

As the months wore on and the sun came out some warmth seeped into their bones, but cold wet weather could often drag on, even into the summer months. To stand on the deck of a ship in the roaring winds and pelting rain, snow, ice, hail, or spray, and to risk one's life and limb every minute of every working day was not for the faint of heart. A shot of grog may have been the only thing keeping them going.

Whether a drop of water or spruce beer went in his rum, a fisherman drank strong liquor to keep the cold out and the warmth in. Add numbing poverty, nagging hunger and miserable weather to this, and we might begin to understand the complex historical relationship Newfoundlanders had with alcohol. For many centuries, alcohol in Newfoundland was more necessity than luxury.

After a day filled with brutally hard work, catching and curing fish from dawn to dusk, a fisherman's well-earned reward was to quaff a jug of ale or something stronger, socialize with other fishermen on shore, gather the news from home, and snatch a short but well-deserved rest.

These fishermen came from all over the British Isles, but mostly from the coastal areas of West Country Britain. They fit into the lifestyle of fish and bad weather with relative ease, perhaps because they had the advantage of a shared culture and language. One group that came over to Newfoundland from the British Isles, however, may have found it more difficult to adapt. When the Irish came to Newfoundland in the eighteenth century, these predominately young, transient, unmarried male fish servants had perhaps good reason to 'take to the bottle.' Not only did they have a sea voyage of more than 3,500 miles to contend with, but when they arrived in this new land, these Irish farm boys had a steep learning curve, handling fish and curing cod. Those that stayed endured much harsher winters than those in Ireland. Many found work cutting wood in deep snow and frozen ground, another unaccustomed task. These young, lonely Irish males spoke only Irish and had to work under English masters of a different faith. It is no wonder they turned to drink to soothe their roiling emotional state.

Since ancient times, intoxicating beverages have acted as a bonding agent for different levels of society, and in Newfoundland it functioned in a similar way, a sort of social lubricant, helping to bring together men from diverse backgrounds and creating in the taverns a home away from home.

In the early years of colonization and the migratory fishery, alcohol could be compared to a knight in shining armour, coming to the rescue in many situations. For those in the fishery or trying to carve out a living on the land, it afforded the very necessary calories for survival, provided medical assistance, and acted as a psychological godsend. It provided a recreational activity and served as a bonding agent for the new settlers and those propagating the fishery. Without it, we may not have stayed here. The concept of booze as a necessity runs like a scarlet thread through our history, thinned almost to invisibility in this century, but perhaps even now there are still those out there who believe in taking a nip for the constitution or a hot toddy to stave off the flu now and again.

TRADE
From Fish to Wine

> *Oh some are for the lily, and some are for the rose,*
> *But I am for the sugarcane that in Jamaica grows;*
> *For its that that makes the bonny drink to warm my copper nose,*
> *Says the old, bold mate of Henry Morgan.*
> —From John Masefield's "Captain Stratton's Fancy"[1]

CLASSICAL WRITERS LIKE LUCRETIUS AND SENECA WARNED
against the use of alcohol, arguing that wine could disturb the soul,
weaken the body and magnify character defects. Perhaps they had
a point, but in the seventeenth century, necessity trumped any negative
ideas. Important for its curative properties, not many thought ill of alcohol. There were, however, some dissenting voices with direct connections
to Newfoundland. English entrepreneur Sir William Vaughan, who
sent the ill-fated Welsh colonists to Renews in Newfoundland, attacked
alcohol use in his 1626 book *The Golden Fleece*. He stated, contrary to
popular belief, that strong liquor was not good for cold climates. Rule
number ten in Vaughan's directions for good health cautions the reader
to drink no more than four times with each meal and to eat and drink
moderately or else they may be caught in the "prison house of gour-
mandise."[2] But despite these dire health warnings, alcohol continued

to top the list of provisions for the voyage to Newfoundland. As traffic increased between Europe and the colonies and populations grew, it became apparent that as the desire for spirits increased, so did the incomes of the individuals involved in its production, shipment, and sale. Alcohol generated big profits, and trade in this highly desirable commodity became a very serious business and one of the engines that drove commerce in the colonies.

In the early Newfoundland fishery, alcohol choices consisted of primarily beer and aqua vitae, but Newfoundland fish soon traded for wine. This created working-class wine drinkers, a practice frowned upon in the seventeenth century. It was considered a threat to the social order to have the plebs living such a rich lifestyle, but these Newfoundland fishermen were simply reaping the benefits of Europe's insatiable appetite for cod.

Since medieval times, the Catholic Church had insisted on several days of abstinence a week in keeping with their religious beliefs, and on these non-meat days, fish filled their medieval bellies. The most popular fish at that time was a rather tasteless, salted European herring. When Cabot discovered Newfoundland's abundant cod stocks, many nations rushed

Scotsman William Buchan wrote in his *Domestic Medicine, or, A treatise on the Prevention and Cure of Diseases by Regimen and Simple Medicines* (1769) "The effects of wine are to raise the pulse, promote perspiration, warm the habit and exhilarate the spirits." He goes on to sing the praises of wine as a base for medicines, an agent for extracting the virtues of other medical substances. *Photo by author; items courtesy of John Wicks.*

to catch cod off the coast and supply it to people in Europe who clamoured for this more flavourful protein-rich meat alternative. On the rocky, seaweed-strewn shores of Newfoundland, the fishermen split, cleaned, and salt-cured the fish. Alternatively, fishermen from nations with plentiful salt supplies transported the fish 'green' (salted without being dried) back to Europe, putting it in the hold of the ship and throwing on large amounts of salt. The people of the Iberian Peninsula and Mediterranean preferred the dried fish, which kept longer in the heat. In response to the large demand for fish in southern Europe, ships came in droves to the *New Founde Land,* and business in the salted, wind-dried cod fish boomed.

In England, Henry vIII's decision to divorce his first wife, Catherine of Aragon, caused him to split with the Catholic Church. This rift produced an unfortunate hiccup in the fishing industry. Having established a new state religion, the Church of England, Henry wanted no part of anything Catholic, including fish and all the traditional fish days. British fishermen suffered acutely from this decision, so when Henry's young son Edward vI came to the throne in 1548, he made the wise decision that "For worldly and civil policy, to spare flesh, and use fish, for the benefit of the commonwealth, where many be fishers, and use the trade of living"[3] fish days would be reinstated. This was also good for the British ship-building industry because fish and bartered goods had to be transported in English ships.

With hard currency in short supply, the barter system prevailed, and fish initially traded for oil, rice, and salt. None of these commodities generated much of a return, so English merchants decided to trade their fish for wine and fruit from the Mediterranean regions. These products brought a higher unit value and converted into much larger profits, giving the fish merchants a better bang for their bartering buck.

English ships fishing off the coast of Newfoundland brought their catches back to the West Country ports of England which, in turn, sent them off to Iberian and Mediterranean ports in exchange for fish. The English then shipped men and supplies back to Newfoundland.

This inefficient system went on for some time until, eventually, the fish merchants just sent sack or transport ships directly to Newfoundland to pick up the fish. The word *sack* may have come from *vino de sacca,* which means wine set aside for export.⁴ These ships came primarily to trade in fish, not to catch it.

On their arrival in Newfoundland, sack ships offloaded supplies (including wine and brandy) and then packed their holds with fish and train oil (oil rendered from cod livers), which they brought back to Portugal, Italy, and Spain. They then returned to England with either specie (money in the form of coins), or bartered goods in the form of wines, olive oil, and fruit, essentially creating a triangular trade between Newfoundland, Iberian and Mediterranean ports, and England. Thus, the fish business became the wine business, not only in Europe and England, but also in Newfoundland.

Some enterprising individuals benefited from the wine trade here in Newfoundland. In 1638, David Kirke, an Englishman from a family of wine merchants, took over as governor of the Colony of Avalon (now Ferryland), with its 100 settlers on the south coast of the Avalon Peninsula. Kirke changed the dynamic of that early settlement. The original plan for the colony had been to create a diversified economy, but in the end, they resigned themselves to the fact that the fishery and selling alcohol (in the case of Kirke and a few other forward-thinking souls) were the only things worth pursuing. Kirke built the Colony of Avalon into an important trading port, exchanging local fish for Iberian wines. A clever businessman, in addition to his fishing business, he received permission to sell tavern licenses at £15 each, a tidy sum in those days. Kirke had his thumb on liquor sales from Trepassey to Bonavista.

Through that century, alcohol continued to pour in. A ship called the *Unicorne*, out of London, arrived in Newfoundland in 1675 carrying a cargo which included three tons (almost 3,000 litres) of French aque vitae (forerunner of brandy) in addition to tobacco, and other food supplies. In 1675, out of 50 sack ships arriving between Trepassey and St. John's, one in every three carried imports of alcohol.⁵

With the population of St. John's hovering around 1,500 at its peak, these imports provided a fairly large amount of booze to support the fishery; although a great amount of it was sold to the crews of visiting fishing ships. At that time, Newfoundland functioned as an *entrepôt* with ships from many nations coming to trade and fish off its coasts.

In 1677 the imports of alcohol exceeded the value of all other imports brought over to service the fishery. Although Newfoundlanders eventually became big rum drinkers, in the late seventeenth century rum imports accounted for only a small fraction of what they would become in the next century. Here's what the breakdown looked like for 1677:

Severall sorts of wynes & Provisions imported this yeare only in St. John's Harbr.
- Rum – 16 tuns from England and 16 tuns from the West Indies.
- Malt – 50 hhds. from England
- Hops – 2000 lbs. from England
- Wines – 110 tuns from England, 15 from France, and 94 from the 'Islands.'
- Brandy (aqua vitae) – 18 tuns from France.[6]

Wine imports and beer-making supplies still outstripped other forms of alcohol at this point.

One wine in particular stands out in the early days of Newfoundland's colonial history: port wine. Its origins can be traced back to Portugal in the late seventeenth century. The earliest wine involved in trade with Newfoundland would have been the 'Red Portugal,' from the Vinho Verde area of northern Portugal. Highly acidic and not very palatable, Portuguese wine had two advantages. It was cheap and, due to its acidity, it travelled well, a strong advantage when the transportation of goods took weeks or months. The English, however, didn't care much for Red Portugal, preferring French wines and brandies, which they sipped with great relish.

Unfortunately, France and England were prone to arguments, and when the French started a trade war restricting the import of English goods into France, Charles II of England retaliated by forbidding the import of French wines. Then the Nine Years War (1688-1697), which some commentators refer to as the first global war, cut off the Englishman's supply of the good stuff. With the Portuguese red no substitute for their customary French beverages, British traders travelled to Portugal to search for something better than acidic Vinho Verde. They discovered it further south in the Mediterranean-like climate of the Douro Valley, where grapes still grew on vines planted by second-century

Pipes of port wine stacked in a warehouse in Vila Nova de Gaia. Port wine was shipped in long barrels called pipes from Porto to Newfoundland. A modern pipe holds approximately 550 L. This is not a strict measure because the barrels are handmade and have slight variations in size. Originally the wine was measured using Arabian measurements, the ahmud (25 L) and the kanadesh (2 L). *Photo from author's private collection.*

Romans. Here, the English discovered a sweet, rich wine better suited to the English palate.

The merchants wasted no time in sending their sack ships to Oporto (Porto in Portuguese), the closest shipping port to the vineyards. The wine from this region soon became known as *port*, named after the city at the mouth of the Douro River. The English abandoned their Vinho Verde headquarters up north in Viana do Castello, where they had been trading cod for Red Portugal, and set up shop in Oporto—closer to the Douro wines.

Newfoundland's connection with port started in 1679, as the legend goes, when a pirate ship chased a vessel belonging to the Newman family. The Newman's ship, loaded with port wine, had left Oporto bound for England when the attack occurred. They were driven far off course, deep into the Atlantic and far from their intended destination. They wisely headed for St. John's, where ship, crew, and cargo spent the winter. The captain arranged to have the port wine stored in caves on the Southside Hills of St. John's. In the spring, the ship, with its cargo, returned to England, and upon arrival, the vintners discovered a marked improvement in the taste of the wine. The merchants soon sent their port regularly to Newfoundland, maturing it in casks for four years and then sending it back to England.

The big sailing ships bringing Newfoundland cod fish to Portugal transported port wine as ballast back across the Atlantic to Newfoundland. When the matured wine made its return journey to England, it was stored for another year before being bottled and marketed as Hunt's Port Matured in Newfoundland. Some suggested the rolling of the ship mixed the different blends in the wine and therefore improved the quality.

From this early start, West Country English merchants like the Newmans, the Roopes, the Hunts, the Goodridges, the Teages, and the Holdsworths all participated in the port-wine industry.

To further strengthen this lucrative fish-for-port-wine trade, the British monarchy encouraged the aristocracy to drink port at court. It soon became all the rage and ladies and gentlemen took their port with dessert or after dinner. In eighteenth-century England some adventurous fellows would polish off three bottles in an evening. It remains difficult to say for certain just how much alcohol these notorious 'three-bottle men' were consuming since the bulbous, short-necked decanters of those days held less port than today's bottles, and were used mainly as transport vessels for bringing the wine from cask to table. By 1775, bottles became more cylindrical and could be stored on their sides. It wasn't until the 1800s that bottles contained a uniform quantity with a regulated capacity.[7]

Newfoundlanders also did their part to support the industry in the nineteenth century. Not as lush as some of their English counterparts, they kept up with the local fashion of drinking at least one bottle of port per man per meal.[8] At the height of the fishing boom in the mid-1800s, port wine cost only a shilling a bottle.[9] At the elegant dinners hosted by upper-class Newfoundland merchant families, the bottle of port always travelled clockwise around the table and was slid gently, never picked up, so as not to stir up the dregs.

This history of the trade in port wine would not be complete without discussing the Newman family, well-known in Newfoundland and in the port-wine industry. The Newmans had a long-standing relationship with fish and wine. The earliest records indicate John Newman shipped a cargo of Newfoundland fish to his home base of Dartmouth, England, in 1589 and later that year a ton of train oil, which he later traded with Portugal. This made the Newman family one of the first to trade Newfoundland fish for wine.[10] Robert Newman acquired the fishing rights off "Newman's Rock" on the south coast of Newfoundland in 1601. At first, they had no permanent stations, as there was little or no settlement in Newfoundland at that time, but by 1672 the Newmans established business premises at Pushthrough, followed by trading stations at Harbour Briton (Harbour Breton), Hermitage Cove, and Gaultois, shipping codfish out and importing merchandise of all sorts. Some people overwintered in Pushthrough in 1679, and by 1700 the trading stations became permanent.[11] In a survey of planter's rooms, a Newman presence appears in St. John's as early as 1701, and the census of 1796-97 mentions them as being merchants and one of the largest property owners in St. John's. By the 1800s they traded in two distinct areas: wine and fish.

When Newman's Port first came to Newfoundland, the company stored it in the cellars of their fishing premises in Harbour Breton and in

St. John's, possibly in the caves in the Southside Hills. The Newman vaults that currently exist on the west end of Water Street may not have originally been built to house wine. Constructed from stone, red brick, and mortar made from seashells, the vaults originally had an outer wooden shed to protect them from the elements. In 1786 there is a mention of wine storage in St. John's, but no location is given. Maps of St. John's dated 1807 show the vaults existed at that time, but there is no proof the Newmans owned the wine vaults until 1845, when their agent, Mr. Morey, wrote a letter referring to the condition of the roof.

An ideal spot for wine storage, the steady temperature in the vaults of between 40 and 60 degrees Fahrenheit (4 and 16°c), helped age the wine. The pipes, long wooden storage barrels, held about 120-126 gallons of wine (550 litres). The Newmans stacked their pipes in tiers, three deep, and matured them for four years or more in the dark, dank 10½-foot-high arched caverns. The stone and brick of these arches, in addition to several feet of dirt above and around the walls, insulated the port from the cold and extreme weather. Grated vents in the stone walls provided some ventilation.

In the 1930s tight security ensured the entrance door to the vaults had three locks and three people held a key each. Management kept a close eye on the contents of the pipes as well, making sure customs officers gauged and measured the volume of each barrel twice: once when they arrived at the wharf and again when they reached the vault.[12]

The practice of aging the wine in the Newman vaults on Water Street certainly began in the early nineteenth century and continued until at least 1893 and possibly until 1914. When T. H. Newman passed away in 1892, the management of his St. John's estate was handed over to Messrs. Baine Johnston of St. John's. This company shipped octaves, quarter casks, and hogsheads of Newman's Port all over the world.[13]

Newman's fish business waned in 1907, due to the increase in competition and the dubious quality of the product. This brought about the closure of all the firm's holdings on the south coast. With the wine business still flourishing, however, they retained their properties in St. John's.

During World War I, the business struggled on. Before convoy shipping became the norm, the Newmans lost many of their valuable shipments of port due to enemy action at sea.

In the hiatus between the wars, prohibition also hampered the local port-wine industry. After prohibition, the Newfoundland government took over control of the liquor industry and the Board of Liquor Control used the wine vaults as a bonded government warehouse from 1937 to 1957, after which they moved to a new facility.

But all good things must come to an end, or at least change substantially, and in 1956, the Roopes and Newmans sold off the bulk of their port firm. The Newman family retained the ancient Quinta da Eira Velha

Inside Newman's wine vaults. In the spring of 1815 the HMS Bellerophon, a Newman's vessel, made the journey from Newfoundland to France transporting a cargo which included rum and Port wine. The vessel picked up the captured Napoleon in France on July 15th, and was transporting him to England, when the officers on board that ship toasted the capture with aged port from the Water Street Vault. They transported Napoleon to Plymouth and from there he was sent into exile at St. Helena. The ship's log for that day states "Broached, rum, 88 gallons; wine, 88 gallons." As they had recently purchased a hogshead of port wine from Newman's St. John's agent, Mr. Teage [Teague], it was probably that port which they opened. (Smallwood and Pitt, eds., The Encyclopedia of Newfoundland and Labrador, Vol. 3, s.v. "Liquor, Beer and Wine.") Photo courtesy of Dale Jarvis and the Heritage Foundation of Newfoundland and Labrador.

vineyard at Pinhão, Portugal, and in 2007 the Fladgate partnership purchased the Quinta, absorbing it into the port houses of Taylor, Fladgate, Fonseca and Croft.

Up until 1996, Portugal still shipped their port wine to Newfoundland to be bottled at the Newfoundland Liquor Corporation. This changed when the European Union required the Portuguese government to stop exporting bulk shipments of port.[14]

Since the EU ruling, Newman's celebrated port has been processed and bottled in a plant in an industrial area just outside the historic centre of Villa de Gaia Nova. Nowadays, Taylor Fladgate continues the nostalgic practice of producing Newman's Port exclusively for the Newfoundland market.

When the fishery moved from a migratory fishery to a settlement-based, inshore fishery in the nineteenth century, the population of Newfoundland grew, and with it came increased profits, more investment, and a boost in the local alcohol trade. Despite some setbacks due to wars, fluctuating prices, and drops in fish catches, there was still plenty of booze around. Newfoundlanders now drank because liquor was pleasant, cheap, and available, and by this time there were plenty of people aggressively marketing alcohol and reaping the profits. Alcohol gave the poor man an illusion of a better life, dealing with work conditions and an environment that had changed very little over generations. In the eighteenth century, a unique form of colonial society evolved in Newfoundland, and alcohol was woven into the fabric of the culture.

ALTHOUGH THE ELITE IN NEWFOUNDLAND PRIMARILY WET their throats with port and other fine wines, rum was the drink of choice for the lower classes. Rum became a major player on the Newfoundland stage not only as an article of trade, but as a beverage that permeated all levels of society and worked its way deep into Newfoundland culture and lore. One might go so far as to say we have rum in our DNA.

With a colourful history, the production of rum started from a simple source—the sugar cane plant. Christopher Columbus first imported the sugar cane into the Caribbean in 1493 and 10 years later, a sugar industry started in Hispaniola (Haiti/Dominican Republic). Much beloved by the Elizabethans, the queen herself apparently had teeth much blackened by the consumption of sugar.

When the juice extracted from this sugar cane came into contact with wild yeast spores, it fermented into an alcoholic beverage. Caribbean slaves soon discovered they could get pleasantly hammered on this raw undistilled liquor. Not long after, plantation owners used it for their own ends, controlling it and doling it out as a labour incentive. When some clever people realized the possibilities of mass producing this liquor for sale, distilleries sprang up.[15]

Rum seems to have been mostly manufactured on the British island of Barbados and the French island of Martinique. Referred to as "kill devil" by the early Caribbean British, it became known as "rumbullion" by the mid-1650s, or rum for short. Rumbullion, a Devonshire word meaning a great tumult, probably reflected the events that often occurred after tossing back a few drams. Giles Silvester, a resident of Barbados wrote, "The chiefe fudling they make in the Iland [Barbados] is Rumbullion, [alias] Kill-Divill, and this is mad of suggar cones distilled into a hott hellish and terrible liquor."[16] Dutch refugees may have introduced the art of distilling to the island, and by the late seventeenth century distillers discovered that molasses, that thick sticky goo that dripped from the sugar molds as the sugar cured, could be used more economically to make rum. This industry by-product had a higher sugar content than raw cane juice and produced a better beverage.

Bellamine bottle for transporting liquor from the barrel to the table. Archaeologists examined remains in a small one-roomed house in Renews, and determined the existence of a 'tippling house' by the presence of alcohol paraphernalia. This included liquor bottles, ceramic and glass vessels and ceramic drinking cups. The vessels found suggested more fortified beverages like wine or brandy were consumed. Alcohol was most often shipped to Newfoundland in staved containers, e.g. puncheons and firkins. The liquor was then decanted into case bottles or ceramic bottles like this Bellamine bottle. *Photo courtesy of William Gilbert Baccalieu Trail Heritage Corporation.*

The Caribbean merchants soon started supplying European trading ships which—having fortified their crew with beer, wine, and brandy on the way over—turned to rum as the liquid refreshment for crews on the return voyage. These same island distillers also saw to the needs of settlers and seafarers on this side of the Atlantic, in exchange for plantation supplies.

New Englanders recognized the excellent potential of this business and began importing large quantities of molasses to fuel distilleries in Massachusetts and Rhode Island. The first distilleries appeared at around 1640, and the New England population got into the rum. It took a bit longer for Newfoundlanders to get their hands on any substantial amounts of the old black rum.

For most of the early 1600s, Newfoundland obtained supplies from England, but by 1670, trade with the New England colonies increased. It was also around this time that larger quantities of rum appeared in Newfoundland.

By 1693, an average of twenty-five sack ships and a half a dozen coasters from the American colonies brought provisions and rum into St. John's. Given their geographic proximity, it was only natural that Newfoundland should trade with the New England colonies. The Americans needed outlets for their primary products, so trading in areas where they could earn good bills of exchange, or trade for goods that could be used to acquire bills of exchange, made sense. Two of these trading areas included the West Indies and Newfoundland.

The New Englanders, at that time still a part of Britain, bought low-quality refuse fish from Newfoundland and traded it for rum and molasses in the West Indies. They soon discovered they could circumvent the high cost of the British products by purchasing the much cheaper molasses of the French and Dutch West Indies. The British were not amused. Refuse fish bought in Newfoundland with American rum fed slaves on the sugar plantations of the Caribbean.

This reprehensible side of the rum trade affected many nations. Cromwell, for example, sold Irish captives to plantation owners in the West Indies as slaves. Indigenous peoples in America were sold as slaves, and of course large numbers were brought from Africa. Some

African traders bought slaves with a variety of goods, including textiles, metal bowls, jugs, and sheets of copper, but it wasn't long before alcohol became the preferred commodity. Newport distillers even produced an exceptionally strong rum for trade with the African kings, who provided the traders with slaves. One wonders if it might have been similar to Screech, Newfoundland's version of strong rum.

The cultivation of sugarcane increased in the eighteenth century, and the New England distilleries happily turned the cheap, plentiful molasses into rum. By 1715, reports show an increase in the rum traffic to Newfoundland shores: 19 ships from New England carried rum to Newfoundland, and 15 ships from the West Indies carried rum, sugar, and molasses. Early Newfoundlanders used molasses to make their spruce beer, which, when mixed with rum, created a drink known as *callibogus*. A popular drink in many early colonial seaports, it is no longer found on present day cocktail lists. Back in 1964 some bartenders at the Hotel Newfoundland in St. John's mixed their version of callibogus with local spruce beer. Probably an acquired taste, this attempt to resuscitate tradition didn't last long.

With the New Englanders getting their cheap molasses from the French and producing large amounts of rum for the Atlantic ring of colonies, the British retaliated by introducing the Molasses Act of 1733, which imposed tax on foreign molasses, sugar, and rum entering North American ports, in particular French Caribbean products. The Brits wanted the colonies to buy rum, sugar, and molasses from them and not get into the rum trade at all. This Act made little difference, though. With lax enforcement and increased smuggling, the New England rum distilleries marched on unscathed, and Newfoundlanders still acquired their cheap rum.

It seems the rough, un-aged rum from the West Indies was considered a superior product, but the Newfoundland fisherman preferred the stronger, cheaper, New England rum. This predilection could only have been due to the price and not the taste, as American humourist Artemus Ward (1834-1867) stated, "New England Rum and the measles were equally disagreeable."[17] In 1750, trade increased with the West Indies and the New England States, and rum from these producers supplied many Newfoundland grog shops. One record from 1708 tells how Robert Holmes, a Salem, Massachusetts merchant, sold five and a half hogsheads of rum (approximately 1,195 litres) at Newfoundland for £60.[18]

Rum barrels on the dock in Barbados awaiting shipment. *Photo courtesy of Jean-Pierre Andrieux.*

Losing out to the "Americans," and in an effort to boost their own rum trade, the British cut back on French brandy and encouraged rum drinking. Rum also made headway on the high seas. Contracts for rum with the British navy helped things along nicely. Naval administrator and diarist Samuel Pepys authorized supplying rum instead of brandy to the West Indies fleet in 1687, but it did not become a regular issue until 1731, when administrators incorporated it in the "Regulations and Instructions Relating to His Majesty's Service at Sea." One-half a pint of neat rum could now be substituted for one gallon of strong ale. This allowance was distributed throughout the day: half in the morning and half in the afternoon. Sailors could add sugar and limes to it if they chose. Boys under 14 received half that ration.

Even though Newfoundland's trade with the American colonies increased in the eighteenth century, they still imported plenty of alcohol from England, in 1731 bringing in seven tons of beer from Bristol, 11 hogsheads from Dartmouth, and just over 20 tons from Poole. A ton equated to about 1,000 litres, and a hogshead to 240-250 litres. Cider arrived as well: a half ton from Bristol and 71½ hogsheads from Dartmouth.[19] Not bad considering the permanent population for all of Newfoundland at that time stood at around 3,000, with about 440 people in St. John's.

New England merchants, like early pushers, traded vast quantities of their rum to the Newfoundland fishermen in exchange for fish. A British Colonial Office report described the effect of the arrival of New England rum on the shores of Newfoundland in 1680, in effect starting a complaint that would be heard over and over again:

> Considerable quantities of rumm and molasses are brought hither from New England with which the fishers grow debauch'd and run in debt so that they are obliged to hire themselves to planters for payment thereof.[20]

And in what was probably very similar to our local situation here in Newfoundland, John Josselyn, an English trader, described the New England ships coming into Maine as mobile taverns. Their captains came ashore and offered free samples of rum and brandy to the fishermen and planters, luring them into buying more. This interfered with business as the men preferred to drink on shore rather than go out and fish. Drinking would sometimes go on for a whole week at a time.[21] This description jibes perfectly with Captain Taverner's observations of the alcohol trade in Newfoundland:

> [The New Englanders] carry great quantities of wine and brandy, to Newfoundland, which is very destructive to that trade [...] those Gentlemen are frequently soliciting to get their wine and brandy sold, by those means every inhabitant's house is a tavern [...] The New England traders bring vast quantitys of rumm, which they retale out of stores and on board their vessels, it is plain that between all those taverns, stores and vessels which retale liquors as aforesd, that drunkenness abounds exceedingly. I have often seen from 100 to 300 men drunk of a Sabath, in the moneth of Sept. at some places when rainy weather, it is rare to see a fisherman sober etc.[22]

In the early 1700s the town and surrounding areas of St. John's had an over-wintering population of about 1,100. Numbers swelled in summer, with St John's, Petty Harbour, Quidi Vidi, and Torbay numbers increasing to about 3,000. In the 1760s it peaked at about 6,000.

Between 1730 and 1770 cheap New England rum, typically one-half to two-thirds the price of West Indies rum, poured into Newfoundland.

Rum imports to Newfoundland from those times looked something like this:[23]

Year	Imports to St. John's	Imports to Newfoundland
1708		• 8 hogsheads (504 gallons) of rum from Boston arrived at Ferryland • 5½ Hogsheads (346.5 gallons) exported to Newfoundland by Robert Holmes of Salem, Massachusetts
1715		• 48,000 gallons from the West Indies • 660 gallons from New York • 4,244 gallons from Philadelphia
1731		• 51,600 gallons of rum from Boston • 8,040 gallons from New York
1741–1742	• 126 hogsheads (7,938 gallons) from America. • 238 hogsheads From the West Indies (14,994 gallons)	• 51,000 gallons of rum from Boston • 880 gallons from New York
1754		• 56,400 gallons from Boston • 3,630 gallons from New York.
1763		• 49,140 gallons of rum from Boston • 6,120 gallons from New York • 2,160 gallons from Philadelphia
1764	• 134,314 gallons from America	• 20,700 gallons imported to Placentia Harbour from America • 14,020 gallons to Harbour Grace from America • 21,700 gallons to Ferryland from America
1768	• 68,801 gallons from America	
1770	• 198,046 gallons from America	• 274,000 gallons from America

Year	Imports to St. John's	Imports to Newfoundland
1771– 1772	• 120,791 gallons from America • 57,343 gallons from the West Indies • 124,753 gallons from America (unknown if this is an additional amount or connected with the stat above)	
1773		• Barbados: 51,930 gallons • Dominica: 11,470 gallons • Tobago: 6,030 gallons • St. George's: 2,349 gallons • Savanna la Mer 35 puncheons (2,940 gallons)
1774		• Barbados: 120,740 gallons • Savanna la Mer: 35 puncheons (2,940 gallons)
1775		• 250,000 gallons of rum imported
1807		• 39,599 gallons from Britain • 284,989 gallons from the West Indies • 829 gallons from British America

Some canny Americans even traded their rum with Newfoundlanders for fish, which they then resold to the newly arriving European ships for other tradeable goods.

By 1750, Boston produced rum in twenty-five rum distilleries, and by 1763, there were perhaps as many as 159 distilleries in New England alone.[24] In the last decade of the eighteenth century, they utilized seven million gallons of imported molasses a year. Researchers Barty-King and Massel claim that, in 1763, Newfoundland ships brought in 280,000 gallons[25] of New England rum to the island, in addition to the more expensive West Indian rum. With an average population of 1,103 in St. John's and an average of about 125,000 gallons of rum imported into town per year from 1768 to 1772 (not to mention other varieties of alcohol that flooded in, i.e. whisky, gin, brandy, wine, and cider), what a time it must have been! To be sure, a good amount of this rum disappeared down the throats of the seasonal fish servants that crowded St. John's during the fishing season. When trade increased with the Yankees, the practice of exchanging rum for cod fish became even more popular. In 1770, Newfoundland became the largest New-World market for rum.[26]

This all changed when the American Revolution began in 1775. British ships blockaded American ports, allowing nothing in or out. Newfoundlanders in need of rum had to get it from the mother country or directly from the Caribbean. As a result, our American neighbours suffered a severe rum drought and the New England rum distilleries foundered.[27] Newfoundlanders took matters into their own hands to get their coveted rum supplies. They traded fish directly with the West Indies for rum and molasses.[28]

In Newfoundland, rum wholesaled for about 25 cents a gallon. By 1789 the price went up, retailing to the fishermen at $1.20 a gallon.[29] They

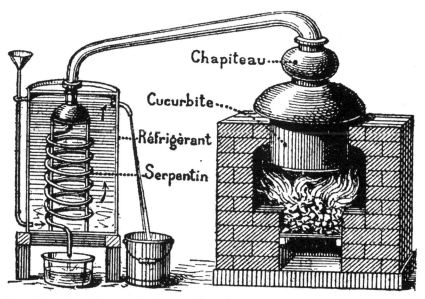

Pot still similar to those used in Jamaica. Rum distilled in Britain from imported molasses never tasted as good as that from the West Indies, perhaps because they rarely cleaned the pot stills in the Caribbean, and the molasses burned onto the sides, enhancing the rum with a superior caramelized flavour. *Image in public domain.* *CC-BY-SA-3.0.*

would, no doubt, roll over in their graves if they knew today's prices. George Smith, in 1729, noted that rum distilled in Britain never tasted as good as that from the West Indies, perhaps because they rarely cleaned the pot stills in the Caribbean, and the molasses burned onto the sides, enhancing the rum with a superior caramelized flavour.[30]

By 1807, rum and molasses came directly from the West Indies rather than from the American continent. In that same year, the imports of rum into Newfoundland stood at approximately 325,000 gallons for a population of around 20,000. That worked out to about 16 gallons per head for every person. This was above and beyond any brandy, gin, wine, beer, and cider imported.[31]

Although rum drinking provided the favourite means of recreation, as can be seen in the table below, it was not the only form of alcohol appreciated by the local population.

Alcohol importation figures for Newfoundland in selected years of the nineteenth century:[32]

Description	Amount imported	Amount exported
1826		
Wine	236 tuns	18 tuns
Beer, Porter	1,604 casks	51 casks
Spirits	271,740 gallons	
Rum	*n/a, see spirits*	552 puncheons
1836		
Ale and Porter	93,176 gallons	647 gallons
Brandy	19,183 gallons	145 gallons
Cider	22,967 gallons	
Geneva [Gin]	8,042 gallons	
Rum	212,345 gallons	5,764 gallons
Wine	41,530 gallons	17,075 gallons
Whisky	2,061 gallons	

1851

Beer and Cider	1894.5 barrels	
Brandy	17,497 gallons	1,335 gallons
Geneva [Gin]	6,550 gallons	30 gallons
Whisky	185 gallons	
Rum	83,009 gallons	
Undefined	64.5 gallons	
Wine	310,182 gallons	212–430 tons

1895-96

Ale, Porter, Cider, Perry	13,473 gallons	
Brandy	2,550 gallons	
Rum	23,809 gallons	
Gin	1,713 gallons	
Whisky	11,388 gallons	
Cordials	48 gallons	
Wines		
Champagne	101 gallons	
Claret	581 gallons	
Hock Burgundy and light Rhenish, Spanish	45 gallons	
Malaga, Mantilla under 80°c.	787 gallons	
Port or Madeira	2,161 gallons	61 barrels + 2,407 gallons
Sherry, Manzanilla	423 gallons	
Figueira, Red Lisbon, Cape, Lisbon Common	1,457 gallons	
All other	10 gallons	

Description	Amount imported	Amount exported
1896-97		
Ale Beer and Porter	14,369 gallons	
Spirits viz. Brandy	3,502 gallons	
Spirits undefined	151 gallons	
Cordials	5 gallons	
Gin	2,163 gallons	
Rum	36,157 gallons	
Whisky	13,907 gallons	
Wine		
Champagne	126 gallons	
Claret	447 gallons	
Malaga	423 gallons	
Port and Madeira	2,334 gallons	61 barrels + 2,407 gallons
Sherry	612 gallons	
Red	1,345 gallons	
All other	7 gallons	

During the War of 1812, enormous quantities of alcohol came ashore in Newfoundland. In 1813, 426,000 gallons of rum and spirits landed on Newfoundland shores. With nearly seventeen thousand men employed in the fishery, this worked out to about 26 gallons per man per year. Easy access to this amount of alcohol must have proven to be too great a temptation for Newfoundland topers.

The higher-ups in Newfoundland society had slightly different tastes as shown in this 1845 list from Commissariat House in St. John's. The list shows the approximate prices for provisions. Note the amount paid for

Port and Madeira far outstrips that paid for rum. The amount of rum is recorded as unspecified, which could suggest the amount was too small to bother recording. They do not indicate the size of the cask, as casks came in many sizes, so it is difficult to ascertain how much exactly they were talking about, but the prices indicate that this elite group perhaps preferred Port and Madeira to the drink of the lower classes:[33]

Year	Liquor	Amount	Price in pounds sterling. £ s. d.
1845	Port	¼ cask	13.10.0
	Madeira	½ cask	24.0.0
	Porter	3 doz. Bottles per cask	1.13.0
	Rum	Unspecified	0.10.0
	Whiskey, Irish	Unspecified	0.7.6
	Brandy (cognac)	Unspecified	0.14.6

Large amounts of alcohol continued to be consumed in Newfoundland well into the nineteenth century. The 1857 St. John's census indicated a population, including women and children, of approximately 30,000. It showed the breweries and distilleries operating in St. John's produced 16,000 gallons of malt liquor and 20,000 gallons of distilled liquor in 1856. This would have been in addition to any imports. The statistics on imports/exports in the tables say it all.

Trade in alcohol introduced a cornucopia of temptations. So much alcohol came into the fledgling country in the eighteenth and nineteenth century that—given the residual belief that alcohol was healthy and combined with a growing psychological dependence on the stuff—consumption skyrocketed. It wasn't just in Newfoundland and Labrador, however. Britain too, in the eighteenth century, had a serious alcohol problem with their gin craze. Gin consumption in Britain in 1743 stood at 8.2 million gallons, without taking into account the illegal gin production. By 1750 consumption had grown to 11 million gallons annually. After 1750, gin production fell for various reasons, one of them being failing corn harvests.

The British gin craze provides one example where Newfoundlanders did not follow in the footsteps of the old country. The import figures for gin in Newfoundland were low, with little mention of it in earlier documents. In 1836, import records reveal approximately 212,000 gallons of rum, but only 8,000 of gin. By 1896, perhaps due to the rise of the temperance movement, the records show a drop in consumption, or at least in importation, with 36,000 gallons of rum and 2,000 gallons of gin coming into the island

In the beginning, there was beer, aqua vitae, and wine, but by the eighteenth century, rum dwarfed all other forms of alcohol. In fact, most of the story of alcohol in this period of Newfoundland history can be told through rum. If cod drove the Newfoundland economy, alcohol came a close second, and trade for one generated trade in the other. With so much booze coming into the island and few restrictions—legally, socially, or morally—on drinking, great problems, general skulduggery, and often great abuse occurred. In some ways, alcohol was pushed upon us by people wanting to up their profits, but in other ways we embraced it wholeheartedly.

WARSH AND KRASNICK STATE IN THEIR INTRODUCTION TO *DRINK in Canada: John Barleycorn Must Die*, "Economics based upon resource extraction have tended towards high levels of alcohol consumption... when social systems fail to meet an individual's needs, a high intake of alcohol and drinking to excess may occur."[34] The resource extraction in the case of Newfoundland was fishing, and in turn, the fish business and alcohol soon became inseparable.

So, from necessity to big business, alcohol wove its way more and more into the fabric of Newfoundland culture, seducing the population and enriching the wealth of many. It was the age of mercantilism, where governments consolidated national power by maintaining an iron fist on their economies, maximizing their own exports, and minimizing imports. They did this, in part, by extracting raw materials from their colonies and then selling the finished goods back to them at exorbitant tax rates.

Profits from taxes on these goods helped fund Britain's war efforts in the seventeenth and eighteenth centuries.

British colonies in the West Indies produced raw materials from the sugar cane and distilled rum. Hence the production of sugar, molasses, and rum, for example, were very important to the eighteenth-century British economy.

Newfoundlanders did their part to support this economy by supplying the fish, which they mostly traded for British goods. Unfortunately, Britain did not give much back except access to a plentiful supply of booze, before the market was partially usurped by the New Englanders. Through the centuries, alcohol in Newfoundland has forged relationships and destroyed households, facilitated political careers, and fuelled riots.

EXCESS

How a Culture of Alcohol
Gave Birth to the Binge

THE AVERAGE NEWFOUNDLANDER CAN PROBABLY COUNT ON less than five fingers the number of teetotallers they know. Only one in four Canadians abstains from alcohol.[1] And at the other end of the spectrum, one in four Newfoundlanders (27.7%) is classified as a heavy drinker—more than any other province in the country.[2] Almost everyone in our society drinks alcohol to some extent. Those who have never taken a drink do so for good reasons, and those who no longer drink have perhaps gone through great pains to stop this often debilitating and destructive habit.

Love it or hate it, alcohol use has been entrenched in many of the world's cultures for millennia. Used in religious ceremonies, in the treatment of disease, and for pure pleasure, it has generously lubricated both high and low society since Neolithic times (10,000–4,000 BCE). When mankind developed a taste for alcohol, they needed malted grains to make their brews. One theorist, Dr. Jonathan D. Saur, from the University of Wisconsin, proposed that man switched from hunting and gathering to the domestication of grains in order to acquire this raw material.[3]

Most of Newfoundland's drinking culture hails from the British Isles, where making fermented beverages may have started in the Celtic Iron

Age. The Celts first brewed with barley, and ale became the beverage of choice in early England. When the Romans invaded Britain, they brought wine, wowing the upper classes but not impressing the average Brit. In Roman Britain, the wealthy cheerfully quaffed large amounts of wine, emulating their Roman counterparts. The average ancient Briton, however, preferred his own form of ale-like drinks, not caring much for Roman wine. This might have had something to do with the way Romans watered down their wine, thinking it uncivilized to drink it full strength. The Romans believed drinking un-watered wine brought on extreme violence or even madness.[4]

After the Romans marched their troops out of Britain in the fifth century, the Northern Teutonic tribes invaded and brought with them their malted liquors, which were much more suited to English taste buds. Then came the Vikings in the late eighth century, big ale drinkers. The preference for wine reappeared with the Normans in the invasion of 1066, and the upper classes did their best to welcome the usurpers. They kept up appearances by speaking French and drinking their wine—anything to distance themselves from the great unwashed, who believed "Ale for an Englyshe man is a natural drynke."[5]

In the Middle Ages, religious houses took on the role of early inns, offering travellers accommodations, food, and beverages. They soon got into the business of brewing ale.

The Abbot of Burton brewed good ale,
On Fridays when they fasted,
But the Abbot of Burton never tasted his own,
As long as his neighbour's lasted.[6]

Ale became a prolific source of income for the church, allowing many opportunities for fundraising. Through events known as church-ales, bride-ales, Whitsun-ales, clerk-ales etc., the church acquired malt and food, profiting from the sale of their ale. The proceeds were administered for the relief of the poor. They also sponsored help-ales, bid-ales, christening-ales, and give-ales in memory of the deceased,[7] perhaps the forerunner of our Irish-Newfoundland wakes. So in a sense, the church at this time encouraged drinking, and these 'ales' essentially evolved (or perhaps devolved) into drinking parties and times of excess. The harder the patrons drank, the more the parish benefitted.

In addition, women known as *alewives* brewed and sold ale. Some added herbs and spices to their brews, others the juices of flowers or fruits. The monks sold a special herb mixture known as *gruit* to the ale-wives. This helped preserve the brew and added further revenue to church coffers.

Brewing good ale was a serious business. Ale testers assessed the quality of all the ale sold. Wearing leather breeches, an ale tester would visit a pub and draw a pint. He would then spill a puddle of it on a wooden bench and sit in it. After thirty minutes of talking, smoking, and drinking, if his leather breeches stuck fast to the bench, the ale would be judged impure with too much sugar in it.[8] The alewife who sold bad ale was promptly put in the ducking-stool and given a good ducking.

Beer came over to England with the Flemish in the fourteenth century and differed from ale in that it included the addition of hops, which preserved and guarded the brew from the contaminating bacteria often left in the barrels.[9]

From the same family as cannabis and stinging nettles, hops have been used since Egyptian times as medicinal plants. In European culture, hops didn't appear until about 700 or 800 CE around the Flanders area, and English-speaking cultures did not use them until much later.

> Hops and turkeys, carp and beer,
> Came into England all in one
> year.[10]

Hops made the ale taste so different that Henry VI (1421-1471)

Mother Louse, an early English alewife.
Image in public domain. CC-BY-SA-3.0.

outlawed the ale brewers from using it, and Henry VII (1457–1509) repeated this prohibition. Obviously both kings remained loyal to the good old spiced, un-hopped English ale.

When they got tired of drinking sour ale, they finally began adding hops to both ale and beer, and the distinction between the two blurred. At first, the brewers hopped ale to a lesser extent than beer, but drinks with less alcohol in them needed more hops to keep them from going off, especially in summer.[11]

Beer and ale remained as separate entities for almost 200 years. Then sometime in the 1500s, the two guilds, the Beer Brewers' and the Ale Brewers', combined into one.

When fishing ships from England first ventured across the ocean to Newfoundland, they brought their beer and ale with them. Once here, they met other nationalities fishing off our shores who brought their own forms of alcoholic beverages. All these fishing ships sought shelter in St. John's harbour well before the English colonization in the seventeenth century.

Sir Humphrey Gilbert cruised into the harbour of St. John's in 1583 to claim the *New Founde Lande* for Queen Elizabeth I. He may have thrown the first Newfoundland kitchen party, inviting all thirty-six vessels in the vicinity to come ashore. After the party, which included musicians and other fine fare, he exclaimed the harbour had serviced him with "all wants commodiously, as if we had been in a city."[12] One can imagine that plenty of alcohol serviced his 'wants' and those of his guests.

Obviously, Sir Humphrey liked a good party, but his half-brother, Sir Walter Raleigh, in his *Instructions for youth, gentlemen and noblemen*, gives alcohol consumption a resounding thumbs down, echoing a few other brave souls who had also panned it:

Take special care that thou delight not in wine [...] for it transformeth a man into a beast, decayeth health, poisoneth the breath, destroyeth natural heat, brings a man's stomach to an artificial heat, deformeth the face, rotteth the teeth, and to conclude, maketh a man contemptible, soon old and despised of all wise and worthy men; hated in thy servants, in thy self and companions, for it is bewitching and infectious vice.[13]

Strong words, but no one was paying much attention to him. Drinking in those days was a very important part of life.

THE FISHERMEN WHO FIRST SAILED OVER FROM EUROPE AND THE British Isles to fish brought their drinking culture with them. With so little else to do besides work in early Newfoundland, drinking, besides being used for mental and physical health, became the favourite pastime. The harsh conditions of life and the strenuous labour paired with the availability of cheap alcohol nurtured this culture of drink, not only in Newfoundland but in other areas of colonial North America.

People drank on board ship, on shore, and in fishing stages, but also in the tippling houses and grog shops. In 1677, of the 30 planters residing in St. John's, 29 of them kept tippling houses.[14]

Sailors Carousing by J.C. Ibbetson, illustrating sailors celebrating their return to land. Drinking and gaming soon emptied their pockets of hard-earned wages. *Image in public domain.* CC-BY-SA-3.0.

And so the entertainment continued, with only a few regrettable interruptions. During Queen Anne's War (1702-1713), between France and England, the French destroyed St. John's on two separate occasions: once in 1705 when they "laid in ashes every house around the harbour"[15] (there go the grog shops) and again in 1708, when the French easily overtook the small English defensive force.

Despite war and destruction, the eighteenth century saw great expansion in the fishery, and the small but stable population of Newfoundland experienced a growth spurt with the mid-century arrival of Irish settlers. These new arrivals definitely altered the drinking landscape of the young country, especially in the St. John's area where many of them settled.

Whereas in previous years Britain had supplied a great deal of the labour force needed to prosecute the fishery, between 1697 and 1732 English ships stopped in at Irish ports for provisions, in particular salt beef and salt pork. They began transporting young Irish males who wanted to work in the upcoming fishing season. Some of these fishing servants stayed, but were not recorded as residents in Newfoundland before 1720.

The Irish might have been few in number in the early years, but the ones overwintering raised concerns. In 1729, Capt. Osborn stated:

> The complaints of the Inhabitants against the disorders committed by the great number of Irish Roman Catholicks who remain here in the winter is the only thing further I have to lay before your lordsp [Lordships]... Those people who very often plunder them if they can't or won't imploy them in the winter, and threaten with their being superior in number.[16]

Complaints about the Irish immigrants continued. In 1731 they were referred to as "felons [...] scum of that kingdom [...]. Papists brought from inland places and many from gaols [are] very ignorant and insolent, and naturally prejudiced against Englishmen and Protestants."[17]

The planters, however, needed Irish labour, so these newcomers kept arriving in Newfoundland. Soon they would form the majority of the year-round residents.

The British saw the Irish as a threat and possible soulmates to the French because of their shared religion. The British commander of the garrison in St. John's ordered his officers to break up any gatherings in tippling houses if they thought them the least bit suspicious, in particular in tippling houses with French or Irish patrons.[18] Convinced the Irish would desert and advance the French cause, the British saw the Irish 'youngsters' as "Treacherous [with] designs" including "not only ye servants of this harbour, but his Majesties servants in ye fort."[19]

Commodore James Story commented that if they didn't stem the inflow of these poor, indebted 'passengers', the country would soon be ruined. Governor Watson (1748) estimated that the Irish represented a quarter of the overall population on the island, with immigration from Ireland exceeding that from England. By 1750 Irish servants formed the majority in most coves and harbours between St. John's and Little Placentia, on the other side of the Avalon Peninsula. Edward Langman, a missionary with the Society for the Propagation of the Gospel (SPG), lived in St. John's from 1752 to 1782 and described the population as being 50-70 percent adult males, with single Irish men outnumbering the women four to one, and in some years, outnumbering them thirteen to one.[20] This state of affairs, with regard to the Irish, worried Governor Hugh Palliser, Newfoundland governor from 1764-1768: "[The country is] crowded with Poor Idle and mostly disorderly People [...] being all dealers in Liquor more than Fish to the great Increase of Idleness, debauchery and every kind of Excess and Vice amongst the Fishermen and others."[21] No doubt the Irish contingent contributed greatly to the number of grog shops in the town.

The English government frowned upon settlement in Newfoundland until the end of the American War of Independence in 1783. After this, the population of Newfoundland increased, with numbers pushing up over 16,000. St. John's turned into more of a small town than a fishing station, and businesses, including many taverns (often referred to as "houses of ill fame" by those who didn't approve of them), lined the lower path (Water Street). With the country awash in alcohol, the very unsettled nature of the fishery fuelled a rough and largely lawless population. The locals and the visiting fishermen had a mighty thirst to quench and the purchasing power to do so.

Both rich and poor drank away their sorrows. Many of the upper classes gambled heavily at card games as they whiled away the dreary winter evenings. They sometimes lost a great deal of money and turned to drink to soothe their souls. This, of course, only compounded their problems.

Drink was both plentiful and, in the case of rum, easy on the purse. In his journal of 1794-95, Aaron Thomas, able seaman aboard the HMS *Boston*, stated:

> Grog shops are very numerous in St. John's. Rum here is very cheap, it being brought from the West Indies and only pays [one shilling] a Gallon Duty. Three Shillings and Sixpence is the common price to the consumer. A person who is fond of malt liquors will find them very dear. One shilling a bottle of London Porter is the price.[22]

Unfortunately, people without licenses sold as much or more liquor than those legally entitled to do so. There's nothing like easy access and a wide profit margin to get everybody on the bandwagon. The local population stayed mum on the matter, and with no informers coming forth to snitch on the unlicensed alcohol sellers, it made this black market very difficult to suppress. In 1799 Admiral Waldegrave allowed the magistrates to grant licenses to 50 additional sellers; perhaps he thought it better to collect the fees than attempt to supress the activity.

By the early nineteenth century, the town consisted of around 2,000 buildings clustering around the waterfront and straggling up what, in those days, were much steeper hills. Crooked, narrow, and muddy roads, with hardly enough room in places for two carts to pass, wove their way through town. By all accounts, a walk in the downtown area at that time was not a pleasant experience, the paths "abounding with dirt and untidiness," manure, wood chips and fish offal thrown in the streets, and multitudes of dogs and vagrant pigs adding to the filth. The houses "were mostly small and nearly all unpainted, and many of them had linneys in which they kept horses and cows," while all around business carried on as usual. Chandlers, haberdashers, coopers, sail makers, blacksmiths, cabinetmakers, ironmongers, and liquor and grocery sellers lined both the upper and lower paths of the old town, where "every shop on one side of the street was the emporium of some merchant dealing in all the commodities here in demand, and every shop on the other was, speaking generally, a grog-shop."[23] For any visiting members of the elite, this state of affairs must have been difficult to take.

SIMILAR TO BRITAIN IN THE EIGHTEENTH AND NINETEENTH centuries, the poor lived in abominable circumstances; their damp and dirty housing stood as invitations to disease. Like many other rough seaport towns in North America at the time, St. John's had its share of crime, but better here than the poor slums of London, where people lived through the gin craze of the eighteenth century. In the nineteenth century the motto of the grog shops was still "Drunk for a penny, dead-drunk for tuppence."[24] The poor sought solace in drink. In those days, a 'moderate' drinker consumed about a half a pint of rum a day.[25] Considering a standard rum and Coke holds only 1.5 ounces of alcohol, this amount equates to about six drinks a day. In Newfoundland, easy access to alcohol changed the drinking landscape, as more people came into contact with alcohol through work and leisure. By 1872 visitors to the town took note of the easy availability of liquor, with a great number of stores licensed to sell "Ale, Wine and Spirituous Liquors." One visitor, David Kennedy Jr., wrote that "every second store" appeared to be selling alcohol.[26]

With so much drinking going on in town in the eighteenth and nineteenth centuries, it must have been difficult to conduct business. To control the problem, the mercantile society of St. John's adopted the old naval tradition of serving up tots not only as a work incentive, but also as a means of controlling the unbridled drinking habits of their workers. In Newfoundland the tot consisted of an unsweetened mix of rum and water. Every *hand*, boy or man, had his brown jug with the yellow strip round the middle, called *a yellow belly*, and when the time for the *mornin*, and *eleven o'clocker* and the *evenin* arrived, "he approached the rum puncheon, and drawing the spile, filled his yellow-belly."[27]

The tot was also known as a *bever*, a drink taken at certain times during the day. A bever/bivver/bibber also means a tremor of excitement (all a bivver). Perhaps this *bever* was in anticipation of the *swalli* (swallow).

Local St. John's firms continued the traditional three to four tots of alcohol per day for their workers well into the nineteenth century and beyond.

Adding to the drinking population were the extra residents in the town, heavy-drinking military men of dubious character, some 700 troops at the garrison in 1806-07. Naval ships and crews that came in the summer season to protect the fishing fleet augmented the military population.

In the next century, if you worked for the military as a soldier, you would have benefited from an alcohol ration. During the First World War, the army received the tot. Soldiers in the Newfoundland Regiment got their ration of thick, dark rum at the rate of 1/16th of a pint per man, per day. Many men complained about the small size of the rum ration.[28]

To Rum

When your feet are like two stones
And your face is pinched and blue,
And you have that "Fed up" feeling,
(We have had it just like you)

What is it will cure your ills,
Put some warmth into your toes,
Make you feel quite fit and chirpy,
And bring colour to your nose?

It's the stuff that is contained
In a simple jar of stone.
tho' it should be given a palace
And be set upon a throne.

For it is a mighty spirit,
To whom we all do homage pay,
Giving strength to weary soldiers,
Fitting them for another day ....[29]

The unconstrained drinking habits that the tots attempted to control came from a drinking culture deeply ingrained in the populace and helped along by the establishment. Planters sometimes paid their sharemen part of their wages in rum, sealing vessels kept a keg of rum on deck with free access for all, school fees could be paid in rum, and fishermen and merchant seamen expected their daily rations of booze. It was not uncommon to see drunks openly rolling down the steep hills of St. John's of an evening at any time of year.

For those who didn't get tots on the job, there were always the taverns, where even non-drinkers ventured out to enjoy the varying forms of entertainment the town so desperately needed. Although mostly seen as dens of iniquity, the taverns were soon appreciated as important fixtures in the community—not just for keeping the drunks out of sight, but also as venues for other types of diversions. Consuming rum at these taverns still constituted the main form of recreation, perhaps because it was so cheap, but taverns also afforded their clientele with a place to disseminate

Interior Tavern Scene by D. Teniers. Tavern life in the seventeenth and eighteenth centuries was rowdy, with patrons drinking, smoking, carousing, and carrying on all manner of devilment. *Image in public domain.* CC-BY-SA-3.0.

information and spread town gossip, as well as carry out their business affairs. In addition to this, they offered up everything from theatrical presentations to cockfights.

With larger spaces than the average home, taverns and inns became multifunctional buildings and important community structures. The extra activities offered helped to make the taverns more respectable.

Billiards, for example, was a popular pastime at Cornelius Quirk's London Tavern. In the late 1890s, George and Elizabeth McKay operated a skittle alley in their tavern at 434 Water Street and for those who longed for a bit more excitement, some local taverns hosted cockfighting. A notice in the *Royal Gazette* stated that a cockfight would take place at Robert Brine's tavern. "A main of cocks will be fought on Tuesday next the 29th inst. at 3 O'clock in the afternoon, for five guineas a battle or five guineas the main or odd battle. Rules in every respect conformable to those practised at the Royal Pit and Newmarket."[30]

As a way to attract customers, many public houses in England became museums of sorts with collections of taxidermy, farm implements, old coins, and other ancient artefacts. Today, mimicking this age-old tradition, Trapper John's on George Street displays farm implements and woodworking tools.

Local taverns hosted reading rooms with books and newspapers for lovers of the written word. The first edition of the *Royal Gazette and Newfoundland Advertiser*, published in 1807, stated, "the work will be published early every Wednesday morning and sent to the houses of subscribers in town, and to such public houses, inns, etc., as the Outharbour subscribers may direct." In 1820, citizens of St. John's formed a library society and set up a public reading room in the Freemason's Tavern. This tavern may have been one and the same with the London Tavern, as the Masons met at the London for fifty-eight years.[31] Another group, the Benevolent Irish Society, met in the London Tavern in 1806 to plan out the formation of their society, and they continued to meet at the London for many years before moving to The Globe Tavern.

In addition to hosting society meetings, The Globe served as a theatrical venue, advertising a local comedy production, entitled "The Poor Gentleman," which was to be put off by a juvenile theatre troop on

Monday, January 31, 1820. The advertisement added "weather permitting." The weather, of course, did not co-operate, and the performance
was postponed to February 7. By 1822, theatre had become so popular
in St. John's that a new theatre house was constructed at the corner of
Duckworth Street and Queen's Road. This area became known as Theatre
Hill. On November 8, 1822, to celebrate the laying of the cornerstone of
that building, a procession consisting of constables, magistrates, clergy,
guard of the military, Masonic officers, and members of the theatrical
committee left the Crown and Anchor tavern and marched up to the
location of the new theatre. After the event, they all retired to the Crown
and Anchor to toast the success of the venture. The Crown and Anchor
must have been a popular tavern because, in 1823, the town's elite held
Governor Edward Morris's farewell dinner there.

In St. John's, postmaster Simon Solomon even operated a post office
out of his St. John's tavern.[32]

A tavern actually stood in as a rudimentary parliament building. In
1832, Mary Travers's Inn, opposite what is now the War Memorial, hosted
the election headquarters for Newfoundland's first representative government. The parliament met there until they ran into a spot of trouble. On
February 3, 1834, Mrs. Mary Travers had a confrontation with the House
of Assembly when the esteemed parliamentarians refused to pay their
rental bill. Her revenge was sweet. Mrs. Travers seized the governmen-
tal paraphernalia, including the mace and Speaker's chair, and advertised
an auction of goods in a local newspaper. The House promptly paid her
expenses and retrieved their belongings.

Many of the St. John's taverns were described by local writers as having
brightly painted swinging signs depicting names like the Jolly Fisherman,
the Rising Sun, and the Three Crowns. Despite their picturesque names,
few could be called attractive buildings, but were, for the most part, low,
dark, dirty hovels where alcohol was sold and fights broke out at regular
intervals.

The upper classes passed by holding their noses at most of these establishments. They preferred to host their own entertainments in the form of
balls, masquerades, dinner parties, amateur theatrical performances, and
dances. Events such as these, held at more respectable public or private

venues, successfully kept the moneyed inhabitants of nineteenth-century St. John's amused. Upper-class gentlemen did, however, frequent the London Tavern, described in 1813 by a visiting Lieutenant Edward Chappell as the only "tolerable Inn" in town.

Perhaps because of its "quality," the London Tavern lasted for many years, while the number of other public houses fluctuated greatly. In 1801, when the population of St. John's was a mere 3,420, Captain Barton ordered that the number of taverns be reduced from 26 to 24.[33] By 1804-05 the population of St. John's had only increased to 4,608, but the following year, Governor Duckworth, concerned about the illegal sales of alcohol (and probably the loss of revenue for the island), requested the number be increased to 36.[34] Selling alcohol was said to be next in line after the fishery as an industry of importance.[35]

IN 1815 THERE WERE FIFTY-ONE GROG SHOPS SERVICING A POPULATION of 10,000 permanent residents in St. John's. For comparison, St. John's currently has more bars per capita than any other city in Canada, with 3.35 bars per 10,000 people[36]—hardly a drop in the bucket compared with the 1812 figures. It must be considered however, that in the eighteenth and nineteenth centuries, during the fishing season, the population of the town swelled with visiting ships and seamen. They too liked to visit the taverns and buy alcohol.

Those who lived outside of the larger centres like St. John's took advantage of all it had to offer in the way of taverns when they came into town. Such was the case for the farmers of Portugal Cove and St. Philips.

At Bakehouse Corner in the mid-nineteenth century, near the "little fort" [Fort William] a new arrival, Lieutenant-Colonel McCrae and his companion, stopped to witness an event. His friend described it as one of the 'events to see' on one's arrival in St. John's. "Wait half-a-minute [...] I hear farmers going home. It's worthwhile to see the style of driving here"

In less time than he named, merry bells and loud voices were heard rapidly turning the corner at the foot of the glacis [ice]. On they came in succession, five or six sleighs, or lumbering catamarans. The occupants, drivers included, were lying full stretch across the bars and backs to the horses, shouting, laughing, or swearing jocosely at one another, as the mood of the instant took them. It was a procession of bacchanalians, foolish, half-screwed, yet intending no harm or mischief. The leading catamaran was going at a heavy trot, right in the centre of the track, the reins dragging through the snow by the side and the owner flat across the bottom of the concern, face, up and most likely asleep which his legs perched across a flour barrel, hitched upwards like a pair of pistons at every forward jerk of the horse. Not one of them was watching the road, yet they followed the leader in the narrow track as skilfully as a London cabman could have done. On they went past the crest of the hill down to the little bridge spanning the river at the head of the lake, till we could see them no longer.[37]

The horses took their inebriated owners home, to a community about six or seven miles past Windsor Lake. These gentlemen would come into town for supplies to find the flour, tea, and molasses on one side of the street and the grog shops on the other.

Not much had changed by the twentieth century. On a Friday night in the 1930s a heavy traffic of farmers came in from Torbay and Outer Cove to sell their products in St. John's. Flush with cash, they headed down to the Cottage Garden or Cameron's for their reward. Leaving their horses and carts out front, they went in for a few drinks. At the end of the evening, they were too drunk to drive, so their faithful horses successfully navigated the route home while the farmers slept it off in the back of the carts.

Not that the smaller towns and villages didn't have their taverns and tippling houses; most did. Lieutenant-Colonel McCrae took a trip to Witless Bay, a village roughly thirty-five kilometres down the coast from St. John's. Here he visited Paddy Carey's hostelry. In the nineteenth century travellers faced a long journey back to St. John's, so McCrae and his party asked to stay the night. The publican promptly shepherded them into the bar filled with fishermen having their evening grog. According to McCrae's notes, the 'inn' consisted of a bar, a dusty parlour, and a garret with two bunks, "the whole highly perfumed with cod-liver oil."[38]

Carbonear also had a rich tavern culture. Philip Toque wrote a vivid description of his father's Carbonear public house in 1897:

> He sold liquor of every description, rum from the West Indies, wines from Spain and Portugal, brandy, gin, ales and beer imported from Liverpool and Dorsetshire, England. Those liquors were retailed by the gallon, quart, pint, half pint, naggon and wine glass up to the hogshead and puncheon. During the spring and fall, the average receipts a week at the tavern were between four and five hundred dollars.[39]

He muses about how they used ropes and parbuckled the great puncheons, pipes, and hogsheads up over the steep hill to the tavern, adding that in those days you could get men to do anything for a drink. The customers at the tavern would sit around drinking punch, smoking pipes and singing songs until the tavern closed at 10 p.m. The publican did not allow dancing or card playing and no liquor was sold on Sundays.

Alcohol was alive and well outside of the taverns and the towns; however, in the smaller centres, drinking and socializing occurred more in the home.

Traditionally, the outport man got his keg of rum in the spring and then had to make it last until the next trip or until a boat with supplies came to the outport. He drank judiciously, having one drink before his meals and one before bed. Necessity dictated moderate drinking. If the supply of alcohol ran out, some made their own brew or wine, or got whatever form of local moonshine was available. Outport people drank their homebrew at garden parties and kitchen parties and tended to drink it in rotation (e.g., when your brew was 'working' beside the stove, your buddy's was ready to drink). At the kitchen dances, they'd all have their keg of beer and if they had a big crowd it wouldn't last, and they'd all go somewhere else and drink someone else's keg. P. J. Wakeham recounted a story of making wine with his uncle in the outport. The process involved filling an empty keg with water and adding blueberries and other ingredients to make up a batch of wine. When they strained the liquid to pour it into bottles, they dumped the residue from the berries in the garden to make compost for the next year's grass. Busy putting on the next brew, they thought nothing of it until their rooster began to crow, followed by a commotion from the hens. When they went to look, they saw the inebriated poultry staggering and falling over each other.[40]

Sometimes, supplies made their way slowly out around the bay and occasionally certain individuals lost patience and made their own hard liquor. A famous case of moonshining occurred on Flat Island, Bonavista Bay, on July 5, 1919, where a lone policeman attempted to arrest seven fishermen. When they resisted, the policeman called for reinforcements. Help came in the form of the warship HMCS *Cornwall*. Under such overpowering odds, the fishermen surrendered and were transported to St. John's and charged with moonshining and resisting arrest. The men were later discharged.[41]

Whether it was rum from the keg, moonshine, or homebrew, Newfoundlanders celebrated life's transitions, whether secular or religious, with alcohol. Weddings, wakes, and baptisms were all causes for celebration. These events were not considered to be much of a success without a good supply of spirits, most often consisting of 'bought' rum, wine, and moonshine. Often, no invitation was needed, and all sorts of people just showed up. At weddings, the feasting and drinking went on all night with guns and muskets being fired off in celebration. Fiddles played and people danced through the night.

Outport people went all out when it came to acquiring alcohol to celebrate the union of two souls, and they weren't shy about drinking it either. Reverend William Marshall, a Methodist minister who initially came to Hermitage Bay as a missionary in 1839, recorded several marriages he presided over on the south coast of the island. He performed a marriage on September 9, 1841, in Mosquito and described it as a scene of drunkenness and riot. He also noted a quieter wedding in Pushthrough and one in Grole the next day with less drinking than he had expected. To this he added "Praise the Lord for this change."[42]

In times of death, the Catholic family waked the corpse night and day for a week. The grieving family and friends made sure all attendees were well fortified with good food, pipes of tobacco, and alcohol. Games and storytelling entertained the mourners.

A year in Newfoundland was not only punctuated with these transitional events, but each season's work and entertainments revolved around drinking alcohol.

In the bleak mid-winter, sleighing parties amused the upper classes. These consisted of up to 12 sleighs all in a row, transporting ladies and gentlemen, with their grog, wine and other goodies stored under the seats. When they came to a smooth spot, a pond for example, they found some shelter and built a fire, heated up soup and picnicked on the snow.

Not that different from today, many young men in 1812 liked to party no matter what the time of day. One cold day in February, a group of them met at 10 o'clock in the morning and set off for Twenty Mile Pond to eat and drink at Thomas Kearsey's house. Here, they ate bread made from locally grown wheat, and drank "fine old Madeira wine." Well into their cups from drinking 'generous libations', one creative young sport suggested they call the village by the pond, Windsor and re-name Twenty Mile Pond, Windsor Lake. They raised their glasses to the future prosperity of the regally named village and shortly after, "proceeded over the immense sheet of ice which covered [Windsor Lake's] romantic surface to the commencement of the New Road on the North side" travelling to George Goff's at Portugal Cove.

> They dined at Mr. Goff's with the great hilarity and leaving his house at three o'clock returned over Windsor Lake renewing their refreshments at Windsor, succeeded by the loyal song of Hearts of Oak reached St. John's at 5 much gratified with the amusements and occupations of the day.[43]

Come mid-February local fishermen got busy preparing for the upcoming seal fishery. The men hit the grog shops on Water Street with a vengeance, often drinking up expected profits with the agreement that the score would be settled when they return from sealing. If the hunt was successful, all would be well, and the night of the return spent in an orgy of drinking. One sea-going officer, who had spent only a few days in St. John's just after the men returned from the seal hunt, when asked the question as to what sort of place it was, replied with "Well, sir, I was only there three days, and they appeared to me to be all drunk."[44]

In the middle of the March seal-hunting preparations came St. Patrick's Day, the most important day of the year for many Newfoundlanders of Irish descent, even though it also fell in the middle of Lent. So how did they manage to get around this dilemma? Back in the sixteenth century, Pope Gregory granted a special dispensation to Irish Catholics that freed them from their Lenten abstinence on this day and they were allowed to celebrate St. Paddy's day in the proper style. As Anspach succinctly put it in 1819, "It is hardly in the power of any priest in the world to hinder an Irishman from getting gloriously drunk, if he is so inclined, on the whole of the 17th of March, as well as the next day in honour of Sheelagh, Saint Patrick's wife."[45] With so many Irish Catholics among the flock, when temperance came into fashion in the mid-nineteenth century, certain compromises and modifications had to be made to the grand ideals of this movement. The temperance pledge seems to have been negotiable and was said to have been sometimes 'lifted' for occasions like weddings or St. Patrick's Day.[46]

For the upper classes an unforgettable event occurred at the Benevolent Irish Society in St. John's on March 17, 1829. After a night of "Splendid entertainment" at Miss Ward's Hotel, with music and toasts to King, country, and generally everyone they could think of, the celebrations continued until the wee hours, without a single circumstance to disturb for a moment "the hilarity and good feeling" which everyone appeared to enjoy. After drinking "bumpers" and "brimmers," the company continued to retire, successively, until six o'clock on Sheelah's morning at which hour, we understand, a few of the campaigners might have been seen, as usual, piously and patriotically employed in "drowning the shamrock."[47] This meant that the wearer of a shamrock, whether on his coat or hat, took it off and put it in the last drink of the evening, while proposing a toast. The drinker then took the shamrock from the empty glass and threw it over his left shoulder. The writer of this newspaper report took several days to recover from the all-night affair.[48] In Ireland, they used a real shamrock and ingested it along with the drink.

In the months of March or April, the first ships sailed for the seal hunt. On the return, about a month later, some very thirsty sealers hit the downtown taverns. If the hunt was successful, they drank to celebrate. Unsuccessful hunters with no profit to share, drank just as much to drown their sorrows as they did to celebrate their successes. This of course made things worse in the long run.

After the seal hunt came the unrelenting work of the summer fishery, relieved in August by the St. John's Regatta, an occasion for drinking and rowdiness since 1818.

Coming home from the races,
Bleeding noses and cut faces,
And we we're all as drunk as blazes,
Coming home from the races.[49]

The regatta was well known for its beer tents that sold mostly homemade juniper beer, or hop beer as it was known. In the nineteenth century, the annual boat races on Quidi Vidi Lake, the Royal St. John's Regatta as it became known, generated a lot of drinking and bad behaviour. From its very inception in 1818 and onwards, lots of liquor circulated by the lake. Mr. Best's tavern, the Bunch of Grapes, which lay on the north side of Quidi Vidi Lake, must have been hopping on race day, as patrons dropped in to quench their thirst on their way to and from the Regatta. At lakeside, numerous possibilities for inebriation presented themselves. Hop beer tents dotted the side of the 'pond'; if you were shy on cash you could bring your own refreshments and get pleasantly hammered while cheering on your favourite team.

WITH THE FALL MONTHS CAME THE END OF A HARD SEASON AND preparations for the long winter. Shorter days and longer nights signalled the approach of the next season for celebration.

Christmastime brought with it many opportunities to overindulge. Just to get the ball rolling, drinking started on the day before Christmas Eve, known to some as Tibb's or Tipsey Eve, sometimes called the first day of Christmas.

Christmas Eve traditions in many communities on the island followed a familiar pattern. Men would gather at a predetermined house on Christmas Eve afternoon and a bottle and shot glasses would be brought out and put on the table along with some small snack. The men, including the host, would have a few drinks and then move on to the next house. If they met anyone along the way, he would be invited along and the group grew larger with each visit. After stopping for supper, usually one family cooked a large pot of beans just for that occasion, and the drinkers would carry on late into the night. If someone got too drunk to continue, they were dragged to a nearby house and deposited on a daybed to sleep it off. If the victim woke before the night was over, he often rejoined the party.

One custom from Placentia Bay called 'dancing out the light' signalled the host and the group it was time to move on. The revellers would do this by stamping together on the last bar of a jig, usually, with enough of a bang to put the lamp out. The party always broke up at midnight, the beginning of Christmas day.[50]

Christmas amusements in nineteenth-century Newfoundland kept the populace happy for the season. Not much work got done, and along with the eating and drinking came mummers and fools, who wandered the streets looking for grog or money.

In Philip Toque's reminiscences of Carbonear, he remembers every house having a decanter of rum and a very large Christmas cake on the kitchen table for guests to help themselves. Those who could afford it placed brandy, gin, and wine on the table as well.[51] Christmas revelries continued unabated until necessity forced the inhabitants back to the serious business of earning a living, and the yearly cycle began again.

By the nineteenth century, in response to the bacchanalia of the gin craze in Britain, a temperance movement spread across the British Isles and eventually found its way to Newfoundland. They certainly had their work cut out for them. The newspaper *Evening Mercury* printed statistics in 1885 that in the decade between 1873 and 1882, Newfoundlanders drank 1,826,073 gallons of liquors, which included 871,642 gallons of rum.[52]

CONTROL

Between the Devil and the Deep Blue Sea

I N 1633, ENGLISH MERCHANTS WITH BUSINESS INTERESTS IN Newfoundland, noticing the undesirable effects alcohol was having on their labour force, lobbied the court of Charles I to ban the sale of liquor in tippling houses:

> noe person doe set up any Taverne for selling of wyne, Beere, or stronge waters, cyder or Tobacco, to entertayne the fishermen, because it is found that by such meanes they are debauched, neglecting thar labors and poore ill governed men not only spend most part of their shares before they come home, upon which the life and mayntenance of their wife and Children depende but are likewise hurtfull in divers other waies, as by labour, by purloyning and stealing.[1]

The Star Chamber of Charles I took action. Members drew up rules, the Western Charters, to try to keep things in check. And while this looked great on paper, it accomplished little. So the merchants continued to agitate for stricter controls, with successive rulings appearing in 1634, 1661, and 1671.

Alcohol flooded the colony, and increased use led to increased abuse. From the very beginning, the fishery in Newfoundland was seen as a resource to be harvested and the island only as a convenient station from which to process the product. And because it was all about the money, this valuable resource had to be both protected and controlled for maximum profits. The first objections to drinking had little to do with concern over the actual health and welfare of the drinker, but rather with the smooth execution of the fishing industry. It was important the fishermen did not overindulge to the extent that they spoiled the product and impeded the profit-making of their merchant masters.

Great care had to be taken to process the fish in a timely manner, and servants who failed to show up for work, or who worked poorly due to intoxication, created problems. The merchants, who were often the ones supplying alcohol to the fishermen, did their best to control access, but if a fish servant abused the privilege by getting intoxicated and neglecting the fishery, the employer soon cut him off. The existence of tippling houses and taverns outside the merchants' control only served to compound the problem.

Another major concern was that of class distinctions. It was all right for the working classes to drink as long as they didn't try to live like their betters. The seventeenth-century English merchant class viewed wine and brandy as upper-class luxuries, not something one would equate with the diet of a fisherman. But Newfoundland planters enjoyed a standard of living comparable to tradesmen or lesser yeomen in England. Large amounts of alcohol and tobacco would never have been available in the English working-class home, but in Newfoundland, with easy access to these goods through the triangular trade, fish servants enjoyed luxuries well above their social status. The economies of fish and wine intertwined to such an extent, it is no wonder working-class wine drinkers developed.

Most of the men who manned fishing ships belonged to the lower classes, and in British society of the seventeenth and eighteenth centuries, the classes kept a good stiff distance from one another. The lower classes had to know their place, and any move towards emulating their betters would set a dangerous precedent. But young men in the Newfoundland fishery, now far from the constraints of their homeland, often got out of control. As a result, the authorities stepped in to limit this behaviour and the alcohol said to encourage it. Endangering upper-class profits or a merchant's livelihood would not be tolerated.

The wealthiest classes, however, were not always unified in their attempts to control alcohol consumption in the colony. Upper-class investors of early seventeenth-century Newfoundland had no love for David Kirke, governor of the island from 1638 to 1651, who established a tavern in the Colony of Avalon. Archaeological evidence shows Kirke enjoyed a fine lifestyle. Along with wine bottles, earthenware jugs, pitchers, and individual drinking glasses, archaeologists found evidence of tin-glazed earthenware vessels, Agateware and Delftware punch bowls, syllabub pots, decanters, jugs, and two posset pots, suggesting beverages like punch, possets, syllabub, caudles, wine, aqua vitae, and other strong spirits and beers played an important thirst-quenching role at the colony. Kirke even went so far as to produce his own currency in the form of tokens in multiple denominations, which the fishermen could cash in

Sailors overindulging in a tavern. *Image in public domain.* CC-BY-SA-3.0.

for drinks at the tippling houses. The West Country merchants accused Kirke of being responsible for fishermen "wasting their estates" and being disorderly. They also accused him of being a corrupt blasphemous drunk himself and injuring the commonwealth's interests in Newfoundland.

In a less-than-flattering account, the West Country merchants wrote to the court of Charles I complaining that Kirke:

> hath pleased to licence to keep Tippling Houses for the selling of Wine, Beare, Brandy and tobacco [...] Debauching our men, Tempting them by wine and women not only to unfaithfulness but to common Drunkenness [...] butt especially by his continuall support of rude, prophane, and athisticall planters, whoe hee not only licenceth to keepe taverns att sevrall yearly rents in most of the choysest fishing portes & harbors, butt furnisheth them with wynes, att his owne rates & prises, to the debauching of seamen, who are thereby taken off from theyre labors in the principallest tymes of fishinge.[2]

These strong words may have been an attempt on the part of the merchant establishment to keep Kirke and his alcohol sales in check and to exert social control over the fishermen.

CRITICISMS OF DRINKING IN NEWFOUNDLAND COINCIDED WITH criticisms of working-class drinking establishments in colonial America. For example, in February of 1733, the *Pennsylvania Gazette* added its voice to the chastisement of heavy drinking by suggesting that "spirits and strong waters" when consumed by "people of inferior rank," renders them "unfit for useful labour, intoxicating them and debauching their morals, and leading them into all manner of vices and wickedness."[3] This sums up both of the main arguments against the drink in Newfoundland: the enforcement of patriarchal moral values and the protection of colonial mercantile profits.

Still, the fishing industry and the alcohol industry continued to work at cross purposes in Newfoundland. Despite attempts at controlling consumption, some merchants were making their fortunes not on fish, but on alcohol sales. In the late seventeenth and early eighteenth centuries, certain ships making the trans-Atlantic journey had a creative way of increasing profits. Their masters forced planters to buy alcohol supplies they did not necessarily need or want:

> Those ships can carry nothing to Newfoundland from those parts but wine, brandy, salt, sugar and oyle. When salt is scarce, they generally use this method: when the planter comes to buy a certain quantity of salt, yes says the ships master you may have it, but you must take a butt of wine, and a quarter cask of brandy, with every ten hogsheads of salt, this the buyer is often obliged to do, otherways his men must sit still and catch no more fish.[4]

Ten hogsheads of salt made about 100 quintals of fish. But some boats in a good season might catch up to 400 quintals. The brandy and the ten hogsheads of salt needed might cost the planter seventy-five to eighty quintals of fish. Having to buy alcohol, along with the salt, left some planters destitute, and the only way to get rid of the accumulated stores of wine and brandy, and the debt, was to open up a tavern or tippling house. So it was no surprise that "At least nine of ten planters in each harbour operated a tippling house from their homes selling alcohol and tobacco."[5]

All the attempts to control drinking in Newfoundland by reducing the numbers of grog shops and tippling houses seemed to have had little effect. Taverns and drinking establishments sprang up again like mushrooms in a cow field. Enterprising individuals sold liquor from their homes, from the decks of New England sloops, and from fishing stores.

Much of the drunkenness in the population occurred on Sundays when the men had more free time. Drinking during the week became problematic and interfered with work. One visitor described drinking on Sundays, and drinking in general in Newfoundland, like this:

> I realy believe, that for profanation of the Sabbath, swearing and drunkeness no place in the world is like it[6] [...] the great decay of the fishery being generally ascrib'd to the disorders that arise from drunkeness, to which that people are very much addicted.[7]

Another problem with Sunday drinking came from a different quarter. The population in St. John's included fighting men as well as fishermen. By the later years of the eighteenth century, Sunday drinking had grown to become a major problem for everyone, but in particular for the constables who had troubles with a particular set of drinkers. They had to request that the officers in the Newfoundland Regiment forbid their soldiers from walking through town on Sundays while toting their side arms. The constables reported that they thought it very unsafe to interfere with armed, intoxicated men.

Constables initially came from the ranks of local tavern owners, who were deputized and entrusted with peacekeeping. These tavern owners, including several women, did duty as police officers, making arrests and tracking down criminals. This arrangement remained in place until 1833. The military in town attempted to control drinking among their ranks by the administration of wise council in 1797. When the soldiers of the garrison at Fort Townsend received a slight pay raise, those with wives and children were given a strong warning to put the extra money toward their family's welfare, and those without families to put it toward paying down debts.[8]

The officers cautioned the rank and file not to spend wages on alcohol lest they end up like the hapless Sergeant Dayley. The good sergeant went out one Sunday in August 1797, and drank 10 glasses of brandy. Well into his cups, he met up with two other seamen and supposedly complained about the unfair treatment of the military. His companions viewed these complaints as mutinous and reported this to the authorities (no doubt to curry favour). Dayley claimed that because he was drunk, he could not remember the conversation, but assured the authorities that he never had reason to complain of his situation as a soldier nor a desire to encourage any man to mutiny or sedition. Dayley ended up in prison in the guardhouse trying to use drunkenness as an excuse to get out of charges of mutiny: "James Dayley wishes to assert his innocence of the charges laid against him regarding his alleged dealings with the *Latona* [crew members]." Dayley pleaded drunkenness again in response to what was now being purported as a planned mutiny.[9] A general order from Fort Townsend warned that "drunkenness is not enough to clear a soldier of an offence." They spared his life, but discharged him from the regiment only after he uttered a public oath of atonement.[10]

With so much alcohol floating around, there was bound to be trouble. Rules and regulations out of England constituted the earliest attempts at keeping the fishery running smoothly. The fishing admiral, the title given to the first captain to arrive in a harbour in the spring, administered justice with regard to the fishery in an ad hoc manner. Naval governors acted as a backup for the fishing admirals, but had not taken a strong hand until Captain Josias Crowe, in 1711, naval commodore of the annual convoy to Newfoundland, organized the first legislative council and public meetings on the island, creating, "several laws and orders made at St. John's for the better discipline and good order of the people and correcting irregularities."[11]

Sixteen provisions came out of these meetings, including a ban on selling liquor on Sundays "upon a fine or forfeiture of two pounds for the first offense, eight pounds for the second, with a fine of one shilling for each person found in a disorderly house."[12] Crowe commented that "the Lord's day was nothing at all regarded neither by the inhabitants nor the common sailors who spent it generally in houses of entertainment in drinking and swearing and the most disorderly actions."[13] The commodore dealt with debauchery "by threats, punishments and other necessary means."[14] When one reads the later reports of drinking on the island, they suggest that Captain Crowe's short stay from August to October of 1711 had little lasting effect.

It was all very fine to pass laws limiting the number of drinking establishments and the amounts of alcohol sold, but the impracticality of the situation soon became apparent. With little in the way of a permanent justice system in place, if anyone broke the law during the winter season for offences which sometimes included rape and murder, they had to be incarcerated somewhere for months before they could be shipped back to England to stand trial. Justice lasted only as long as the fishing season while the naval commodores resided on the island. When they left in the fall, law and order went with them.

Awash with taverns and tippling houses, in the early 1700s Commodore Bowler, commander of the Newfoundland convoy and temporary governor (1724-27), estimated that in 1726 sixty-five of the 420 families in Newfoundland kept public houses with "forty-six of them in St. John's and vicinity, ten at Ferryland, four at Bay Bulls, four at Trepassey, and one at Bonavista."[15]

There was obviously a need for more than military boots on the ground to provide law and order and solve various problems connected with the fishing industry. Captain Henry Osborne became Newfoundland's first commodore-governor in 1729. He appointed four justices of the peace and four constables. After the naval officers had gone home for the winter, the justices of the peace took over. Not always well-suited for the job, these gentlemen did not have an easy time of it. The old fishing admirals still wielded power and jealously guarded what they considered to be their turf. They walked all over the newly appointed magistrates, thwarting them at every turn. The laws of the Act stated the admirals should limit themselves to disputes in the fishery, but fond of power, the admirals overstepped their bounds. In 1730, they ridiculed the appointed justices of the peace and set up public houses themselves without obtaining the proper permits.

In the early 1770s, St. John's offered a choice of 46 taverns to visiting patrons, and by 1775, 80 dotted the landscape. The Grand Jury, in 1785, requested the number of taverns be limited to 24. The merchants countered, asking for 64, and the governor compromised by granting 40 licenses.[16]

By October of 1787, the citizens of St. John's wrote to Governor Elliot expressing concern over the reduction in the number of public houses, fearing this might cause problems for maintaining the peace.[17] Governor Elliot brought the matter to the attention of the appropriate authorities in England. He requested that more public houses be built in St. John's, showing the petition signed by 22 principal merchants and stating their view that the present number of public houses could not accommodate the number of patrons wishing to use them. They requested an extra 12 public houses be added to those already there.

Waiting for replies from England on matters concerning the number of taverns allowed was inefficient, and so in 1789 the decision was made to allow Newfoundland's Governor Milbanke to grant licences for the operation of public houses. His only restriction was that he could not exceed 24 in number in St. John's.

Just when things seemed to be getting somewhat under control, another event occurred to upset the balance. The New Englanders began to show up more frequently in Newfoundland with rum and other products. This annoyed the British who, thinking it bad for national unity, didn't want to encourage a close relationship between New England and Newfoundland with regard to trade and provisions.

Normally, the Newfoundland fishermen received most of their provisions from English merchants and repaid these merchants with fish caught that season. If the credit extended surpassed the payment in fish, the fisherman went into debt, which he carried forward each season. This became known as the 'truck' system.

The arrival of the American traders interfered with this established order. In a bad run of seasons, already deeply indebted to his English master, a fisherman might secretly sell a portion of fish to the New Englanders for much needed supplies. The English merchant, however, still expected to be repaid, so tensions naturally arose. Obviously, the English merchants had no love for these traders.

Under such stressful circumstances, Newfoundland fishermen found rum too great a temptation, and they dove deeply into the drink. This created several problems. Intoxicated fish servants did not always take the great care needed to cure delicate fish, and if the finished product failed to meet a high standard, the merchants suffered a loss which in turn they passed on to the fishermen. This financially drained the fishermen and mired them deeper in debt. For many of these men, their financial needs grew so great the American ship masters easily persuaded them to come to New England and work off their debt in a new land. This created a shortage of fish servants in Newfoundland.

With regard to the Yankee traders, they went up and down the coast selling supplies to fishermen and collecting fish, which they sold in St. John's. They too carried unpaid debts, and left collection agents behind on the island to overwinter and cause trouble in their attempts to collect those debts, all while continuing to push alcohol on the livyers.

No wonder Captain Caleb Wade described the population as being "increased by men of broken fortunes and idle fellows." The New Englanders who overwintered in Newfoundland caused "riots and disorders," insisting on selling alcohol to the planters. When the planters couldn't pay them, these New England ships' masters seized their fish and tackle. With their gear seized, the planters couldn't pay their servants, who were also in debt. The servants, caught between a rock and a hard place, quit the planters to go work off their debts. The masters on these New England vessels were given 40 shillings by their government for each man and boy they brought back. In this way the overwintering New Englanders, in addition to their general bad behavior, increased the residents' debts and depleted the island of fish servants, affecting the long-term viability of the fishery and ruining many of the planters. In some cases, the situation became so dire planters were forced to work as fish servants themselves.[18]

Locally, and throughout the island's colonial history, other clever individuals used liquor to their advantage. In addition to being an important commodity, alcohol became a tool and was used to manage Newfoundland's unruly population of workers and residents. This, unfortunately, encouraged further substance abuse.

Captain Sir Robert Robinson used it as a labour incentive in 1680 just as the ancient Egyptians had done to entice their workers to build the pyramids. Robinson paid for the improvements at the St. John's fortifications with very little cost, "except some small gratuity to the seamen in time of labouring, in brandy or the like."[19]

Once again in 1700, Captain Michael Richards reported, "An expense of £206 12s for liquor" which he was obliged to serve up to the local manpower to entice them to work on the construction of Fort William."[20] With brandy at five shillings sixpence per gallon, and rum a little cheaper, £206 bought a substantial amount of alcohol.

To bolster the morale of military troops, commanders supplied their soldiers with plenty of rum, brandy, and other liquors as repayment for the hardships of a posting in St. John's. Alcohol, however, greased the wheels of discontent, and with rivalries between the army and the navy, there were plenty of drunken brawls.

On the civilian side of things, Governor Edwards (1757-59/1779-81) also found alcohol indispensable. He established a force of a few hundred volunteers for the defence of the town. When they were under arms, he paid them and gave rations, which included a half a pint of rum per day. He gratefully acknowledged the loyalty of the Newfoundland population in their defence of the colony and their cheerful submission to military rule and discipline. Cheerful might be the operative word here, brought about by the half pint (equivalent to about eight shots) of rum ingested per man per day.

Adding to the manipulative use of alcohol, men and boys often received alcohol as payment for work, augmenting the deprivation of many families who lived in terrible poverty, with disease and high child mortality.[21] Early accounts of life in St. John's reported sightings of drunken children staggering around the streets in public view, enslaved by alcohol at an early age.

Alcohol was used even more nefariously with regard to the Indigenous population. For example, Sebastian Cabot, the son of John Cabot, instructed the English soldier and explorer Sir Hugh Willoughby that "The natives of strange countries are to be enticed aboard and made drunk with your beer and wine for then you shall know the secrets of their hearts."[22]

John Guy and his men introduced alcohol to the Beothuk when they first encountered them at Trinity Bay in November of 1612, perhaps out of the kindness of their hearts, or perhaps following advice similar to Sebastian's. Colonist Henry Crout recounts their reaction to alcohol during an impromptu picnic with Guy and his crew:

> And so they made much sport together by the fire, making signs and tokens one to the other. So, afterwards, the governor went ashore and some three more carrying with him some biscuit, butter and beer. But they liked not very well our beer—they did drink very little of it—but the aquavitae did like them well.[23]

IN LABRADOR A SLIGHTLY DIFFERENT SITUATION WITH ALCOHOL evolved. Of course, the visiting seamen from Newfoundland, Quebec, and America brought their alcohol with them, doling it out freely to fishermen and sealers on board the ships, and no doubt selling some to the white settlers. The Indigenous peoples of Labrador, however, initially had no alcohol of their own and, when first introduced, had "an aversion to it," according to Governor Palliser in 1765. He issued a proclamation ordering the settlers not to trade strong liquor with the Indigenous population. Certain factions kept up their efforts to sell the product on the coast, however, and the American traders pushed their rum and other goods in exchange for fish in places like Labrador Harbour, Red Bay, and Cape Charles. Despite the best efforts of the Moravian Missionaries to preach about the dangers of alcohol use, Indigenous people travelled south in the summer to acquire the forbidden fruits.[24]

When the migratory fishery transitioned into a more domestic inshore fishery in the late eighteenth century, settlement increased, and with it came more economic diversity. Due to the scarcity of cash, the truck system, which had been in place since the early days of settlement, allowed merchants to fix the price of fish and trade goods to fisherman in exchange for their catch. Many fishermen found themselves deep in debt to the merchants. Other times, if the fishery failed, fishermen still had to rely on merchants for the necessary supplies. The fisherman's habit of depending on the merchant for everything made him vulnerable, so it would have been easy for certain merchants to push alcohol on fishermen to increase their own profits. With the scarcity of coin and alcohol's portability and easy accessibility, it could also be used to pay for fish or labour. Planters sometimes took advantage of their sharemen and fish servants, paying out part of their daily wages in rum.[25] There is no doubt fishermen suffered financially and spiritually, often victimized by a corrupt system.

Despite attempts to control drinking, liquor offences were not always taken too seriously. First of all, very little in the way of law enforcement existed at that time, and secondly, many of the merchants made good money off the alcohol trade and had no wish to see anything curtail their sales. So, it is no surprise that in mid-1700s St. John's, after Charles Patten was charged with illegally selling liquor, he was immediately given a licence to do so legally. A blind eye was often turned in cases concerning alcohol and alcohol sales.

Corruption abounded, and those who had curried favour with local officials received land grants and other privileges. One of the local publicans, a man by the name of Stripling, had friends in high places and received a nice package of land, just outside of St. John's on Quidi Vidi Lake. Although completely illiterate, he was appointed a justice and a sheriff. He, along with two other St. John's judges, made a tidy fortune selling liquor licenses and fining drunks. They sold a total of 108 licences in 1784. Since the magistrates and constables had no set salaries, they kept instead a portion of the fines and licence fees. This situation allowed for great abuses. In one case they levied a large fine on one man for being drunk and using improper language. The three magistrates then divided this money between themselves. Licenses sold in 1784, at four and a half guineas apiece, were split 50/50 between themselves and the public fund. Anyone with enough wealth who committed a crime in the town could usually buy off the justices,[26] but the poor had no hope.

Four justices of the peace wrote a letter on October 23, 1794, stating that some of the small business people in town requested permission to sell alcohol in quantities less than the regulation five-gallon amount, and without coming under the designation of keepers of public houses. At that time, liquor could only be sold in quantities greater than five gallons if you didn't own a pub with a liquor licence. These businessmen agreed to pay the same sum as that paid by the licensed public houses, provided the justices of the peace waived their constabulary service. The authors of the letter felt it would "not have any evil tendency" and thought that since these businessmen had agreed to pay for the privilege, it would greatly help the public purse. The country's debt at that time stood at an oppressive £912 1 shilling 5 pence. These same magistrates stated that they would give up any claim they might have, by custom, to any of the monies raised by these new 'licenses' until some other source of money could be found to provide these urgently needed public funds.[27]

The authorities acquiesced, stating that to help service so oppressive a debt, permission could be given to those that "shall be well recommended for their orderly behavior and good conduct and who would wish [to] obtain it upon these terms, but an express condition that no less than a

Pint be sold to any one person and that no Liquer whatsoever be drank in their houses."[28]

As time went on, many fishermen, unable to get out from under their debilitating habits and crippling debts, fell more and more to alcohol.

In 1802, Governor Gambier, concerned about the drunkenness and filthy conditions of the old town, declared 36 public houses to be enough. He wanted only "commodious houses to front towards the harbour." Echoing, in even stronger terms, his predecessor Hugh Palliser, in his parting words before he left Newfoundland in 1808, offered up some other charming aspects of the town:

> I cannot take my departure from Newfoundland for the season without ear-
> nestly enjoining you to enforce with the utmost rigor the Laws made against
> Blasphemy, Profaneness, Adultery, Fornication, Polygamy, Profanation of
> the Lord's day, Swearing, Drunkenness and Immorality.[29]

What Gambier's harsh appraisal of Newfoundland failed to admit was that the laws set to control the population were often undermined by lucrative profiteering. While the powers that be berated the settlers for their drunkenness, they simultaneously sold the source of that drunkenness right back to them. This damaging paradox heightened as consumption went beyond moderation, threatening the social order and the stability of the workforce.

Up to this point, alcohol abuse was recognized as a dilemma affecting peace, order, and profitability, and there had been little concern for people's actual well-being. In the coming century, as settlements grew and social systems developed, attitudes changed greatly, and temperance became the watchword for many.

TEMPERANCE
The Rise of a Social Conscience

We are but few, toil tried, but true
And hearts beat high to dare and do.
Oh! There be those that ache to see
The day dawn of the Temperance victory.

—E. Doyle Wells[1]

ALCOHOL CONSUMPTION IN BRITAIN IN 1743, DURING THE infamous gin craze, reached 8.2 million gallons. This was without taking into account illegal gin production. By 1750 consumption had grown to 11 million gallons annually. Gin was all the rage at every level of society, but particularly among the poor. The burgeoning middle class began to take notice of the open drunkenness all around them, and by the nineteenth century, many public commentators openly opposed alcohol. Having developed a social conscience, they attempted to effect changes that would alleviate or at least minimize the hardship and suffering they witnessed in their towns and cities. Alcohol was recognized as a prime contributor to poverty, and a movement arose to moderate consumption—the Temperance Movement.

A Northern Irish Presbyterian preacher, John Edgar, started his temperance campaign in 1829 by pouring his whisky out the window onto the cobblestone street of Belfast. A little unnecessary perhaps, since the churches in Ireland initially preached moderation rather than total abstinence, not wanting to offend their drinking parishioners. But when Theobald Mathew (1790-1856), a Catholic priest from County Cork, opted for total abstinence and launched a major campaign, he won over about half the Irish population to the cause.

The news soon travelled to this part of the world, and one local St. John's newspaper, the *Newfoundlander*, reported that Father Mathew had enrolled 150,000 Dubliners in his movement and, perhaps as a result, 200 Dublin public houses had shut down.[2]

Theobald Mathew, a famous Irish cleric and temperance advocate. Father Mathew took his campaign to America in 1849-1851. We know that he had planned to visit Newfoundland to spur on the cause, but there is no evidence that he actually came. *Photo from author's private collection, Jubilee Volume of the St. John's Total Abstinence and Benefit Society 1858-1908.*

In nineteenth-century Newfoundland, tavern culture and drinking were firmly entrenched in daily life. Along with the many licensed establishments, 181 unlicensed shebeens (illegal public houses) crowded the few streets in St. John's, a town of about 12,000. This allowed one tavern for every 66 men, women, and children.[3] With no restrictions on clerical drinking until 1830, even clergy frequented the taverns. According to one visitor, Newfoundlanders—although good, honest, industrious people—would often get into the rum and be drunk for weeks on end, or as he put it, "fou for weeks thegither."[4]

The first ripple of temperance hit Newfoundland in 1833 when a contributor to the *Times*, a St. John's newspaper, wrote a letter to the editor suggesting the success of temperance societies in Britain and Ireland might be repeated in Newfoundland. The letter sparked a swift reaction. Just a week later, a notice of a public meeting to found a temperance society appeared in the same paper. On February 20, 1833, a group of local citizens formed the Newfoundland Temperance Society.[5]

Congregational and Methodist preachers gave the first fiery speeches, denouncing the heinous effects of evil alcoholic spirits from their church pulpits. It wasn't long before the Catholic Church picked up the banner. On October 2, 1841, during Mass, Bishop Michael A. Fleming, the newly appointed Roman Catholic bishop, stated the need for a grand temperance movement. Having witnessed the destruction on homes and families back in his birth country of Ireland, he spoke at length on the evils of alcohol. After Mass, to start the ball rolling, he administered the 'pledge' to many of both sexes. Within a month, over 3,000 had spoken these words: "I solemnly swear not to consume alcohol for a period of [a duration particular to the parishioner] from this day forward. I will seek the powerful intervention of Mary Our Mother of Perpetual Help that God in His divine mercy will help me daily to keep this solemn oath."[6]

By 1844, ten thousand people had signed up. This vow, taken before the priest, was known as *caging*, promising not to touch rum or spirits, either for a year or two, for the rest of their lives, or perhaps only while they stayed on shore.

Newfoundland temperance smouldered, at first, but burst into flame by mid-century, producing an army of very devoted followers.

At one meeting of the new Temperance Society, a zealous member even suggested renaming Newfoundland "Temperance Island." But how could they begin to change centuries of culturally ingrained alcohol consumption? One of their members, George Garrett, proposed that "the labouring man in this island, at certain times in the season required a stimulant in time of hard daily labour and the use of spruce beer or tea and coffee might [...] be quite useful and far more safe than the spirituous liquors now in use." Another member, William Johnston, recommended that, in an attempt to break old habits, coffee with grated nutmeg could be used as a substitute for alcohol. This had been "tried on several vessels within his knowledge, even at this bitter season of the year [February], with the most encouraging effect." As the meeting rolled on, sad stories on the debilitating effects of alcohol poured out and no doubt strengthened the resolve of all in attendance.[7]

To understand just how popular the movement had become, one need only read the report on a temperance parade printed in the *Newfoundlander* of January 1843, which paints a vivid picture of the time:

> It was therefore with no little degree of satisfaction that we witnessed the grand display which the Temperance Procession of Thursday last presented. The day would seem to have come on purpose to give éclat to the demonstration—so beautiful it was—so unusually mild for the season [...] The Procession could not have numbered less than 8000 persons, men, women and children whose respectable appearance and good and orderly demeanour were highly credible. They all wore the medals suspended by a ribbon and seemed each of them proud of the association in which they were placed. The procession moved through Water Street, Cochrane Street round Government house (where they were greeted by his Excellency) through the Military Road and through Duckworth Street accompanied by the band of the Newfoundland Companies and one or two Amateur Bands whose lively airs tended much to the invigorating character of the proceeding.
>
> The Rev. K. Walsh [the apostle of Temperance] and the Rev. J Forrestal headed the procession on horseback; the Farmers followed as equestrians, and then came the Fishermen, Mechanics, etc. in distinct bodies— the women bringing up the rear—the post of honour being very gallantly assigned to them.[8]

The fight for moderation or abstinence would turn out to be quite a battle, as many still rejected the cause. The centuries-old custom of using alcohol as a work incentive and manipulative substance had worked more in the name of upper-class profit than as a benefit to society. Bishop Fleming expressed a particular concern for the boys in the fishery drinking tots three times a day. Fleming preached about the need for a religious order to come from England to teach and care for these boys, putting them on the straight and narrow path rather than in the workforce and on the bottle.

The use of alcohol as a work incentive on land also thwarted the temperance cause. Serving up daily tots continued to encourage alcohol usage, although several people bravely tried to change this aspect of the town's drinking habits. A Scotsman by the name of Mr. Wullie [T. William] Johnston, a managing partner of the old firm of Baine Johnston, tried watering down the grog. This worked for a while, but when he took it too far, his employees rebelled.

The merchant and politician Robert Job was the first business person to take a firm stand against this serving of daily tots. In time, many of his fellow merchants followed his example. Newfoundland dock workers still took their 'rum break' up until the late 1800s, and the Newman firm may have been the last in St. John's to discontinue the practice of serving the daily tot to employees.

Another churchman, Anglican Archdeacon Edward Wix, complained of seeing girls on the west coast of the island given their rum ration before breakfast: "Girls of 14 may be seen taking their 'morning' of raw spirits before breakfast and then repeated a second time before a 7 am breakfast."[9] This cavalier employment of alcohol as a form of motivation was widespread in the mid-nineteenth century and suggests that the state of the working-class in Newfoundland at this time was very much in "an altered state."

Beyond the workplace, politicians consistently plied the common folks with distilled spirits in an effort to sway votes. As the words of a popular ditty attested, people in positions of power used alcohol to their own advantage:

To win the political battle I've come,
And to win it, I'm certain, there's nothing like rum.[10]

Even after Newfoundland gained responsible government in 1855, politicians continued to use booze shamelessly to buy votes, often at great personal expense and, in some cases, financial ruin for the candidates whether they won or not. The candidate with the most money to spend treated his constituents to a stiff drink as voting occurred, and this could often sway the vote. In those days, before secret ballots, the tellers counted votes according to what side of the room you stood on. Those favouring a particular candidate stood on one side of the room while those favouring the other candidate stood on the other side. Voters could change their vote and walk to the other side if a politician enticed them over with liquor.[11] It soon became evident that alcohol and politics made for a bad marriage, often fuelling religious-faction fighting. In the way of small victories, the statutes of 1892 prohibited the sale of alcohol on election day.

At the dawn of the new century, in 1909, Archbishop Michael Francis Howley took on the monumental task of trying to stop the custom of *treating* within his Catholic flock. Treating meant to buy friends and acquaintances a round of drinks. They, in turn, reciprocated, creating an ongoing series of mutual exchanges until all members of the company were sufficiently legless. From the pulpit, Howley suggested that great benefits might be seen by establishing an "Anti-Treating League." The Archbishop hoped that eliminating this practice would stave off the excesses of intoxicating drinks and encourage sobriety and moderation. He encouraged his parishioners to turn down a drink if offered one by someone else. He didn't say they couldn't buy one for themselves, but simply encouraged them to avoid the treating trap.[12] Changing this well-ingrained social habit proved to be a very difficult task. Alcohol acted as a sort of social currency, strengthening or mending relations over a drink or two. In the all-male establishment of the tavern, treating and drinking, socializing, and sharing the news enhanced male solidarity.

The press played an important role in the decline of public drunkenness as well, with some newspapers even banning ads for spirits of any sort. They raised awareness of the evils of drink by publishing articles like the *Morning Courier*'s report in 1844 on 22-year-old John Boyle, who "came to his death by intemperance." These reports probably coloured public opinion, especially when they included particularly foreboding statements: "That should serve as a warning to all who happen unfortunately to be addicted to this vile propensity."[13] The printed media of the time employed various ways and means to inform the public of the risks of heavy drinking. A somewhat tongue-in-cheek ad appeared in the 1849 Harbour Grace *Weekly Herald*:

100 pounds reward: Run away from the subscriber, his whole estate, consisting of a good house, store and trade and above all, a good name. They gradually disappeared, being decoyed by a demonic fellow named INTEMPERANCE. Any person who will restore the aforesaid property and bring the offender to justice, shall receive the reward. If the gratitude of a broken-hearted wife and the joyful thanks of half-starved children are of any value, they will be given with the reward.[14]

Later, in the *Weekly Herald* of March 8, 1854, "A friend of Temperance" wrote a letter to the editor stating:

I am happy to hear the temperance cause is making such rapid progress in St. John's and in Conception Bay and although we have had no soirees, tea meetings, processions etc. yet we have been endeavouring to propel onward this grand engine of moral regeneration. Many in their place and neighbourhood have rallied around the standard of temperance.[15]

The "friend" reported that 2,800 people had signed a petition to bar transportation of liquor to the colony and that 500 more had taken the pledge. He added that among those who signed, "Many [are] largely engaged in the trade, but who seem disgusted with their business and who would gladly see its importation prohibited."[16]

Despite small gains from the temperance movement, *The Banner of Temperance*, a temperance newspaper printed in St. John's, published statistics for 1850 stating that 100 people were incarcerated each month for drunkenness. In the first month of 1851 alone, thirty were incarcerated.[17]

While most of the historical records documenting the temperance movement in Newfoundland focus on St. John's, the movement spanned far beyond the island's political and economic power centre. In Labrador, Sir Wilfred Grenfell travelled around the coast by ship, giving medical care to people, settling disputes, and condemning the drink. With no liquor licenses allowed in Labrador, selling liquor was technically illegal, and Grenfell took great pleasure in hunting down offenders, remarking to an acquaintance that "soon there would not be a bottle left in Labrador, much less anything in it to drink." But the battle continued with the

"Jersey firms" doling out brandy 'on tap.' The firm of De Quettville employed about 250 men and served out five glasses of brandy to each man daily. The Hudson's Bay Company gave rum to members of the various Indigenous nations as payment for work.[18]

AMONG THE MANY TEMPERANCE SOCIETIES AND LEAGUES THAT EMERGED in Newfoundland, perhaps the longest running was the Total Abstinence and Benefit Society, with branches in communities all around the Avalon Peninsula. A St. John's blacksmith by the name of William McGrath

William McGrath initially proposed the idea of an abstinence society and held a meeting at his forge in 1858. *Photo from author's private collection, Jubilee Volume of the St. John's Total Abstinence and Benefit Society 1858–1908.*

initially proposed the idea of an abstinence society and held a meeting at his forge in 1858. Keen to work for the cause, William had taken the abstinence pledge under Father Kyran Walsh, "The Apostle of Temperance in Newfoundland." Along with John Donnelly, John Myrick, John Sheehan, Patrick Reardon, Philip Hally, Thomas O'Brien, William Vinnicombe, Henry Hewett, and Charles Kickham, who all came to the forge that day, they formed the Total Abstinence Society (later to be renamed the Total Abstinence and Benefit Society or TABS for short). Kickham, a carpenter by trade, became the first president of the society. One friend, a barrister named John Little, drafted the rules and regulations. Open to men, women, and children of all religious persuasions in Newfoundland, and bent on being beneficial, the society sponsored literary, musical, and theatrical events as alternative entertainments to drink. To change a culture that for so long had done very little else but drink as a form of entertainment would be no mean feat.

The object of the society was to "Shield its members from the use of all intoxicating drinks and to afford relief in case of sickness or death: to elevate their individual characters as men and Christians."[19]

TABS went by the motto "Be sober and watch." Its members came from "the very best classes in the community" and were composed largely of men who had been abstainers all their lives. Its members swore the following oath:

> I pledge myself with the Divine Assistance that as long as I shall continue a member of this Society I will abstain from all intoxicating liquors unless for medical or religious purposes and that I will discountenance intemperance in others.[20]

Many shades of abstention existed in the various groups. The Daughters and Sons of Temperance, the Good Templars, and the Women's Christian Temperance Union (WCTU), favoured total abstention and prohibition, while other groups preached moderation.

Women weighed in heavily on the side of temperance, perhaps because they were quite often the victims of violence and abuse caused by drinking. In the past, women were encouraged to follow advice similar to that provided by this anonymous 'conduct manual' from eighteenth-century England. *The Whole Duty of a Woman: Or, An Infallible Guide to the Fair Sex*, offered guidance for women living with heavy drinkers: "It will be no new thing for a Woman to have a Drunkard for her Husband [...] and yet a Wife may live too without being miserable." It goes on to suggest that no one's life is perfect and that if a woman finds herself on the worst side of a drunkard, terrible as it is, she should look on the bright side and be thankful her husband has faults, because "A Husband without Faults is a dangerous Observer. He hath an Eye so piercing and sees everything so plain." In fact, the author proposes the benefit of drunkenness since a husband will fail to see his wife's faults through the "veil of

A cartoon from the 1800s showing women as warriors in the battle against drinking and its evils. *Image in public domain. CC-BY-SA-3.0.*

wine." It advises women to greet their inebriated husbands with kindness. Because men wrote most of the books for and about women at the time, this must have seemed either quite plausible or exceedingly hopeful from a male perspective.[21]

With those days long gone, women were free to speak out, and they exerted a strong influence on the temperance movement. They certainly made their point when it came to the St. John's Regatta, viewed by many as an annual orgy of alcohol. Many men looked on the Regatta as an excuse to overindulge, and drinking binges sometimes continued for weeks after the big day. This resulted in men skipping work and wasting away money meant to feed and clothe their families. The women left at home to deal with the fallout smouldered with rage, and business owners sputtered when workers did not turn up for their shifts. So great was the problem of drinking and rowdiness at the Regatta, that the ladies of St. John's boycotted the event in 1828. A journalist in the *Newfoundlander* offered this interpretation of the women's refusal to attend:

> About the hour appointed for starting, we felt rather disappointed that the banks of the beautiful sheet of water were not lined with so brilliant an assemblage of female beauty [...] We do not, however, imagine for a moment that the disagreeable weather was the sole cause of the non-attendance of so many of our fashionables. No: we feel assured that it was a just and necessary retaliation upon their parts for the inattention with which they have been treated for the last three or four years; and, certainly, they

could not adopt a more effectual mode of punishment than by absenting themselves from *every* scene of amusement, and proving to the beaus how joyless and dim, such places are, when not enlivened by their smiles [...] We would strongly recommend the Ladies, until a proper return (and such a one as they are led to expect) be made for all their kindness, to persevere in this line of conduct, and they will soon be enabled to dictate their own terms.[22]

Other temperance types soon joined the fray and made their views known about the Regatta. Opposition grew, and the future of the races became less secure. By 1846 the opposing parties managed to stop the event completely. Revived again in 1851 by staunch Regatta supporters, it ran a scant few years before officials cancelled it again for ten years in 1860. The Regatta returned in 1871, but the drunkenness continued, and calls came to increase the police presence at the event and restrict the number of liquor licences.[23]

Everyone seemed in agreement that liquor sales needed to be curbed in some way, and the temperance groups successfully lobbied government for change. The consolidated statutes of 1871 stated that people wishing to sell alcohol had to have a licence issued on a yearly basis, and that licence had to be placed, visible for all to see, over the door of the retailer's premises. Those who sold intoxicating liquors without this licence displayed would be fined $25. The government defined intoxicating liquors as all ales, wines, malt, brewed or spirituous liquors containing two percent or more of alcohol by volume. This included Bavarian beer and botanic beer as well.[24] Things were tightening up.

In the northern and western regions of the country, the introduction of the 'local option' brought victories to the temperance cause. The Newfoundland Temperance League, a Protestant group, had convinced the governor to pass the Temperance Act of 1871. This Act gave voters in each electoral district the power to control, by a two-third majority, the number of licenses issued to sell spirituous liquors within the boundaries of that district. By limiting the number of licenses, they hoped to remove the social temptation to drink.

BY THE 1880S, MANY TOWNS OUTSIDE OF ST. JOHN'S EXERCISED these local-option rights and prohibited the sale of intoxicating liquors. These included communities in Trinity Bay, Bonavista Bay, Twillingate, Burgeo and LaPoile, Fogo, Burin, St. George's including the whole of the Bay of Islands, and the districts of Carbonear, Harbour Grace, and Port-de-Grave.[25] St. John's, however, voted the local option down.

The next step in the efforts to control alcohol use was to regulate the opening hours of taverns. In the nineteenth century, the 'take-out' method meant you could send someone down with a jug or a tankard and have the publican fill it up and send it back to you. If you had the time, you would simply buy it on the premises and consume it wherever you pleased. The only way to regulate this free-for-all was to enforce set opening hours for the supplier.

The License Act of 1875 decreed that public houses could open at 6 a.m. and close at 10 p.m. between April 1 and December 31 (the fishing season), but in the winter, from January 1 up to and including March 31, public houses had slightly reduced hours, opening from 7 a.m. until 9 p.m. No alcohol could be sold on Sundays, Christmas Day, or Good Friday. With the drinking age set at sixteen, tavern owners could be fined fifty dollars for allowing underage drinkers on their premises.

Things seemed to be changing for the better. In his address to a public meeting at the Temperance Hall on December 27, 1879, Judge Prowse stated:

> Last Christmas Eve as I watched the numbers of drunken men and half tipsy boys that I saw about our streets, I felt almost inclined to despair. It seemed as if all the lifelong exertions of my friend here, the Chairman, all the good work done by the Sons of Temperance, the Temperance Journal, the Total Abstinence Society and all the other Temperance organizations in this town had been labour in vain; but that seeing was only a momentary feeling. I feel and shall be prepared to prove by and by that temperance has made a great progress in the colony.[26]

Prowse went on to provide statistics of arrests in St. John's and some of the outlying harbours. Including foreign sailors, the number of arrests for drunkenness and for disorderly conduct came to only 527 for the year of

1879. But he hastened to add that the communities out west and north who opted for the local option reported no arrests for drunk and disorderly conduct.

Temperance followers believed if men's drinking habits could be controlled, more money would be freed up to care for families. They made use of an abundance of anti-drinking material such as magic lantern shows, which spread the message with tragic stories of alcoholic fathers and suffering damsels. The wildly popular *Ten Nights in the Bar-Room* played at the town hall in Twillingate in 1888. Many of these temperance stories had maudlin but happy endings (once the offender had sworn off drink), others ended in predictable tragedy—the death of the drunkard or some close family member.

To further the cause, advocates of temperance advised women to refuse any intemperate young men entrance into their drawing rooms and advocated the mantra, "Lips that touch liquor shall never touch mine," reasoning that romantic banishment would soon make drinking unpopular.

And local women, often the victims of alcohol abuse, wholeheartedly supported this. In 1890, The Women's Christian Temperance Union formed to put an end to public drunkenness and the domestic abuse that often came with it:

> Women are the greatest sufferers by strong drink and if there is any enjoyment in it, it is the men who are enjoying the gilded saloon. The poor woman is often found freezing over the fireless stove or listening to the cries of her poor hungry, cold, ragged children, and not knowing the moment she will receive a blow from the wretch she is forced to call husband.[27]

The women's movement started on a moderate platform, but soon became more audacious in their attempts to curb consumption. A women's temperance publication, the *Water Lily*, printed the names of politicians who abstained and those who didn't. It stated that those who did not abstain supported and even profited from "spreading death, destruction, ruin and degradation."

Leading temperance adherent Elizabeth Neyle claimed that the working and labouring classes, men and women, spent two thirds of their hard-earned wages in public houses. Her counterpart, suffragist and leading member of the WCTU, Jessie Ohman, asserted that alcohol and tobacco usage caused two-thirds of the city's poverty.[28]

The temperance cause had found a strong ally in the women's movement. Women had found their voices and they were putting them to good use.

And so the faithful struggled on. With slogans reminiscent of communist and labour movement calls for solidarity—"Trade, Industry and Happiness," "Triumph of Temperance," "Piety, Union and Peace"—the advocates of abstention continued to preach the idea that temperance brought prosperity. This consistent forward march—which included education, regulation of sales, and the local option for prohibition—substantially reduced alcohol consumption on the island from 270,000 gallons per year to 98,000 gallons by 1888,[29] but the war raged on.

Alcohol had always had its detractors, but the advancement of Enlightenment ideals, the belief in individual freedom and a wish to improve human existence, helped empower the Temperance Movement in Newfoundland. This movement, backed by the church and forward-thinking citizens, discouraged the decision to drink, not so much as a moral choice based on the damnation of the individual soul, but focused instead on the health of the community. The Temperance movement ushered the country into the twentieth century, and with it came more voices, louder voices, calling for a complete ban on the sale and importation of liquor.

PROHIBITION

Extreme Measures

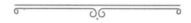

Hark ye voters, hear the bugle
Calling to the fray
Prohibition is our watchword
Right shall win the day.

—Frank J. Sibley.[1]

THE TEMPERANCE MOVEMENT HAD ALREADY MADE GREAT gains convincing people to drink moderately, but for some, this was not enough. The local option system already existed in many areas in Newfoundland, but St. John's continued to be a sticking point. The vote for local option came to the districts of St. John's East and West for a second time on March 3, 1909. Again, it failed to pass. In other areas of the island, the option passed by majority or with no opposition at all.[2] For the common person around the bay, local option made little difference. Public houses were few and with limited policing, homebrew could fill the need. In St. John's, however, tavern culture dominated the town's social life and a good part of the local economy. Any attempt to limit the industry in the capital was met with resistance. The dream of eradicating alcohol from our society, championed by prohibitionists, created a bitter debate. Moderates fought back hard, and it took some time for the prohibitionists to see their legislation passed. Eventually, those who were against the act were talked into and, in some cases, tricked into allowing it to pass. The end game of prohibition was certainly attractive. The abolition of alcohol from society painted a utopian picture of happiness and prosperity for all, particularly for the women and children in Newfoundland society.

When the first vote to introduce prohibition to the whole of Newfoundland was held on April 18, 1887, the speaker of the house, J. A. W. McNeily, cast the deciding vote, breaking a 17-to-17 tie, and defeating the bill. Undeterred by this defeat, the prohibitionists' fervour raged on.

A corresponding fire burned in the breasts of the anti-prohibitionists as well. The merchant class and the captains of St. John's, whose livelihood depended on the transport and sale of rum, stood to lose a lot of money. In addition, many prominent merchants held shares in the Bennett Brewing Company, and prohibition would have eliminated their incomes from that venture. These groups openly campaigned against prohibition. It is also probable the working class of St. John's would not have found prohibition too thrilling, especially not the thought of losing any daily tots.

To resolve what had become a contentious public issue, the government held a plebiscite (an advisory referendum) on November 4, 1915. Prohibition would become the law of the land as long as the majority of voters in the referendum supported it and as long as that majority represented 40 percent of the total registered voters on the island. The 1913 electoral list had set the number of possible voters in Newfoundland at 61,473, so the prohibitionists had to both win the referendum and achieve a vote total of at least 24,589.

But the licensed liquor sellers, who organized a committee to fight prohibition, somehow misunderstood the process and encouraged people not to vote. The head of the committee convinced his followers that refusing to vote would be the same as voting no. They misunderstood the criteria of the referendum, thinking that the prohibitionists had to achieve a majority of the entire population of the country. As a result, all the licensed premises put out signs that read, "If you don't want prohibition, don't vote"! This gave the prohibitionists an upper hand. The "wets" followed instructions and didn't vote; the "dries" (prohibitionists) came out in force.

During the campaign, convinced by the power of their convictions and to ensure their victory, the dries played on the well-established enmity between "baymen" and "townies." There are reports that, in their travels around the outports, prohibitionists misled potential voters, telling them prohibition would only apply to St. John's residents. They assured baymen they would still be allowed their half-yearly allowance of a keg of rum. Unfortunately, this would not be the case.

In the end, there was a low voter turnout of 30,324—less than 50 percent of registered voters. Of those voters, 24,977 elected for prohibition. The dries had achieved both of their objectives: they won the referendum and reached, just barely, 40 percent of voters.[3] Sixteen electoral districts voted yes, and only two voted no.

The prohibitionists rejoiced. A newspaper editorial of January 1, 1917, summed it up: "Today [Newfoundland] enters a new era that will be fraught with increased prosperity to her people, because money that was wasted [on alcohol] will be diverted to provide comforts and necessities of life."[4] Unfortunately, it did not turn out that way.

The anti-prohibitionists did not give up without a fight. They filed petitions in the Supreme Court alleging irregularities in the conduct of the election officials. They claimed that no returning officer had been duly appointed; no legal counting of the votes had taken place; no proper returns of the number of votes polled existed; persons purporting to be returning officers improperly counted the ballot papers; and persons under the age of 21 had voted.[5] All to no avail. Powerful people in the pro-camp included the likes of Sir Richard Squires, an ambitious justice minister in the government at that time, and William Coaker, founder of the Fisherman's Protective Union and staunch prohibitionist. Coaker, a total abstainer, helped keep the prohibition flame burning brightly from 1917 until 1923.

When prohibition came into effect on January 1, 1917, all the taverns and saloons closed, and owners with stocks of liquor to sell had until August to get rid of them. Outside of this, the law stated that any individual with alcohol in his possession—bought, manufactured, or imported into the colony after the first day of January 1917—would be liable to a penalty of not less than $50 and not exceeding $500 or, in default of payment, imprisonment not exceeding three months.[6] In our currency today, this would translate to a hefty sum: approximately $1,100 and not exceeding $11,000.[7] The government, through an appointed controller, assumed authority over the greatly reduced trade in spirits, permitting only alcohol for medicinal or sacramental purposes to enter the country.

This really threw the liquor importers into a tizzy. Letters flew back and forth as to whether Port wine could be brought into Newfoundland and held in bond. The request went to the Minister of Justice on August 15, 1916, where it was denied, stating that, under the act, no intoxicating liquors could be imported except for medicinal and sacramental purposes. The high commissioner of London wrote saying they had been approached by Hunt, Roop, Teage and Company of Oporto basically asking the same question. The letter from Hunt, Roope, Teage and Company, penned by Robert Newman, pointed out that "It seems a pity that a business that has been going on for so long—some hundreds of years anyhow, should come to an end for really no reason because it will not affect Newfoundland itself in any way except detrimentally, as the handling of the wines requires labour, hence wages." The matter didn't get settled until October 28, 1919, when the Newfoundland government finally stated that "Port wine could be imported in bond for sacramental purposes and for use of the Controller, in transitu."[8] That meant it was okay as long as it was stored "in bond" at the government warehouse to be shipped on after its maturation.

The British Consul General of Philadelphia inquired as to whether or not whisky could be shipped to Newfoundland in bond and then exported out of bond. He was given permission to do so with a storage limit of two years and the rates of 15 cents per barrel for the first month and 10 cents for each succeeding month.[9] These accommodations were to have far-reaching future consequences and led to great abuses in both high and low echelons of society.

After prohibition passed, things went well for a while, and the police reported a sharp decline in the number of arrests for drunkenness. But this was a society that, since the 1600s, had had alcoholic beverages built into their meal plans. From small beer to the daily tot, pulling the plug left a landscape so arid that many in the population went to great lengths to re-establish the status quo. Individuals found many creative ways to access alcohol through both the medicinal and sacramental supplies of liquor.

For the most part, the churches behaved themselves, and the sacramental use of alcohol remained sacred. The act stated that each religious denomination could appoint one person of that faith to act as importer of alcohol for religious purposes. The controller allowed each denomination to import its own wines. The import invoices were then initialled by the controller when shipments arrived. A nice system, but certainly not foolproof, as shown when R. S. Frelich embarrassed the Jewish community by selling large quantities of the sacramental liquor he had acquired. During a search of his premises, the police turned up several gallons of rum and two bottles of whisky. Mr. Frelich explained the whisky was for sacramental purposes. He didn't mention his plans for the several gallons of rum. He stated that the controller held a document signed by a number of individuals from the Jewish community, granting him authority to procure liquor for religious purposes.

Mr. Israel Perlin, who founded the synagogue in St. John's, confirmed that a request had been made to the controller for an amount of spirituous liquor for sacramental purposes, but the controller objected to each person getting an amount, and when certain individuals appointed Samuel Frelich to oversee distribution, Mr. Perlin refused to add his name to the controller's document as he did not consider Mr. Frelich an appropriate representative of the Jewish community in this matter. He stated that he was aware the liquor received by Mr. Frelich was not used for the purposes intended.[10]

Such instances within the religious community were rare, but the medical use of alcohol provided numerous opportunities to take advantage of the system. Still clinging to the belief that alcohol could cure certain ailments, the government allowed doctors to prescribe it for medical conditions. The controller granted licences directly to medical practitioners and druggists. Both parties could dispense alcohol, but only doctors could write up the prescriptions. Doctors and druggists had to keep written records of the prescriptions issued and those that had been filled. Each party had to submit a monthly report to the controller.

Prescriptions for alcohol cost from $1 to $2 each. These "scripts" or "scrips" allowed the recipient to obtain spirits. The legal limit for a script was eight ounces of spirits, one dozen pint bottles of stout, porter, ale, or beer every two weeks, or 24 ounces of port wine, claret, sherry, or even champagne.

Doctors could keep their own stores of liquor and dispense it, some keeping supplies of only a few gallons, while others kept puncheons. Pestered to insanity day and night, doctors had to deal with not only legitimate patients, but also with friends, acquaintances, and every Tom, Dick, or Harry looking for a drink. Certain doctors confessed to writing scripts just to get rid of the individuals plaguing them with requests.

If an individual had the financial means and could find a liberal doctor, they could buy up to a dozen allowances. They just had to say they had eleven sick friends, give the names to the doctor, and then walk away with 12 eight-ounce bottles.

Local law-abiding citizens, not too pure to sully their hands, bought alcohol through the local bootleggers as well, but if you were having an event and needed alcohol in larger quantities, you could still use the script method to take advantage of the controller's stockpile. Organizers for a local banquet, involving many respectable citizens, sent out a letter which came to be known as the *Medicine Circular*, in order to procure the necessary libation for the event. It read:

> An effort will be made to obtain for members attending the dinner such medicine as each member may require [...] Members' individual orders will be supplied in packages addressed to them upon arrival at the scene, and positively no medicine can be supplied unless ordered one week before the dinner. The price charged for the medicine will be the usual drug store prices and cheque or money must accompany all orders [...]. Write what you require on back of this form and send same to Secretary.[11]

Some went beyond the bending of rules into outright criminality. If the doctor stood his ground and refused to provide a script, other opportunities sometimes arose. Legitimate scripts could be stolen from the doctor's office. The perpetrator then forged the doctor's handwriting and signature and made scripts out to innocent individuals such as outport clergymen. They then cashed them in for that individual. For those who lacked the nerve for such bold thievery, it was possible to simply buy counterfeit scripts from obliging printers who could print copies of the real thing. It wasn't long before the generous number of prescriptions began to raise a few eyebrows.

The earliest version of the act allowed a physician to prescribe the medicine "in larger quantities if necessary" to a patient. This left it wide open. It soon became a national joke about who was really sick and who was shamming. Doctors were hauled into court on charges of abusing the script, but the Act did say "8 oz or larger quantities if necessary." This made a mockery of such cases. The defence was simple. "Who but a doctor is the best judge of what is necessary for his patient [...]. It would be a rank injustice and most unfair if the court could step in between a doctor and his patient and deny the doctor the right to prescribe what in his opinion was necessary for the patient."[12]

Something had to be done. On August 8, 1917, the Governor in Council appointed three people to a newly created Board of Liquor Control. On October 23, 1917, this board submitted changes to the act to deal with prescription abuse. Under the new changes, doctors and druggists could only prescribe alcohol that was 20 percent under proof (about 11 percent ABV, alcohol by volume), and they could only give out eight ounces per patient in St. John's and twelve ounces outside of St. John's with no more than one prescription per week. Doctors could only prescribe up to the aggregate amount of three gallons (about 13.6 litres) per month of hard liquor in St. John's and four and a half gallons outside. Of wines, beers, ales etc., they could prescribe up to five gallons in a month.

In further attempts to tighten the system, new regulations dictated that prescriptions had to be written on printed, numbered forms supplied by the controller. The controller now had to keep a separate record for each practitioner or druggist, and they had to submit a statement to the board on Monday of each week showing the number of prescriptions given out for liquor. Even this system had problems.

In one humorous instance, a certain local doctor with notoriously bad handwriting gave out a script and a payment receipt for treatment to one of his patients. When the patient handed in what he though was a script to the druggist, he received his bottle of Scotch unchallenged. Only when he got home did he realize he had passed in his payment receipt and not the script in his pocket.[13]

Another rather ridiculous situation arose in the case of gin. Because gin had not been popular in Newfoundland before prohibition, the controller was unsure whether it should be classed as a spirit or a wine, and so it became possible to get a 24-ounce bottle of gin as a substitute for wine, instead of the eight ounces allowed for spirits.

The amendment also stated:

> In acute illnesses such as pneumonia, typhoid, septicaemia, etc. medical practitioners will be able to prescribe any amount necessary for such patients subject to the discretion of the Controller. Extra amounts may be added, but must be marked "Special Case." If an aged person needs an extra amount above the 8 oz. prescribed, the practitioner may prescribe up to 14 oz. a week. The prescription must be marked "aged person."[14]

Despite these additional regulations, sales of liquor for medicinal purposes during prohibition climbed from $60,462 in 1917, to $467,583 in 1921.[15]

The prosperity promised by the prohibitionists never came to pass, and disillusionment soon set in. Instead of alcohol disappearing, even worse abuses started. Although many thought of prohibition as a great reform, others thought it a great mistake, a great annoyance, and an opportunity for the government to interfere with private behaviour.

When the regulations on scripts tightened, the next domino in the game fell—patent medicines. Along with hair tonics and flavouring essences, these products were freely available over the counter and contained alcohol, which acted as the medicinal ingredient in some, as a preservative in others, and as a flavour extractor in the essences. The bay crowd had known about this for years, using these handy alternatives when other sources of alcohol dried up.

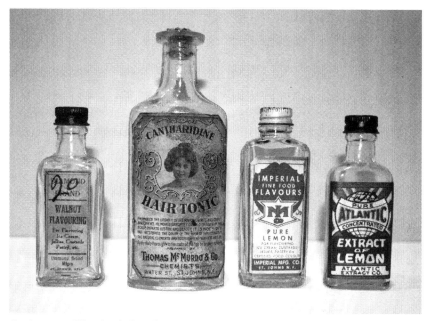

A selection of 'dope' including flavouring extract, hair tonic and patent medicines. *Photo by author; items courtesy of John Wicks.*

For a time, retailers experienced a boom in business for these products, but it did not go unnoticed. The consumption of dope, as it was known, gradually grew in spite of the partial blacklisting of particular products.

A Constabulary Diary entry from September 13, 1920, says "Within the past week two drunks was arrested and on each of their persons was found a bottle each of a brand of flavouring Extract of Vanilla, known as (Red Feather) Tincture [...] Mr. Davies the public Anilist informed me that he have found 29 1/2 % of Alcohol in this brand."[16]

Government analyst James Davies found that a bottle of Brown's Bronchial Elixir, confiscated from one Alice Walsh, contained 70.46 proof spirit, or 40.20 percent alcohol by volume. Probably a popular choice.[17]

A letter from Inspector General of the Constabulary, M.H.C. to the Deputy Minister of Justice, Mr. P. J. Summers reported that "The Assyrians on Gower Street were selling large quantities of Nervilene, Essence of Vanilla and similar articles." Head Constable Byrne found over fifty empty cases and bottles on the floor of the Tompkins hop-beer

shop on a visit he conducted one night. Displaying a common racial bias
for the time, he unabashedly wrote:

> The Assyrians are purchasing wholesale and selling at a price that is bring-
> ing them in large profits." He continued with "This class of business is not
> been done by our own people, but by these Foreigners, who take advantage
> of any and every situation to coin money regardless of results to our people,
> and particularly to our men returning from Over-Seas.[18]

During Constable Byrne's visit, he learned, according to the owner of the
hop bar, that men would purchase the extracts of vanilla and Nerviline (a
brand-name liniment claiming to remedy a host of ailments from aches
and pains, to colds and flatulence) elsewhere and then go to the hop bar
where they would purchase hop beer and pour the extract into it, and this
he was powerless to prevent. He said he did not see them put the extract
into their beer, but afterwards would find the empty bottles on the floor.[19]

In certain cases, people selling legal extracts and patent medicines
obtained new labels from local printers and attached them to the banned
substances in an attempt to hide their real contents.

Some creative types concocted a prohibition special called Hard Up,
a mixture of patent medicines: Beef, Iron and Wine (a patented "nutri-
tious tonic"); Bay Rum (an aftershave); Nerviline; and molasses. This
was so potent that "after a couple of glasses of the above mixture we
would recommend the services of a doctor, a minister, an undertaker and
a grave digger."[20]

Other enterprising individuals tried manufacturing their own intoxi-
cants with some concoctions containing as much as 16.2 percent alcohol.
Others contained no alcohol at all. One homemade mixture named Royal
Household sold for $1.50 a bottle, but contained nothing more than vine-
gar and water with a little artificial colouring. Some of the truly addicted
were reduced to drinking shoe polish diluted with water, and some even
drank wood alcohol, with deadly results.[21]

The government soon banned importations of these items except
under a licence given by the controller. No essence, tincture, compound,
or preparations described as a flavouring extract or essence containing

alcohol could be sold in quantities greater than two ounces to anyone at any time, and a record of any sale, with name and address of the purchaser, had to be kept by the seller. In addition, no peddler or trader by schooner entering Newfoundland could sell or dispose of any of the above.

The medical board was tasked with determining which drugs and medicines should be on a no-sell list. Dr. Rendell, the registrar for the medical board, referred to it as a very "knotty problem" as these patent medicines had long been referred to as the "poor man's physician" and it would be a great hardship to deny the poor this consolation. The board's solution was to label all patent medicines with the percentage of alcohol they contained. If the patent medicine had more alcohol than allowed under the prohibition act, then open sale would be prohibited. "Such preparations as Beef, Iron, & Wine, Wincarnis and Tincture of Ginger, are nothing less than an undiluted curse,"[22] Rendell stated. He added they should only be sold by prescription.

In the following years, many patent medicines made the intoxicating liquors list, including toilet waters, flavouring essences, or all other substances containing two percent alcohol or upwards. Some of the more popular products to make the list were:

Aftershaves	Patent medicines	Essences	Other
Bay Rum	Nerveline	Essence of Vanilla	Lavender water
Florida Water	Alvina	Essence of Lemon	Cologne
	Tanlac	Extract of Ginger	Nitrous ether
	Beef, Iron & Wine		Sweet spirits of nitre
	Wincarnis		Aromatic spirits of ammonia
	Hall's Balsam of Honey		Alcoholic perfumes
	Brown's Bronchial Elixir		Perfumed spirits

Moderates expressed opposition to these corrective measures. In the "As We See It" section of the *Daily Star*, the unnamed author blamed the extremists for pressuring the government towards continual amendments:

> Extremists—rather than trying to keep on amending the law to encompass all the mediums that contain alcohol (most contain from 50 to 75% alcohol for preservation purposes), their time would be better spent chasing the real offenders, the known drinkers and sellers of alcohol.[23]

The *Evening Telegram* of July 21, 1917, printed this complaint:

> There are dozens of intoxicating (and more or less poisonous) liquors with which a dipsomaniac can kill himself by degrees if he wishes; that is no reason why the rest of the public should be forbidden the benefit of their use.[24]

But for all those against it, many more were in favour of banning these products. Judge A. Penny of Carbonear wrote to the attorney general of Newfoundland enquiring as to whether Jamaica Ginger or Beef, Iron and Wine had been placed on the no-sell list since large quantities were being sold there as a beverage to "confirmed drunkards to the injury of families and themselves."[25]

Initially, some improvement came about after authorities blacklisted most of the essences and medicines. The number of people drinking dope seemed to decrease. But by 1919, when police began to keep a record of the causes of drunkenness, 20 percent more arrests for dope drinking occurred in that year than in 1917 and 1918. Of the 228 cases of drunkenness in 1919, 160 were due to dope, and of the 276 arrests in 1920, 198 were dope related, an increase of nearly 25 percent over 1919. Figures showed that in 1916 less than one-third of those arrested were disorderly. In 1920, about half of those arrested were disorderly. The assumption was that the use of dope or moonshine created far more disorder.[26] Moonshine production became so popular that, at one point, confiscated homemade stills filled a cell in the St. John's courthouse to the ceiling.[27]

The American term *moonshine* referred to the fact that the illegal production of liquor usually took place at night, away from prying eyes.

Moonshiners used all sorts of repurposed articles in the construction of their stills in Newfoundland, including automobile parts and even canisters from soda shops. Some of these parts added the delightful flavour of lead solder. Perhaps not very healthy for the drinker, but not as bad as some moonshine which, when analysed, showed the presence of poisonous fusel oil, a substance that could cause blindness.

Although the prohibitionists rejoiced when the Prohibition Act passed, their glee was short-lived. They discovered a general lack of sympathy for the cause amongst those in administration, combined with lax enforcement of the law. This apathy on the part of the authorities sabotaged their hopes and dreams of an alcohol-free society. It was easy to acquire liquor and easy to avoid punishment by the law. Laws that are not fully enforced often do more harm than good.

A July 2, 1919, letter to John R. Bennett from the minister of justice revealed how lenient the law could be on alcohol offenders. The courts convicted Arthur Sweetland, James Miles, and Jonathan Fifield of Bonavista for selling beer containing over two percent alcohol. Each was fined $100, and after having paid one-third of the amount, they protested against paying the balance. The government analyst came to their defence, suggesting additional fermentation may have taken place between the time when the men were taken by police at Bonavista and when he analyzed the samples. He stated that he could not swear under oath as to whether or not the alcohol was over the two percent allowed at the time they were arrested. The analyst stated that, when analyzed, the samples contained very little alcohol over the maximum allowed by law. This effectively quashed the case and the minister of justice recommended that the portion of the fines already paid should be repaid to the persecuted gentlemen.[28]

In another case, Gideon Bown, James Hefferton, John Hefferton, James Tulk, Alexander Perry, Edgar Norris, John Sainsbury, Kenneth Hoddinott, William Bungay, Joseph Parsons, Daniel Bungay, and Jacob Bungay were charged with having liquor in their possession. They were fined $100 each or one month in prison. Five of them paid their fines while the others claimed inability. They pleaded ignorance of the law and claimed they had been brewing for their own personal use. After surrendering their distilling equipment to the police, Mr. Warren, the minister of justice at the time, displayed sympathy for the men:

> I am of the opinion that much of the liquor distilled or brewed in this section of the country was for personal use and not for sale, and that if the prohibition law is harshly or strictly enforced it will become of very little value. If it becomes necessary to send them all to jail at Greenspond that building cannot accommodate such a number, besides the building is not heated, as owing to the stormy weather, and the loss of the "Dundee", that section of the country is without coal.[29]

He also stated that he thought they did not wilfully break the law and recommended a remission of $95 to each who had paid and that the others pay $5 each.

SMUGGLING, AN ADDITIONAL CRACK IN THE PROHIBITION ARMOUR, presented yet another means of procuring liquor. A letter of June 23, 1920, reports on the capture of smuggled liquor in Shores Cove. The constabulary received a letter from Cape Broyle accusing Mrs. Essey Carew of hiding liquor, which had been smuggled in on the schooner *Hagger*, in her house.

Constables O'Neill, Simmons, Dempsey, and Hutchings and Detective Tobin of H. M. Customs drove down the shore, and while one constable watched Arthur Carew's house, the other three went to search Mrs. Essey Carew's residence about 200 yards away. Two constables went in the front door, while the third constable entered by the back, where he found Mrs. Carew about to serve rum to three men sitting in her kitchen. When asked if she had any more liquor, she replied she did not. On searching the house, the officers turned up ten kegs of rum and eight of whisky under the floor boards. Thomas Carew (Essey's son) confessed to owning the liquor, but complained that he was now out a lot of money on the transaction! The constables transported the alcohol to St. John's, but rather than sending it to the bond store, they stored it in the police station as evidence.[30]

Among the local population, there was great sympathy for people caught breaking the liquor laws. A judge, sympathetic to one offender, displayed his bias on the subject:

> I am sorry that the law leaves me no choice but to impose this penalty; but my good man let it be a lesson to you; always remember that there is no sin in smuggling unless you're caught.[31]

Local law enforcement agents actually benefited financially from the confiscation of alcohol. When the police seized sixty gallons of rum and over three dozen bottles of whisky, all illegally imported, the inspector general of the constabulary asked that $200, a quarter of the value of the alcohol, be awarded for distribution amongst the members of the force who had been involved in the 'bust.' This was approved, and a sum of $200 was divided among the enforcement officers. Perhaps realizing this was not the best use of public funds, the situation changed in 1920, and they divided the fines collected from prohibition confiscations three ways: one-third to the Constabulary Widows and Orphans Fund, one-third to the informer, and one-third to the treasury.[32]

With all these complications, loopholes, and misapplications, the time for change had come. The two sides, pros and cons, squared off again and presented two petitions to the House of Assembly in 1920. A tug of war ensued between the moderates and the strict prohibitionists. The dries wanted the government to clamp down on every aspect of alcohol, prohibiting it in all shapes and forms, and wanted tighter controls on dope, scripts, smuggling, and the manufacture of moonshine.

The moderates felt prohibition had spawned these myriad abuses. They suggested the solution to the problem was to modify the act to enable people to obtain, under strict control, limited quantities, and to punish sellers who operated without a licence. In their opinion, the majority of people did not support the present act. The moderates had the foresight to see that "the tighter the noose, the more the abuse."

In response, the government appointed a Royal Commission to sort out the dog fight and suggest remedies for the situation. On September 18, 1920, the commission presented their report on the Prohibition

Plebiscite Act of 1915 and the amendments made to it. They gathered evidence from sworn testimonies, answers to interrogations, and police records. Well-informed and well-prepared, they presented their recommendations, but took the side of the prohibitionists, suggesting tighter controls on prescriptions and an augmented police force to deal with smuggling. They did suggest allowing the local manufacturing of beer and stout as long as it was sold only by the board of control. But no one took them up on this suggestion. At this point in time, they were unaware of just how bad things could get. The smuggling problem was about to increase exponentially.

Several factors brought about the growth of the illegal trafficking industry. Because of trade and local business interests in Newfoundland, prohibition regulations allowed alcohol to be stored "in bond" for periods of time before being shipped out of the country. These regulations created a wonderful loophole for smugglers. When the United States passed the Volstead Act, starting their prohibition (two years after Newfoundland), things began to get interesting. This big, thirsty nation to the south came looking for alcohol, and they found a wonderful supplier in the French islands of St. Pierre and Miquelon. The smuggling industry in Newfoundland bloomed. There was no more need of scripts, patent medicines, or moonshine. For those who could afford it, getting hold of the good stuff was suddenly easy and, for those selling it, very profitable. With the onset of the smuggling trade, large quantities of rum and whisky arrived in St. John's and the outports, making those obnoxious alcohol substitutes unnecessary. Gentlemen of all walks of life took part in the smuggling. Civil servants and even justices of the peace plied this illegal trade.

Between the years 1920 and 1933, at the height of rum smuggling to the USA, Newfoundland customs did not consider goods in transit or held in bond as imported goods and so charged only a small amount of duty. This helped to create a rum-runner's heaven, especially since Newfoundland had only one inspector of customs, one registrar of shipping, and one customs office with one enforcement officer. Business for Al Capone, Legs Diamond, and the Torrio Brothers never looked so good.[33] The colony acted as a transhipment port, with storage warehouses, little ability to enforce customs laws, and a Newfoundland government uninterested in interfering with international smuggling operations, with some members even taking part in the industry.[34]

The French islands of St. Pierre and Miquelon, off the coast of Newfoundland, discovered that they could make a small fortune selling liquor to the rum-runners who supplied product to the large American markets. St. Pierre shipped out an estimated 300,000 cases of liquor each month during prohibition. Conveniently, rum-runners could, at any time, store and withdraw whatever they needed of their contraband liquor in the St. John's bonded warehouses.

Prohibition presented excellent opportunities to make money for the local population, too. Most people living on the south coast had never thought of travelling to St. Pierre for alcohol, but when prohibition arrived in the States, many fishermen turned away from the fishery and took up the lucrative trade of smuggling liquor. Stories of large profits to be made, along with bad prices in the fishery, at that time, lured many fishermen into the rum business. At first they used their sailing vessels, but soon changed to high-powered motorboats for increased speed and stealth. It was a risky business fraught with thievery, violence, and murder. Run by gangsters and criminals, our local men received very poor treatment, and they soon asked for the money first before they handed over the liquor, learning to be wary of their employers, who were not fellow countrymen and certainly not trustworthy.

St. John's was abuzz with gossip about visits from famous American gangsters. Al Capone visited both St. Pierre and St. John's, staying at the Hotel Robert in St. Pierre and at the Hotel Newfoundland in St. John's. Legs Diamond spent time in St. John's and befriended a St. John's taxi driver, Jack Johnson. Some say Legs got his name because he was always on the run, others, because of the argyle socks he often sported. Johnson ferried the famous Chicago gangster and rum-runner all around town. And Diamond was well liked by all the drivers, being known as a big tipper.

Crime and corruption in Newfoundland, with regard to smuggling, went all the way to the top. In 1923 the auditor general openly accused the Newfoundland government of being in league with the rum-runners, allowing them to supply American citizens with illegal alcohol and denying their own citizens access. Thomas Hollis Walker, a British Lawyer,

Legs Diamond spent time in St. John's and befriended a St. John's taxi driver, Jack Johnson. Some say Legs got his name because he was always on the run, others, because of the argyle socks he often sported. Johnson ferried the famous Chicago gangster and rumrunner all around town. Diamond was well liked by all the drivers, being known as a big tipper. *Photo from author's private collection.*

was commissioned to investigate the liquor controller and found evidence of large-scale bootlegging, directed by the acting controller, to the tune of about $100,000. The real amount may have been twice as much. The lawyer discovered that $22,500 of that money was paid to an accountant in Prime Minister Richard Squire's office. In the words of Mr. Walker, it was little more than a "legal front" for a far-reaching bootlegging operation.[35] The whole prohibition thing was going to hell in a handbasket.

With the scripts, patent medicines, moonshine, and smugglers, it became obvious that prohibition had failed its social goals miserably. In actual fact, it had created far worse problems in the form of crime and illness than could have ever been imagined at its onset.

Thus the 'Great Reform' backfired, and the smuggling, brought about by prohibition, resulted in large amounts of alcohol coming onto the island again, without the government benefitting a whit from tariffs or taxes.

The futile attempts to make the Plebiscite Act work continued under a pro-prohibition government even though, all around them, other Canadian provinces had started to question their own prohibition policies. Quebec, in 1921, introduced the first government-controlled liquor system and set the model for the rest of Canada. When Mr. Monroe won the Newfoundland election in 1924, his Liberal Conservative government abolished the Prohibition Act and railroaded through a new liquor law, much to the severe discontent of the prohibitionists. The line had been drawn in the sand, however, and the great experiment that began on January 1, 1917, ended with the repeal of the act on August 12, 1924. It lasted exactly six years, seven months, and twelve days.

Prohibition produced major changes in the drinking habits of Newfoundlanders, but not for the better. The temperance movement's attempts to improve society by moderation or elimination of the drink was certainly a noble cause, but extremists pushed Newfoundland into a prohibition which seriously backfired. With the repeal of the Act, more sensible controls were introduced, and people were allowed to drink moderately. Unfortunately, the controlled sale of liquor did not completely eradicate the moonshining, smuggling, and illegal shebeens.

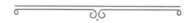

CHAPTER SEVEN

POST-PROHIBITION
Loosening the Noose

ROHIBITION, INSTEAD OF CURING AN ILL, ACTUALLY CONTRIB-
uted to the problem in Newfoundland society. In an attempt to
regulate the situation, the government-established liquor board
adopted a system of controlled alcohol sales. The new Liquor Act permitted Newfoundlanders to buy one bottle of liquor a week from a
government agency. Your weekly bottle could only be acquired if you
purchased the necessary 50-cent permit. The board had permission to
refuse to sell alcohol to undesirables (i.e., those in the habit of purchasing liquor beyond their reasonable needs, any person who the board
suspected of selling liquor without a permit, or any person who was in
receipt of public charity or relief). The Act also banned sales to "any
Esquimaux, or Indian; to any constable on duty except by authority of his
superior officer; to any inmate other than an employee thereof a hospital,
or lunatic, or poor asylum."[1]

In an attempt perhaps to shame local drunkards, the police created
a "drunk list" containing the names of people arrested on liquor-related
charges. They posted the list in liquor outlets.[2] Such attempts to humili-
ate reveal that this was still a moral and social issue at the time. It would
be years before sustained campaigns appeared that advised against drinking in the name of personal health.

People out around the bay, in areas connected by rail, could go to the railway station with their liquor book and order their bottle of rum from the railway agent. He would send the order in to the Liquor Board and they would ship the goods out express by train, in a box the size of the bottle. The whole process took about a week to complete. *Image courtesy of Archives and Special Collections, Queen Elizabeth II Library, Memorial University of Newfoundland.*

Despite the concerns for drunken behaviour, controlled alcohol sales had monetary benefits. In 1926, two years after prohibition ended, the Board of Liquor Control reported profits of $285,259 in legal sales.

To get your bottle a week you had to go to the controllers, as it was then called. There were always lineups, and sometimes the wait could be as long as an hour, especially around Christmas or other special holidays. A policeman stood at the door letting people in and out. It was not self-serve at that time, but a closed counter with clerks and the liquor on shelves behind them. The clerk took your order and then your permit, on which he wrote all the details, including the type of liquor you wanted. He then had to calculate the amount of money the customer owed. In these pre-calculator days, if you had a batch of permits, it took a while. The three controllers—one in the east end, one central, and one in the west end—sold the only hard spirits, beer, or wine in town. Not only did the controller sell liquor, but they also bottled liquor for domestic consumption.

Inevitably, the tight noose of prohibition provoked people to go around the law, and Newfoundlanders, again, found ways to beat the system. They acquired their booze on the cheap and managed to obtain the desired amounts of alcohol. If a man wanted a dozen bottles, he could borrow his friends' permits. His friends could then do the same with their friends and so on. This was against the law, but there was no way to stop it, and even the most law-abiding citizens took advantage of this loophole. Meanwhile, adherents to the temperance movement continued to preach moderation in drinking, which was probably a good thing.

Some unscrupulous characters went into the permit-buying business, purchasing permits from family, relatives, and friends to buy legal booze for resale. The permit owner might sell his permit outright, or go buy the liquor for the entrepreneur. If he sold the permit, he could simply write a note saying, "Please give the bearer spirits as required," or something along those lines.

Under this new system of limited access, many of the abuses introduced with prohibition continued, including, of course, the smuggling. In a case from the 1930s, a ship with a cargo of liquor, the *Monarchy*, ran aground near Cappahayden. Salvage hunters went to work, but because of the regulations around liquor, the police kept an eye on the alcohol, all of which was supposed to go to St. John's. The cargo consisted of ten-gallon kegs of malt whisky, ten-gallon metal drums of alcohol, two-gallon tins of alcohol in wooden cases, five-gallon kegs of rum, and brin bags filled with bottles of various liquors. The temptation proved too great for many local fishermen. The crews on the small boats, used for transporting the liquor onto larger ships, managed to "spirit away" amounts of the liquid gold in the general confusion. In one case, reported by Edward P. McCarthy in his personal reminisces, one crew managed to acquire three kegs of liquor, two ten-gallon kegs of malt whisky, and a five-gallon keg of rum—twenty-five gallons in total. They placed the alcohol in a temporary hiding place, waited till dark, and then, retrieving it, brought it into the woods to bury it. With the ground hard and rocky, a shallow hole was all they could manage. They returned the next evening to the heartbreaking site of an empty "grave."[3] Someone else had been there before them and made off with the stash.

Across the island, police struggled to control smuggling. The diary for 1932 recorded the many unsuccessful stakeouts of officers Cahill, Ivany, and Dwyer watching for smugglers. And sometimes raids worked out well for the police:

> January, Tuesday 12th, 1932—Const. Kelland & Fleming searched the Premises of Annie Jackson and Pa. Kavanagh New Gower St. for Liquor. Found two bottles of rum at Jacksons, defaced label. Three full, and one part-bottle of Rum at Kavanaghs.[4]

The government amended the Liquor Act in 1933, and again in 1935, hoping this might diminish some of these illegal activities. But even three bottles a week proved not enough for some. The general thirst in the city meant bootleggers could still sell their wares for twice the price of a legal bottle. They kept regular customers and even offered free delivery. Bootlegged stashes were well hidden and rarely discovered during police

Illegal liquor on its way from St. Pierre to Newfoundland. *Photo courtesy of Jean-Pierre Andrieux.*

raids. A bootlegger often stored his rum with his next-door neighbour. The neighbour probably enjoyed certain perks with the job.

In 1935 the Board of Liquor Control was allowed to establish "such number of stores as the board sees fit"[5] in the St. John's area. Getting a liquor store anywhere else on the island was much more complicated and involved petitions from the majority of principal residents and certificates from local magistrates approving and authenticating the signatures of petitioners. It wasn't until 1934 that the first liquor store appeared outside of St. John's, opening in Curling, a small community adjacent to Corner Brook on the west coast. The situation finally changed radically in 1966 with "Come Home Year," when permits were no longer necessary.

Beer under the prescribed alcoholic limit could be brewed, however, and a certain amount of business was allowed to carry on in the form of hop beer shops. Hop beer, like spruce beer, varied in its potency, so the police kept a close eye on these sometimes unsavoury locations, looking for drunks, and monitoring the strength of the beer.

One evening in the 'dirty thirties,' the police made a visit to one of the popular hop beer shops. A report by Constables Dwyer and Roach on December 28, 1934, on their 9:45 p.m. visit to the beer shop of Charles Ahey of 23 Princes Street, described the typical dark and dingy atmosphere of the hop beer shops. They noted one large room and one small, closet-sized room. When they asked Mr. Ahey if they could enter this small room, he said no because his wife was "relieving nature" there. She came out minutes later with a parcel of "nuisance," which she threw in the stove. That was the extent of the sanitary facilities in many of the beer shops. Other patrons using these beer shops relieved themselves in the dark alleys out back.[6]

On a return visit to the same hop beer shop on August 8, 1935, the constables reported that they found two part-tierces of hop beer with 8 to 10 gallons of beer in each part-tierce (*tierce* was an archaic unit of measure of about 42 wine gallons when full). They described the sides and heads of barrels as coated with slimy mould and the bottom of the barrel as covered with a "foul smelling sediment which must have taken years to form." They also found unappetizing pieces of spongy scum which floated on top of the beer and went through the tap.

When they brought a sample back to the police station for analysis, they found the brew to be acid in reaction with a definite "putrefactive" appearance and smell. Considering they suspected this beer of killing a man from Donovans, the majority of the clientele frequenting this beer shop must have had cast-iron constitutions.

The health inspector recommended the barrels be cleaned twice a year. He went on to say the shop was "not in an unclean condition," but did not have a bathroom, which was not important since beer was sold and not consumed there.[7]

Richard O'Brien operated beer shops in St. John's from 1934-38. He had to make the beer strong to keep his customers and sold his product at five cents for two pints. Some patrons spent as much as 25 cents in one sitting. Mr. O'Brien made the beer in the morning, and sometimes, depending on the thirst of his customers, sold out by evening.

The police visited his beer shop on George Street in 1938 when they saw four drunk men leaving the premises. Inside, they found two men sitting on the floor too inebriated to stand and five more in a similar condition. The policemen threatened to "pull out the lazy stick," but these men could not even sit up straight. After throwing some of them out, they found another in the bathroom relieving himself on the floor, apparently too drunk to hit the target. They threw him out along with three others, a total of seven extremely drunk men.

The beer found on the premises had a foul froth spewing from the top of the barrel, and when they tested for alcohol content, it was found to be well above the limit. The police charged the beer-shop owner with brewing over-proof beer, closed his shop, and sentenced him to 30 days in jail. This was his eleventh conviction in four years of operation. After that, Dick O'Brien gave up beer shops and opened a grocery store.[8]

Inspections for sanitation in some of the hop beer shops in 1937 reveal most of the shops had no toilet facilities or running water. While some had buckets, others used the great outdoors of the backyard. At one shop, people had to go into the adjoining backyard, which was enclosed by a high board fence, and use a water bucket. This bucket was enclosed by a makeshift wooden structure for privacy. The authorities described this arrangement as very unsanitary because the fumes and odours arising in warm weather would make it very annoying to the people living in the house and their surrounding neighbours.

The constables inspected the premises of Francis Breen on Water Street West, Mrs. Catherine Hurley on Hamilton Avenue, John March on Hutchings Street, John Ronayne on Brennan Street, Mary Simms on Buchanan Street, and Malcolm White on New Gower Street. The Hurley, March, and Simms premises were described as being clean and tidy, and Mary Simms' establishment as "one of the most respectable beer shops in the city,"[9] despite the lack of water and sewage.

In another inspection of these licenced premises in May of 1938, officers could find no hop beer on the premises. The occupant/owners informed the inspecting officers, Constable W. G. Williams and Sgt. Leo Roche, that they had gone out of business.

In 1938, there were 26 known unlicensed beer shops in St. John's:

John Street	Blackhead Rd.
John Francis	Blackhead Rd.
Uriah Taylor	Blackhead Rd.
Frank Breen	Water St. W.
John O'Neill	Water St. W.
Catherine Snow	Hutchings St.
Catherine Hurley	Hamilton St.
Mrs. Thos. Ronayne	Brennan St.
Philip Conway	Adelaide St.
Gerald Jackman	Prince St.
Walter Howell	Prince St.
Augustus Martin	New Gower St. W.
Michael Lacey	New Gower St. W.
Thomas Kennedy	New Gower St. W.
John Dawe	New Gower St. W.
James King	Brazil Square
Mrs. Mary Kelly	Barter's Hill
Clifford Rumsey	Barter's Hill
Thomas Myler	Sandpits
Richard Whelan	Newtown Rd.

Solomon Anthony	Mundy Pond Rd.
John Stapleton	Signal Hill
Mrs. Stewart	Water St. W.
Peter Quinlan	Duckworth St.
Charles White	Cochrane St.
Mrs. Mary Simms	Buchanan St.[10]

Hop beer shops declined after the start of World War II. In 1940, 17 of these shops[11] dotted the landscape in St. John's, down from 22 in 1938 and 1939.[12]

Up to this point, the drinking and rowdy behaviour had been mostly well managed by the constabulary, but the outbreak of World War II changed Newfoundland society completely: modernizing it, urbanizing it, and changing its drinking habits. During the war, many young men roamed the streets, both locals and visiting military, looking for diversions and entertainments to relax and relieve tension. Drinking and disorderly behaviour abounded with the newspapers reporting property damage, broken windows, and big fights, often between the locals and the military.

1941 was a busy year for the police: "From the beginning of the year up to the end of June, 230 cases for drunkenness were heard in Magistrate's Court [...] an increase of about 50% over the number of cases heard in the same period last year." This included many charges for disorderly behaviour due to drunkenness.[13]

One measure that helped restrict the heavy drinking in the 1940s was to only allow the taverns that served food to get liquor licenses. You were not permitted to buy a drink unless you bought food to go with it. At Mammy Gosse's, during the war, the same sandwich was served over and over again with your beer. Apparently, there was only one on the menu.[14]

In October 28, 1943, inspections by Constables Freake, McCormack, and H. Symonds included the Ritz Tavern, the Queen Tavern, the Green Lantern, the Hamilton Club, the Belmont Tavern, the Cottage Garden Tea Rooms, and the bar at the Crosbie Hotel. The 1944 tavern inspection list included those above in addition to the Hilltop Inn, Gosse's, Riviera, Cameron's, and the Park Inn.

The number of taverns increased in the 1950s. These establishments, along with the liquor sales at the controllers where you could buy your "bottle of buck-fifty," kept the residents of the province well lubricated. And if after-hours found you craving a drink, there was always the bootlegger. It is said that by the late 1940s and early 1950s, nearly every house on or near Princess Street bootlegged liquor.

The local police soon found a clever way to catch some of the local bootleggers. They simply watched the horses. These clever delivery animals knew their routes well and knew exactly where to stop with their wagons. One of the soft-drink companies had a delivery wagon with a driver who was less than hard-working. In the middle of his deliveries, he would regularly scoot down to Princess Street to visit a bootlegger. Here he would stop the horse and pick up his drink. The fellow soon lost his job for various reasons, and the company hired a new driver. They never bothered to train new drivers because the horses knew the routes so well. So when this new driver steered the horse and wagon in the direction of New Gower Street one day, the horse went about its business "training in" the new driver by turning onto Princess Street, where it stopped at a house. The driver looked around confused, but soon realized what had been going on. It was said that the horses showed the police the location of every bootlegger in town. This helped the police apprehend many of them.[15]

Horse-drawn delivery wagons on the west end of George Street before the time of bars. *Photo from author's private collection.*

The bootleggers, hop beer shops, and legally obtained liquor allowed residents who were so inclined to continue their overdrinking and rowdy behaviour. This, along with the heightened presence of the armed forces, frequently led to dust-ups. The unarmed constabulary must have had a very difficult time keeping the peace.

Various measures were introduced to control the consumption of alcohol both inside and outside the city. In St. John's, no new permits were issued, and prospective bar owners had to open their nightclubs outside city limits. Revellers and service men often took taxis to the Club Commodore in the east end, the Piccadilly on Topsail Road, and the Old Colony on New Cove Road.

The results of having so many drunk men around were not always pleasant for local residents. Householders found drunken soldiers and sailors everywhere: in their gardens, in their doorways sleeping it off, or engaged in other activities. The 1940 Department of Justice files hold a letter from Mrs. Mary O'Reilly, who voiced her concerns to the mayor and councillors of St. John's:

No doubt you're now saying to yourselves that a woman's place is in the home—Well I agree with you, but when that home is in grave danger it is time to come out of it and appeal to those in charge to grant justice [...] Our two residence doors are daily and nightly being used as public lavatories. On Saturday night at 8:30, mind you, two of the armed forces used each door at the same time, and to make matters worse, another entered the hall and used it for a different purpose. Is it fair to have to clean such things, and to wash our way out most every morning, but particularly Sunday mornings, our doorstep is strewn with objects of a very questionable nature. Queen Street at one time was respectable, but I am sorry to say now that to use such a word would be insulting Mr. Webster. At the moment we have panels of plywood in our two residence doors instead of the lovely heavy stained glass heretofore used. In our side windows on the ground floor we have galvanized tin painted over. Surely, gentlemen, not one of you here present would put up with such happenings. At one time, some months ago, I saw a prominent gentleman (God help us) who told me, after I stated my case, "That when one lived in the Slums one must expect the actions of the

Slums." No doubt that gentleman was more used to slum districts than I was, but it was news to me that the Corner of Water and Queen Streets was regarded as Slums. From the Health point of view, that drain is filthy; the odour from our doors is nauseating; we are ashamed, yes positively ashamed of conditions. More or less a fracas is occurring at all times: the language isn't fit for human ears to hear, and the congregating of service men and girls of ill repute adds to the difficulty [...] I pay my taxes regularly and what do I get? The way matters stand now the Council is indebted to me for providing Public Lavatories free of cost.[16]

Mrs. O'Reilly then wrote a letter to the Minister of Justice on October 13, 1940, pleading for relief from the nightly torments and the "disgraceful conduct," as she referred to it, caused by the activities at the beer parlour. The Queen Tavern, run by Mrs. Truscott, was located near her apartment in the Byrne Building on the corner of Water and Queen Street. The city suggested they could increase the illumination in the area (the full blackout didn't take effect until 1942) and station a constable on that part of Queen from 7 p.m. to 1 a.m. to keep an eye on patrons of the Queen Tavern. The Board of Liquor Control ruled that because the "conduct" took place in the street and not in the tavern, no fault was found with Annie Truscott's establishment.[17]

The Queen wasn't the only tavern causing trouble on the street. Right around the corner on New Gower, the infamous Green Lantern produced its own share of troublemakers.

After the war, things slowly returned to a form of normal. By 1949, 72 drinking establishments served the people of the province. By 1974, the number had increased to 587.[18] In the 1940s, bars closed first at 11 p.m., and then 12 a.m. By the 1950s, the liquor board extended closing time to 1 a.m.

Old habits die hard though, and smuggling, moonshining, and bootlegging continued for quite a while after the freer access to booze. Cape St. George, on the west coast of Newfoundland, had a reputation as a major centre for moonshine. Some evidence points to the fact that their knowledge of moonshine making may have come from Quebec to the French Shore of Newfoundland, and from this region, the technique spread to the rest of the island.[19]

When a Memorial University student conducted a study of homebrew in Western Newfoundland in 1974, he interviewed a couple of elderly gentlemen who brewed their beer with the addition of a plug of chewing tobacco. "They were very friendly. In fact, they laughed throughout the interview. Neighbours tell me they've been laughing continuously since they sat down to their first 'tobacci brew,' fifteen years ago." When asked what facilities they'd like to see for alcoholics, one gentleman promptly answered, "We wants more taverns."[20]

With regard to smuggling, in 1983 the RCMP estimated that smugglers brought about 300 to 1,000 cases of booze into the province. Not as lucrative as in prohibition times, but cheap liquor always sells well. A dozen 40-ouncers of rum coming in from St. Pierre and Miquelon went for $156 dollars—a steal for sure at $13 a bottle (the liquor store price at that time was $28 a bottle). Mostly restricted to the south coast, modern day smugglers must have had enough local customers to make it worthwhile.[21] Now in present-day Newfoundland and Labrador, with penalties so high, smuggling has slowed to a trickle, at least around the Avalon Peninsula. So times have certainly changed. Sources in central Newfoundland maintain that smuggling is alive and well with plenty of smuggled alcohol still available to those who know where to look.

In the twenty-first century, drinking habits have changed yet again. The old neighbourhood taverns have mostly disappeared, and where once the taverns stretched the length of Water and Duckworth Street, now many of the bars are clustered together around the George Street area or sporadically show up on Water and Duckworth and the small alleys running between them. Drinking in bars is now highly controlled and legitimized as part of the tourist and entertainment industries.

Throughout this span of Newfoundland's history, drinking has remained common at all occasions—funerals, births, baptisms, weddings, Christmas, New Year's, Easter, dances, political meetings, etc. So what has changed in 400-plus years? Well, we no longer suffer from the physical discomforts of our ancestors; therefore, alcohol is no longer seen as a necessity. Perhaps the only argument for consuming it today is a certain aesthetic pleasure in the taste of a cold beer, a good wine, or a favourite rum or scotch. As an aperitif, very few of us need to stimulate our appetites, and as a reality changer there's always cannabis. Perhaps the biggest argument for drink now is to boost our economy. Booze is a money-maker, not only for the small businessman, but also for government charging taxes and duties on its sale and importation.

Even with increased education on the negative health impact of alcohol consumption, it is still difficult to go anywhere and refuse to drink unless you are the designated driver. But with the latest research showing alcohol is harmful in any amount, people may think more carefully about what they are imbibing.

We still enjoy our drinks as a social activity, a way of breaking down barriers and, for some, as a doorway to a different reality. With the legalization of marijuana, alcohol may face some stiff competition, or it may simply be another substance in our stable of mood-altering recreational drugs. The important thing to remember is moderation in all things and that the ugly beast of addiction can raise its head with anyone at any time. Some studies have been done that suggest people of Irish descent are more prone to alcoholism than others, possessing a "lazy form" of a certain gene which lessens the ill effects of drinking alcohol.[22] If this is the case, many Newfoundlanders may be wise to drink with great care. We've all seen that relative, so fond of the drink, fall victim to it and oftentimes lose their spouse and children, lose their jobs, destroy their lives, or simply waste away from disease.

As far as restrictions go, nowadays, we are mostly left to police ourselves. Rarely, if ever, do you see father come home for a drink before supper or have a drink at lunch, as was common in the 1960s. A cocktail after work for the ladies? Pretty rare these days. Granted, there are controls to restrict drinking and driving: with steep fines and penalties, few people risk having more than one drink and climbing into the driver's seat. Meanwhile, the disappearance of neighbourhood taverns means driving or taking a taxi to a bar or tavern are the only other options. Most people have a designated driver, or drink very little. The rest of us, who do not frequent bars or restaurants on a regular basis, cocoon at home with our tipple.

The bars on George Street are now facing tough competition from the big national restaurant chains, where many people spend their evenings eating and drinking. Hopefully, however, that part of our culture, the small locally owned bar, will continue to thrive.

The Newfoundland Liquor Corporation's financial statement from April 2017 to April 2018 reveals they made $268 million in alcohol sales in Newfoundland and Labrador (pop. 526,000).

Consumption amounts in litres look like this:

Spirits	3,706 L
Wine	4,556 L
Ready to drink and cider	2,250 L
Beer, including imported and low alcohol	6,378 L
Total consumption of alcohol in one year	16,890 L[23]

When it comes to beer and rum, Newfoundlanders continue to outpace most other Canadians. It isn't difficult to understand why. After 500 years of colonial history, alcohol has become firmly entrenched in our culture. And while there are organizations devoted to addressing the symptoms of alcohol use and abuse, and while producers inform us to drink responsibly, the old war against alcohol has long since subsided.

TAVERNS AND BARS OF ST. JOHN'S AND BEYOND

S OME OF THE WELL-KNOWN BARS AND TAVERNS HAVE LONG disappeared into the dust of time, while others are still with us today. Water Street, Duckworth Street, New Gower Street, and the small streets in between hosted an interesting variety of drinking holes over the years. In some cases, it can be difficult to pinpoint the former locations of various establishments. Before 1946, Water Street was divided into East and West, starting and ending at Springdale Street. Each section had its own numbering, so old addresses for the bars and taverns can be confusing. And over the years, civic numbers have naturally changed due to development and the city's ongoing evolution.

110 WATER STREET

James White operated a tavern at 110 Water Street for many years. Known as Jim's Tavern, it ran from at least 1951. Initially owned by John Thomas White, his son, James, took it over sometime before 1954. He then passed it to his sons, John and Patrick, in 1959. They renamed it the East End Club in 1964. Alice Druken, Patrick's sister, began working in the tavern in 1954, at age nineteen. She and her husband, Ed, took over in 1984, and ran the business until 2007. Renamed Turner's Tavern in 2008, it remained in business for only one more year.[1] Some claim the tavern may have originally opened as early as 1946.

A description of some of the local taverns published in the *Muse* described Turner's Tavern as smaller than the Georgetown Pub, very quiet, and really only suitable for patrons in their senior years. They described the interior as having one wall in brick and the other three decorated with a log-cabin look.[2]

164 WATER STREET

The name Scanlan has been associated with liquor sales since the 1800s when Irishman James Scanlan carried on a large grocery and provision business at 164 Water Street. He kept an adjoining shop in the lane, from where he sold spruce beer of the very best quality. Men, women, boys, and girls would sit on the ground on both sides of the lane, eating their lunch and drinking what came to be known as the national temperance drink of Newfoundland, "the cup that cheers but not inebriates." This beer was made of spruce tops, spruce buds, and good West Indian molasses. From 1864, Ellen Scanlan had a tavern at the rear of 164 Water Street, until Mr. James Phaelen took over from the Scanlans around 1868-72. He named the tavern the Sunburst, and crowed it was a place that "all the sports of the east end frequented."[3] In the latter years of the nineteenth century, Michael Scanlan operated a wine-merchant's shop on the east corner of Scanlan's Lane and lived in the house behind it.

Other businesses took over as the years went by, but the building returned to the bar business in the 1980s under names like Nightcap, Alley Pub, and, in 1984, as Kibitzers. One of the longest running names for the bar was The Spur. From 1990-1994, it was known as The Silver Spur Country Bar, and from 1995-2005 it became simply The Spur. Another bar called Bar None occupied the upper floor, and for many years a speakeasy operated out of the apartment on the top floor. From The Spur, the name changed to The Victory and then back to the ancient name of Scanlan's for a short period, before it was renamed The Black Sheep.

The East End Club on Water Street, circa 1984. *Photo courtesy of Archives and Special Collections, Queen Elizabeth II Library, Memorial University.*

Running a bar comes with its own unique set of challenges. Don Maher, owner and bartender of Scanlan's, tells the story of one large unruly patron, who, already quite drunk, was causing a disturbance:

> I'm a pacifist at heart, and there was a guy here, a great big guy, and I served him, and as soon as I did he started bugging the patrons, so I took his beer and said "You have to leave now." Well he stood up and looked down at me and I looked up at him and I said to myself, "oh...oh." Now the only way I knew how to handle it was to freak out and start yelling and cursing at him to get out of my bar. And when I came out around the bar I was on his left and sort of in his blind spot. He started walking towards the door and whenever he looked back I got behind him so he couldn't see me and when he got up by the bar he looked behind and I sort of slipped around the corner. Well he went out and he slammed the door so hard the building shook.[4]

186 WATER STREET

Erin's Pub, at 186 Water Street, has been around for many years. From 1962-79 it was the Capitol Cocktail Lounge and then the Golden Spike Lounge, Skyways Lounge, Martin's Lounge, The Oil Patch, and, by 1987, Erin's.

Ralph O'Brien, an Irishman born in Dublin and a member of the well-known Newfoundland band Sons of Erin, emigrated to Newfoundland in 1967 and bought the lounge in 1986, renaming it Erin's. O'Brien claims to be the first to bring Guinness beer to the city in the twentieth century.

Owned now by former Great Big Sea band member Bob Hallett, Erin's Pub is still going strong, and has existed under that name for thirty-two years. Hosting many local bands such as the Irish Descendants, Connemara, the Fables, and Great Big Sea, many of these bands claim to have got their start here.

208 WATER STREET

In 1963, Gerry Stephens opened the El Tico at 208 Water Street. It began as a "beautiful Lounge with a Spanish atmosphere." In addition to the

Morocco lounge on the first floor, it had a steak house on the second floor and a dance hall called the Embassy on the third floor:

> The Chalet Steak House [is decorated] in an Old Fashioned Continental Style [and features] the best Charcoal Broiled Steaks and Chalet bar-B-Q Chicken [...] The Exciting Embassy, Plush and Elaborate, for your Dancing Pleasure, Open Daily 12 Noon is located in the Heart of St. John's Business District.[5]

The decor boasted "Two lamp posts with three globular lamps in shades of red blue and gold, standing over the gold fabric chairs and tables [...] French paintings hang on the wall above each table."[6] An advertisement in another newspaper touted the bar/restaurant as a must-see: "To see St. John's means visiting El Tico [...] visitors of all countries welcome." With no cover charge, it served highballs for 80 cents, beer for 50 cents, and dinners in the chalet were $1.25. For unescorted ladies, highballs could be had for the discounted price of 50 cents; "ladies" in those days did not drink beer. The El Tico also organized events: "In the new year the El Tico will be catering to the women-folk with such things as fashion shows, ladies teas and light luncheons, so it'll really be the spot to see."[7]

By the 1970s the El Tico had become an interesting old club with a reputation for spectacular nighttime fights among the patrons. Under new ownership, the name changed to The Rose and Thistle in 1990 and still exists under that name today. An urban legend suggests Ron Hynes wrote the song "Sonny's Dream" at The Rose and Thistle.

288 WATER STREET

On the corner of Water and George lies the YellowBelly Brewery and Public House. Located on what used to be called Yellowbelly Corner, it is situated opposite what was once called Kent's Cove (now Beck's Cove), a spot where young Irishmen gathered to drink and brawl. At that time, they may have frequented Edward Brennan's public house on the east corner of Beck's Hill.

The name YellowBelly is derived from the boys from County Wexford who wore yellow sashes in hurling matches. A yellowbelly was also the name given to the jug from which St. John's workers and fishermen took their daily tots.

When archaeologists carried out a dig in the area, they found evidence of eating and drinking—plates, cups, tea cups, and bottles including wine bottles and champagne bottles from the 1730s to the mid-1800s. They also found a piece of a spigot used to decant spirits or ale from a barrel cask, along with several pipe bowls for tobacco. A significant percentage of the collection gathered showed alcohol consumption from a tavern or several taverns formerly located on this site.

392 WATER STREET

The Green Lantern, at 392 Water Street, and several other taverns like it, saw to the needs of many visiting Canadian and American armed forces in the 1940s. Even though recreational facilities existed on the various bases around town, many of the servicemen socialized off base. The officers had the Crow's Nest at their disposal, but the common soldier went elsewhere. With as many as 15,000 Canadian and American service personnel in St. John's, recreation facilities such as the Soldiers and Sailors Club on Queen Street, the Red Triangle Club on Water Street West, the Terra Nova Club on LeMarchant Road, the Knights of Columbus Hostel on Harvey Road, and the Caribou Hut on Water Street East saw to their off-base socialization needs. These venues were alcohol free, however, so as a result, many servicemen frequented taverns and restaurants like the Green Lantern and the Queen Tavern. Alcohol could be acquired from local bootleggers, and men drank on the street, casting their empties away. This created a hazard for pedestrians. Well into their cups and looking for trouble, these soldiers and sailors caused all sorts of problems in town.

When the blackout came into effect, the constabulary could hardly walk on New Gower Street or Duckworth Street without crunching on the broken glass strewn everywhere. The rowdies smashed store windows out every night, forcing property owners to board up the damaged ones and put shutters up to protect the rest. Known as the worst beat in town,

At the intersection of Water Street and George Street, the restored YellowBelly's building is a popular spot for pub food and beer. The large window allows a peek at the inner workings of the brewery also located inside. *Photo from author's private collection.*

one purveyor of justice commented, "If you couldn't fight like the devil, you had no business in there."[8]

448 WATER STREET

The Riviera Tavern started life quietly. In 1908, Margaret Fennessey, widow of Sgt. Thomas Fennessey, sold temperance drinks at 12½ Water St. West (modern day 448). These were the first beverages served at that location. Later on, at 16 Water St. West, the Riviera Tea Rooms, run by Mrs. E. LeMee, served up a different type of beverage in 1936. By 1939 advertisements appeared for the Riviera Hotel: "A Home from Home" and "Wines and Beers." When the numbering system on Water Street changed in 1943, the Riviera Hotel's address became 452 Water Street. In 1948, Hotel Riviera moved or re-opened, under the steady hand of Elizabeth Foote, a few doors down at 448. She operated it from 1951-54 under a new name, the Riviera Tavern. Michael F. Power bought the property from Mrs. Foote in 1954 and continued to run it as the Riviera Tavern. Pronounced by the locals as the "Rivera" or the "Riv," by 1979 it had changed ownership again. From 1976-86, the Key Club operated upstairs and then the Midstream Lounge until 1998. The Riviera remained as a tavern until 1995.[9]

Newfoundland author Helen Porter remembers when Anastasia English, the niece of writer Statia M. English, worked there in the early 1940s. A very properly run sort of place, Anastasia kicked Helen's father out of the hotel once for drinking too much. You were supposed to drink, but not supposed to overdo it, and you certainly weren't supposed to argue. She says her father, John Porter, would "get a bit saucy when drinking and he'd argue with the devil!"

The old sign from the Riviera now hangs on the wall of Stanley's Pub at the Bellavista just as you enter the porch. A tattoo shop now occupies the site of the old tavern.

456 WATER STREET

The Porthole, a well-known bar at 456 Water Street in St. John's, started life in 1948 as the People's Restaurant with food and drink. It changed its name to the Station Grill in 1952, and then in 1960 it became the Artillery Club at 458 Water Street with Edwin J. Learning as manager. The Artillery Club operated as a private club wishing to build up a clientele consisting of the "better class of St. John's citizens." In a letter dated July 16, 1960, the club's executive wrote to the Board of Liquor Control to ask permission to sell their alcohol at a higher price, beer at 38 cents and liquor at 48 cents (plus two cents tax), than that of the Riviera Tavern down the road. They requested this so as to discourage the undesirable types from frequenting their club.

From 1963-1970 it operated as the Porthole, complete with a round porthole-like window in the door. An advertisement from 1963 states that proper dress is required and in brackets adds, "This means a tie." By the 1970s the Porthole had garnered a reputation as a hard spot, but earlier on in its career, the Porthole tried hard to create a sophisticated impression.

Entertainment tonight—Marksmen Trio entertains. No cover. No minimum. Fully licensed. Proper Dress Required. (This means a tie) Monday: Leo Michaels; Tuesday: Johnny Francis; Wednesday: Leo Michaels; Thursday: Sam Harnum; Friday: Marksmen Trio; Saturday: John White—Porthole 458 Water St.[10]

Other musicians playing at the Porthole included the Tommy Byrne Band, the Barry Hope Band (this may have been Joe Murphy and friends), the Cabot Trio, and the Mickey Duggan Band. Mickey Duggan was a barber and had a shop on Long's Hill in the 1950s and '60s.

In the late 1970s, a reincarnation of the old Belmont sprang up in the former Porthole building on Water Street. David Devine leased the club from Ed Learning in 1978 and renamed 456 Water Street the Belmont in January 1979. Tucked in amongst the tattoo shops, it was located across the street from the dockyard. In the window, a twisted rope of red wire glowed "Labatt's Blue" and on the walls hung a collection of life preservers, the names of their ships written on them in big black letters. Also on the walls were various brass portholes illuminated to show off the photographs of ships and seascapes placed in them. A large club, it incorporated two buildings creating two sections. The smaller section housed the bar and the larger one opened up into the dance floor and bandstand. The bar section served the customers in the daytime, mostly the dock-workers coming in after work for a quick one, and the larger section with the dance floor and bandstand opened up at night. Friday and Saturday nights featured the live music of one of several bands that played here.

In addition to the locals, a host of foreign seamen frequented the bar. With the Spanish and Portuguese sailors came the ladies of the night. Devine tried his best to "clean up" the clientele, but this part of the bar's ambiance continued to darken the doors. Customers enjoyed hanging out and having a drink, watching the various characters, and dancing to the music of the Belmont Rovers on a Friday night. This new Belmont—formerly Paddy's Inn and before that the Porthole—had always been a seaman's tavern. Cyril "Curly" Power, the doorman, regulated the traffic in and out of the bar, denying entry to known troublemakers or habitual drunks. His wife bartended there for seven years and then their son eventually took over as manager. Open every day at 11 a.m., except on Sunday when it opened at 1 p.m., it was pretty quiet during the week, and the bartender passed the time reading or talking to customers, some from the dockyard or others who may have just come in to try to sell something either second-hand or stolen. Some of the ladies came in the afternoon, ordered a beer, and sat alone at a table. If they spied a single man, they would approach and start up a conversation.

The club developed some interesting customs. A big brass bell hung behind the bar, and tradition had it that if anyone rang the bell it was a

OPPOSITE: One popular entertainer in the downtown bars in the '60s was musician John White. A character in every sense of the word, John could tell a funny story, sing like a lark and drink like a fish. He had a phenomenal memory for songs and would perform cold, without any rehearsal. When playing at the Belmont, appreciative customers would buy John a beer, so that it was nothing to see as many as 20 beer lined up waiting for him. He could never drink them all, so many were given away to the Portuguese sailors who frequented the Belmont and the Porthole. Both these bars let them in, while many others would not as these poor sailors generally had no money. As a result, the Portuguese loved John and the musicians he played with. John lived on Patrick Street and could be seen many an evening at the nearby Park Inn, his favourite hangout. John passed away from cancer at age sixty-eight. *Image courtesy of Archives and Special Collections Queen Elizabeth ii Library, Memorial University of Newfoundland.*

signal that he wanted to buy a round for the bar. If anyone entered the bar wearing a hat, he had to buy a round for the patrons, perhaps a throwback to when "gentlemen" frequented the bars, and it was considered rude to enter wearing a hat.

On a Friday night, the place came alive. The women at the Belmont sat together near the dance floor and waited to be asked to dance. Many sex workers frequented the bar, but most of the men and women were just working-class people out for a good night. The band played old familiar songs, and the patrons sang along, treating each other to drinks all night long. Dancing included modern dancing and the old-fashioned step-dancing. Billy Penney often came in wearing a black vest and salt-and-pepper hat and step-danced or played the spoons along with the band. Patrons drifted off by 1 a.m., tired but happy.

The Belmont, certainly one of the last of the old-time bars, closed its doors for good in 1986.

643 WATER STREET

The Dawson family originally owned the property at 643 Water Street, across the road from Victoria Park. They lived upstairs and leased the lower floor out to various entrepreneurs, including D. J. Williams and his wife, Annie, who ran the Park Inn at this location from April 1938 until 1951.

An advertisement in the *Evening Telegram* of April 16, 1938, showcased the establishment in a very positive light:

> A high class Dining Room designed on the most modern principles will be open for business at 6 o'clock this afternoon. Prompt and courteous service will be our motto, and a share of your valued patronage will be appreciated. [11]

Newfoundland author Helen Porter remembers being in the Park with her father as a child, even though children were not allowed in the dark smoky bar. The men were nice to her, and someone brought her down a plate of cheese, plain biscuits, and a soft drink. She remembers the sounds of boots clomping on the wooden floors and calls from the men entering the bar: "Hello Mr. Porter...Hello Mr. Dunbar." The men rarely called each other by first names in those days but referred to each other by title and surname.

Michael F. Power took over the lease in 1951, operating it as the Park Inn until 1956. The Dawson family returned to the bar business and took over the tavern once more, changing the name to the Park View Inn because Mr. Power owned the rights to the Park Inn name.

In 1984-90 the name changed to the Jolly Roger, still run by Tom and William Dawson, and then Christine Meaney opened up Christine's Place Restaurant (1991-92) at that address. By 1993 the building had been torn down.

20 NEW GOWER STREET

The Ritz Tavern was once located at the present site of the City Hall parking garage. Owned by Toby Jackman, and at one point managed by one of St. John's most prominent athletes, wrestler Tom 'Dynamite' Dunn, it first shows up in the city directories in 1942. In the '40s, with only about four legitimate taverns in the town, when you went out for the evening you didn't just go to one but made the rounds of all. Each tavern had regulars and you could catch up with all your social groups if you moved around. The Ritz was torn down after 1966 to make room for new development.

53 NEW GOWER STREET

Mammy Gosse of Gosse's Tavern opened her tavern early in the old days, at 7 a.m., to serve the fishermen who had just come back in from fishing. Gosse's Tavern was across the street from the Ritz, and a door or two west of where the skywalk goes over the street today. Gosse's Tavern became known as 'Mammy Gosses', perhaps because Anastasia Gosse ran the place for so long. 'Mammy' lived above the tavern and ran it from at least 1908 until the early 1960s. Anastasia had taken over the running of a tavern on New Gower Street from one David A. Gosse, her husband. Mr. Gosse first shows up in the directories selling wines and liquor in 1898.

Mammy Gosse played host to men from all walks of life. Well-known as a kind but firm lady she had a "back room" for special clients. Once Mrs. Gosse reprimanded the mayor for cursing in her bar and threatened to throw him out. He retorted "You can't do that. I'm the mayor." Undaunted, she promptly kicked him out.

Mrs. Jean Long (widow of James Long) took it over by 1963 and then several other managers/owners took their turns at running it. Gosse's Tavern continued at its same location until 2005.

When some local university students went on a pub crawl in 1981, they jokingly mention it sold Geritol on tap—probably a reflection of the average age of the clientele. Mammy Gosse's used to be the oldest pub in St. John's.[12]

164 NEW GOWER STREET

From 1941-43 the original Belmont Restaurant on New Gower Street served beer favourites like Dow's Black Horse and Jockey Club, big sellers at 25 cents a bottle. Located opposite Waldegrave Street where the Delta is today, the Belmont first occupied the Regal (Little Star) Theatre. City Hall now stands on the site of 162 New Gower Street, where Jim Byrne first opened his restaurant.

Byrne changed to another location in 1967, 164 New Gower Street, two doors away from the theatre building. In this much smaller space, he started out with only a few chairs and tables. By 1970 it had a small dance floor, a jukebox and a bar on the right side of the room. Jack Manning, an ex-policeman, worked as a bouncer there, and Ed Scurry and the Belmont Rovers played the regular weekend entertainments. The old Belmont sold mostly beer, and opening hours ran from 10 a.m. to 1 a.m., with the band starting at about 9:45 p.m. Joe Murphy, Willy Walters, Joe Cook and Ed Scurry made up the members of the band originally known as the Beachcombers, who then became the Belmont Rovers. Regulars from town frequented the Belmont as well as patrons from the outports staying at the nearby Brazil Square boarding houses. Most of the regulars, ranging in age from 30 to 50 years, came from New Gower Street and the Pleasant Street area or from the dockyards. In the days of the foreign fishing fleets, Portuguese sailors often tried their luck at the club, but with so little money to spend, the bouncer usually turned them away, allowing only the ships' officers inside. No women were allowed in the bar until the mid-'70s. The Portuguese sailors, though poor, did not cause problems; when they did get in, they danced with the women and nursed their drinks all evening without getting into fights.

Other patrons, known troublemakers, always managed to gain access despite their reputations, and ensured that fights broke out towards the end of the evening.

The Belmont did not have as many fights as the Porthole down on Water Street, another rough spot where the bunch from the Brow (Shea Heights) used to come down, meet up with the bunch from Mundy Pond and always start a racket. Some academics from the university discovered the rich possibilities for research at The Belmont Tavern. People showed up with their instruments and played for free. This was a veritable gold

	RUMS (IMPORTED) (Continued)		
Brand			Price
1O/2	Young's Old Sam (Demerara)	12 oz.	2.80
1OO	Appleton Estate Special (Jamaica)	26⅔ oz.	5.00
1P	Favell's London Dock (Demerara) Proof	26⅔ oz.	6.20
1PP	Jon Canoe Navy-Reserve (Jamaica)	26⅔ oz.	5.50
1PP/2	Jon Canoe Navy-Reserve (Jamaica)	13¼ oz.	2.80
1Q	Favell's Royal Oak (B.W.I.)	26⅔ oz.	5.50
1QQ	Jon Canoe Amber (Jamaica)	26⅔ oz.	5.50
1QQ/2	Jon Canoe Amber (Jamaica)	13½ oz.	2.80
1R	B.L.C. — Screech	25 oz.	3.95
1R/2	B.L.C. — Screech	12 oz.	2.00
1R/4	B.L.C. — Screech	6 oz.	1.15
1SS	Appleton White (Jamaica)	26⅔ oz.	5.00
1TT	Coruba Blanca (Jamaica)	25 oz.	5.50
1TT/2	Coruba Blanca (Jamaica)	12 oz.	2.80
1UU	Watson's Trawler	25 oz.	5.50
1VV	Captain's Choice (Trinidad)	26⅔ oz.	5.50
1X	Big Dipper	25 oz.	3.95
1X/2	Big Dipper	12 oz.	2.00
1X/4	Big Dipper	6 oz.	1.15
1YY	Old Oak	25 oz.	5.50
1Z	Big Dipper Light	25 oz.	3.95
1ZZ	Big Dipper (Proof)	25 oz.	5.50
1ZZ/2	Big Dipper (Proof)	12 oz.	2.90

7

All Prices subject to 6% Sales Tax.

Price List from the Board of Liquor Control. *Author's photo taken with permission at Rock Spirits.*

mine for the folklore crowd, when they discovered that for the price of a couple of beer they could collect some pretty interesting material in the way of old Newfoundland songs.

Not the most sanitary place, one patron mentioned that if you went to the bathroom there, you rolled up your pants because the floor could sometimes be disgusting. The Belmont was known as a longshoreman's place in the old days with beer selling at 70 cents apiece. The tavern stayed at 164 New Gower Street until it burned down in the 1970s.

125 QUEENS ROAD

Tom 'Dynamite' Dunn owned and operated the Ringside Tavern, now JayDee's Lounge. Mr. Dunn left St. John's and went down to Boston when he was 17 or 18 years old. Working as a clerk with the United Electric Company in Boston, he regularly visited the local gym where he trained as a boxer. He boxed for a few years until his coach decided his right arm wasn't long enough. Boxers need long arms, so Dunn switched to wrestling. As a young man, he wrestled all up and down the eastern seaboard. When Dynamite Dunn's father fell ill, he retired from wrestling, and came back to Newfoundland where he worked at the Ritz Tavern as a bouncer in the mid-'40s.

Well-known as a strong Liberal supporter in the time of Premier Joseph R. Smallwood, the former World Wide Wrestling Federation (WWF, now WWE) wrestler became Joey's body guard. Once when Mr. Smallwood was down talking in front of the Colonial Building to an increasingly agitated crowd, Dynamite had to pull him indoors and out through the back door before people lynched him, a good example of the bitterness in the fight for Confederation. Not only a bodyguard, he involved himself in politics as well, campaigning for Joey for many years. In those days political campaigners often bought votes, so when Dynamite campaigned out of town, he left in a car with a loudspeaker on top and a trunk full of liquor and cash. He'd go to a town, get a room in a hotel, unroll his huge wad of bills, and wine and dine the mayor and prominent citizens of the town. That's the way campaigning was done then and lots of big money people backed Joey.

In that tight buddy system of patronage, people who supported the premier got the jobs. It was common knowledge that if you were a bar owner and you crossed the Smallwood administration, you might suddenly be 'inspected' the next day and found guilty enough of something to have the place closed down. Stories of favouritism abound. Old-timers say you had to be on the Smallwood side to get a tavern licence (beer and wine) or a bar licence (bars could sell anything). Many people say that's how Dynamite Dunn got his licence on Theatre Hill.

In 1952 Dunn opened his own tavern, the Ringside, up on Theatre Hill (Queens Road). Tom didn't allow any political discussion in the bar unless it was pro-Liberal! Unfortunately, that still didn't stop the fights and the Black Mariah could be seen regularly rolling up to the tavern door, as Tom turfed out the drunks. Not without a heart, though; he often let those who had over-imbibed sleep it off in the back garden rather than out on the street.

Young Tom Junior, Dynamite's son, watching from the upstairs window, often found his fun at the expense of the drunks. He would wait until a drunk came out, stumbling over himself in an attempt to get down over the three steps to the street. Young Tom would then pour a glass of water over the unsuspecting patron. The poor guy would quickly pull up the collar of his jacket, thinking it was pouring rain outside, and stumble his way back up the stairs into the bar again.

Regular customers routinely dropped in to the bar and spent the whole day. Bars and taverns in St. John's in those days were more about socializing than drinking. Clients filled the hours with lots of chat and games of darts or pool. Many regulars lived nearby while others worked in the Water Street stores. In those days fewer people had cars, so the Water Street crowd walked up after work, dropped into the bar for a drink or two, and then continued up to the bus stop at the bottom of Long's Hill to catch a ride home.

Dynamite Dunn ran a tight ship at 125 Queen's Road, from at least 1952 to 1980. Many visiting Fort Pepperell military men, fancying themselves fine boxers, sometimes challenged Mr. Dunn to a match after a few drinks too many. If Dynamite's attempts to ignore them failed, the hopeful contenders would find themselves out on their derrières in no time flat, much more sober and wiser for the encounter. In 1981 the bar was renamed JayDee's.[13]

203/207 DUCKWORTH STREET

This location originally housed Bristol's Dining Hall with Beer and Wine Dispensaries from 1931-51. Bristol House (tavern), as it came to be, was owned and managed by Arthur Priestman Cameron, also known as "The Man from Yorkshire", and his wife Ethel P. Cameron. He loved to sing and one of his favourites was the "Cock-a-Doodle-Song":

> "When poor old father tried to kill
> The Cock-a-Doodle-Do
> they all shouted 'coward'
> He's not as big as you."

Too bad the lyrics to one of his favourites seem to have disappeared, "Locked in the Stable with the Sheep," a take-off of "Locked in the Cradle of the Deep." In 1936, Mrs. Ethel P. Cameron (probably Arthur's wife) is listed as the proprietor of 148 Duckworth. In later years, the Bristol became known as the 'Bucket of Blood' because of all the fighting that occurred there.[14]

The Bristol had changed location by 1942 and 148/150 housed other businesses. The Hillview Inn served drinks at 148-150 Duckworth Street from 1953 to 1989. From 1990 to 2011 the Brass Rack Lounge occupied the premises. The building has now lain vacant for many years.

207 DUCKWORTH STREET

Mrs. W. Penney worked at an iconic St. John's tavern located at 207 Duckworth St. She took over the tavern, calling it the Campenn Inn, a combo of Cameron, former owner Mrs. Ethel P. Cameron of the Bristol House, and Mrs. Penney. Ma Penney and her two girls lived above the tavern in the three-story house. Well-respected and well-liked by the public, Ma Penney retired and sold the tavern after Newfoundland joined Canada in Confederation.

It made the papers in 1952, with a story about the ships' captains complaining about the new neon signs that graced some of the taverns on Duckworth Street. They claimed it caused a hazard to shipping. These bright signs interfered with the 'range lights' the captains used for navigating into the harbour. Both the Campenn Inn and the Cross Key(s) Tavern on Duckworth Street were named as principle offenders.

Name changes for the Campenn after that time include the Sting Lounge, Sir Humphrey's Pub, the Terra Nova Lounge, and the Welcome Lounge. It is now a parking area.

WAR MEMORIAL

The Crow's Nest, located to the east of the War Memorial, became the official name of the the Seagoing Officers' Club in the 1940s. A club exclusively for naval officers, it opened during World War II and sat high up on the fourth floor of an old warehouse. Vice-Admiral Edmund Mainguy instigated its creation with the help of Lady Outerbridge, who offered the vacant space in Sir Leonard Outerbridge's warehouse for the duration of the war. As for the naming of the club, one story maintains that a certain Canadian Army officer, after huffing and puffing up the many steps from street level to the top of the old warehouse, mopped his brow and remarked, "Crikey, what is this—a ruddy crow's nest?" The Club closed on June 13, 1945, after the war ended, but reopened in May of 1946 when it became a Newfoundland Officer's Club, rented from the Outerbridges for one dollar per year or until revenue exceeded expenses. They redecorated it then to resemble an old English pub.

The original 59 steps must have been tortuous both ascending and descending after a few drinks. One would think many visitors would have taken a tumble, but apparently the only one recorded was that of a Norwegian Lieutenant Commander who "crept down the 57 steps successfully, fighting a ground swell every inch of the way, and in a sudden burst of confidence tripped over the last two."[15] Originally it was men only, with just one evening a week where the ladies were allowed in. "With the hope they would not clutter up the bar...." Built in 1892,[16] the

Old Butler Building occupied the same ground where an old inn called "The Ship" served up drinks two centuries before.

373 DUCKWORTH STREET

In 1960, a Federal Service Club occupied 373 Duckworth St. By 1962-64 it became the Caribou Lounge, and in 1965 the owners renamed it the Horse Shoe Club. The Horse Shoe Club could be entered from the corner of Duckworth Street, but on the floor below another entrance opened onto the eastern corner of George Street. In an interesting mix of fire risks, this lower floor operated as a forge. Musician Ray Walsh remembered the building as three stories high, a treacherous narrow building with stairs going up the side. It could get quite crowded at times. In 1974 this lounge was renamed the Continental Lounge. Figgy Duff played a gig featuring Dave Panting at the Continental Lounge with a $1 cover fee. The advertisement called on people to "Go on down and scuff with the Duffs."

Folklorist Peter Narvaez described the Continental as a "tacky room replete with blue fluorescent lighting and the kind of filthy thick sticky carpet that makes me cautious about walking too fast for fear of stepping out of my moccasins."[17]

The usual clientele at the Continental were younger working-class men and women.

GEORGE STREET

And then came George Street, originally a street of blacksmiths before it became a street of pubs, restaurants, and bars. In the nineteenth and early twentieth centuries, it was home to cooperages, animal feed and hay stores, and O'Keefe's wholesale groceries. It now has over two dozen bars and pubs lining both sides of the street.

One of the oldest buildings on George Street now houses a bar, but its history goes back to the nineteenth century when it was utilized for a variety of purposes. The Cornerstone Building, erected in 1861, was a fisheries hall, served as St. Peter's Church, housed the Sisters of Mercy

Rob Roy's on George Street, circa 1984. *Photo courtesy of Archives and Special Collections Queen Elizabeth II Library, Memorial University.*

Catholic School for girls, and was used by several local businesses before it opened as the Cornerstone Sports Bar in 1985, followed by the Cotton Club in 1999.

Christian's, the Rob Roy, and Trapper John's (originally called The Bull and Bear) were the first bars on or near George Street in the late 1970s. The distinction of the oldest bar on George goes to Christian's.

The Rob Roy Pub, at number 8 George Street, occupies another of the oldest buildings in St. John's, built around the time of the great fire of 1892. It has been a grocery store, a marble works, Fort Amherst Sea Foods, and in 1976 Steve and Frank Taylor purchased it to open as a furrier business. Steve Taylor moved and continued in the furrier business on Water Street, but Frank stayed and opened the bar Rob Roy's in 1977. Due to a technicality, it cannot claim to be the oldest bar on George Street because when it first started the entrance was on Duckworth Street.

Christian's Bar, the oldest bar on George Street, opened on July 25, 1979 and marks the beginning of George Street as a street of bars. It gets its name from the original owner, Christian Decker. Back in those days, a beer cost $1.75, and a drink came to you for $2.25. Christian's served, as it

Christian's Bar on George Street. *Photo from author's private collection.*

does now, a clientele of working professionals, the university crowd, and people from the arts community. When Christian's first opened, George Street was basically a side street to Water Street with a few back entrances and several businesses on it.

Each of the bigger bars on George Street comes with some sort of interesting historical connection. Many can remember The Rock House as former health-food store Mary Jane's. The Sundance moved into the basement of the old Adelaide Motors building, opening up as a bar in 1979. Dusk Ultralounge stands on the site of a former bus depot, last stop for people coming in from rural Newfoundland to the big city, and Christian's occupies a space that was used as the O'Keefe Grocery warehouse (O'Reilly's is on the site of the old grocery store). Dick Hancock opened Green Sleeves in 1985 by converting two large old houses into one big building. Bridie Molloy's opened in 2002 on St. Patrick's Day.

When you walk into Trapper John's, you will see a wonderful collection of old work tools similar to the collections of artefacts in the old public houses of England. The original building at this location mostly burned to the ground in the great fire of 1892. The present building was rebuilt on the original stone foundation and reopened in the late 1800s as a blacksmith's shop, shoeing horses and fixing wagon wheels. The building became a bar called the Bull and Bear around 1976. In 1984, Joe Brown renamed the bar Trapper John's and moved the entrance to George Street. The bar changed ownership in 2009 but is still going strong. Trapper John's made its mark on George Street as the home of the Screech-in and has Screeched in such well known characters as Wayne Gretzky and Kiefer Sutherland. Joe Brown came up with the concept for the Screech-in as a way to make travellers honorary Newfoundlanders, starting it as a promotion for the bar. It became so popular the staff at Trapper's still do it today. It consists of four tasks.

1. Eat something from Newfoundland: baloney (named 'Newfie Steak' in the Great Depression). It has also sometimes been referred to as "dog."
2. Say something from Newfoundland: "Indeed I is me old cock and long may your big jib draw."

3. Drink something from Newfoundland: one ounce of Newfoundland Screech.

4. Kiss something from Newfoundland: a codfish or a stuffed puffin's arse.

The general consensus is that Joe Murphy and Joan Morrissey came up with the idea of the Screech-in at the Bella Vista and it was later popularized by Myrle Vokey who performed it widely. Trapper John's has been on George Street for over 30 years now and seven years before that as the Bull and Bear. Several years ago, *Reader's Digest* named Trapper's as one of the 50 most interesting pubs in the world—rating it at number four.

No one created a plan for George Street: one bar just fed off another and it grew organically. John "Bull" Cook remembers 6,000 to 7,000 people on George Street on a busy night years ago, whereas now you might get 2,000.

Occasionally the bar owners close off George Street for various events like the George Street Festival. The street hosts live-music performances on the outdoor stage, charge admission, and bar-hoppers can go from bar to bar with no cover. Patrons can take their beer with them out on the street, which is not normally allowed. The street hosts a Mardi Gras in October, and on Canada Day sponsors a family day. No organized events take place on St. Patrick's Day, but the George Street bars celebrate in the best Irish tradition.

QUEEN STREET

Queen Street hosted a number of taverns in its day. The Farrels kept a public house at number 10 Queen Street from 1864. When Mr. Farrel died, Mrs. Bridget Farrel remarried a man named John McGrath and continued to run the tavern until at least 1898. Next door to her establishment, lots of St. John's men congregated at Frank Trelegan's social saloon. After his death, Mrs. Francis, and later John (Jack) sold liquors at 12 Queen St. from 1864 to 1915.

Mr. G. J. Keough sold wines and spirits from 2 Queen Street from 1894 to 1897.

George Street. *Photos from author's private collection.*

The Queen Tavern appears in the city directories in 1950 to 1956 at number 3/5. Like many of the taverns in old St. John's, it was originally a boarding house, and was run by a C. J. Truscott. After his death, Annie Truscott, presumably his wife, took over as publican. Reputed to be a very small woman, she had to stand on a block of wood in order to serve customers over the bar. Many years ago, taverns would close up so that men would go home and have supper with their families, and then would reopen for a short time later on in the evening. The widowed Annie lived up on Powers Hill, off Gower Street, and after the second shift of the evening, a gentleman friend often had to walk her home.

The clientele at the Queen varied. In the early years, the bar opened at 5 a.m. to serve the old skippers (pensioners) who, after years of habitually getting up at that hour, came looking for a place to socialize. Lots of them had worked on the boats at one time, going off to fish at 4 a.m.

But there were also the people who came into St. John's from around the bay for doctor's appointments or to go shopping. They arrived at the taxi stand just up the road from the Queen and carried out their business in town. After their appointments, the women went shopping downtown and the men whiled away their time in the tavern. In the case of one family, who came in from Trepassey, father would go straight to the bar, always wearing a hat and a full suit. When it was time to take the taxi back to Trepassey, his young daughter would be sent to fetch him. At age seven or eight, she wasn't allowed in the bar but would just poke her head through the door and have someone else give him the message.

In 1959 the tavern at number 5 Queen Street appeared under the name of City Tavern, and through the years changed names a number of times: Heritage Inn, Gus's Tavern, Fiddler's Green, and, most recently, Fiddler's Pub. It is possible these bars shared multiple locations on Queen Street or street numbers changed as the city developers re-worked the downtown area. Today, the former Fiddler's is closed.

FRESHWATER ROAD

The Cottage Garden on Freshwater Road was originally a private residence, belonging to grocer Mr. J. J. St. John. In 1938 a tea room under that name opened in the house. When Freddy Phaelen took over the old, two-storey, peaked-roof building in the mid-twentieth century, he converted it into a bar, opening up the main floor to make one big room. It soon became a well-frequented tavern, serving the drinking needs of everyone in the neighbourhood. A little rougher around the edges than in its tea-room days, business boomed, especially on Friday and Saturday nights after the men got paid. A lot of longshoremen and council workers frequented this tavern. Freddy acted as bouncer as well, and it would be no strange sight to see a couple of bodies each night flying out through the front door. When Freddy gave up the bar business, his son took over.

Like almost all the old taverns, the Cottage Garden had its dart leagues. The *Daily News* of 1959 published the league games, and one often sees Cottage Garden vs. Hilltop Tavern. Some serious dart players came out of the Cottage.

In 1997 the Cottage Garden came under new management. Ed "Relic" Rees took over the club, which advertised dancing, darts, stags, private parties, and meetings. Towards the end of its life, business slowed with the police crackdown on drinking and driving. Consumed by fire in the 1990s, all that remains now is an empty lot next to Tony the Tailor's on Freshwater.

HUTCHINGS STREET

The Station Lounge first opened as the Station Hotel under Gasker A. Rowe in 1930. He advertised "Comfortable Accommodation for Travellers. Reasonable Rates," and no doubt did a very fine business, located at that time opposite the St. John's railway station. Gasker's wife, Annie (Anastasia) Rowe, took over in 1946 and ran it until 1955, and by the looks of it she was a very busy woman. Mrs. Rowe's receipts for the Station Hotel and Tavern (1951-1954) include purchases of Labatt's, Black Horse, Molson's, O'Keefe's, Red Cap, and King's beer. The station sported a jukebox and the pinball machines "Fireball" and "Shuffle Alley." In 1951 total sales from the hotel and tavern amounted to $14,480. Mrs. Rowe had $5,500 left on her mortgage in 1952 and leased the land that the tavern stood on from the Hutchings' estate at $32.52 biannually.[18]

Morley Rowe took over the bar in 1962 and renamed it the Station Inn. The Station Lounge is still operating on Hutchings Street today, and it clocks in as one of the oldest bars in the city.

HAMILTON AVENUE

Another neighbourhood bar, the West End Club on Hamilton Avenue, is very old as well. Number 16 Hamilton Avenue started life as Hamlyn's Forge sometime before 1924. From 1928 to at least 1936, Mrs. Francis Lockyer ran it as Glencoe House, and then Mrs. L. Wilcox took it over, followed by Mrs. S.J. Budden. As boarding houses often served food and alcohol, it may have acted as a sort of a tavern as well. It went through various owners/managers from 1942 to 1990, changing hands and names. First mentioned as the Hamilton Inn in 1942, it remained as such until 1951 with Thomas Brownrigg as owner. Michael F. Power purchased

Comfortable living. The upstairs apartment of the the Hamilton Inn where the owner lived with his family. *Photo courtesy of Michael Power.*

the building that year and hired his brother-in-law, Scotsman Thomas Thomson, to manage the club. Mr. Thomson and his family lived in the comfortable flat above the club.

In 1979 the club was sold and the name changed to the Foxhunt (1979-1983). Sold again in 1984, the club was renamed the Fireside Club. After a period of vacancy in the early 1990s, Mr. Reddy opened it as the West End Club, named after a property the Reddy family had owned on 719 Water Street. In 2017, the club changed ownership again but is still open under the name of West End Club today.[19]

TORBAY ROAD

As early as 1890, Maurice Fennelon had a summer residence on Torbay Road called Bella Vista Cottage. Perhaps close by or on the same property, Mayor Carnell opened a racecourse on the Bella Vista fairgrounds in July of 1934. A place to picnic and drink as well as watch the races, it is listed in the 1936 directory under the rather clinical title of Beer and Wine Dispensary. By the 1940s, P. C. O'Driscoll took it over, seeing to the drinking needs of customers coming from St. John's and Torbay. Drinking times were different back then. Because no one worked on the Wednesday afternoon half-holiday in the 1940s, it became a favourite time for drinking. The regular work week ran from Monday to Saturday, six days a week with a holiday on Sunday and a half-holiday on Wednesday. When workplaces closed at 12 p.m. on Wednesday, the Bella Vista Country Club overflowed with people.

In 1952 the Young family purchased the building and land, which included the racetrack and other buildings. It remained popular with the servicemen from nearby Fort Pepperell until the Americans left in 1961. A fire in the building forced the owners to renovate and remodel. After trying several different businesses, they hit upon a great idea when they opened the disco in 1977—a renovation that cost them a princely sum.

With the disco craze in full swing, Stanley's Steamer disco on the main floor of the "Bell" packed them in with dancing and drinking under the giant flashing disco ball. In 2017, the Bella Vista celebrated sixty-five years as a bar/dance hall/restaurant.

BROOKFIELD ROAD

Three men from the Bonavista area built the Old Mill on Brookfield Road in the early 1950s and opened it in 1954. They hired Jerry Stevens, a German immigrant who anglicized his name, to manage the operation. A good choice, Jerry efficiently ran the Old Mill for many years. Sitting at tables upstairs and down, patrons came to listen to the music of the Ducats, the Michaels, Chrissy Andrews, and the occasional American jazz pianist from Fort Pepperell.

In 1964, ladies in crinoline dresses and gloves and gentlemen in shirts and ties took the romantic drive out from the city for drinks and dancing at the Old Mill. The advertisements of that time describe it as a place to see and be seen, just 10 minutes' drive from the city. If the men didn't wear a shirt and tie, they didn't get in. The management kept a box of ties out in the coatroom to outfit anyone who came without the proper attire. The live bands played there every week, and on Sunday afternoons, crowds lined up to get into the regular afternoon matinee dance. Downstairs, the restaurant served up many a steak.

After Jerry Stevens left, several people took over and unsuccessfully tried to keep the Old Mill going. The business failed, however, until Ralph Neal entered the scene in 1980 and took over the bank-owned, vacant building. Along with a few friends, they rented the place to run bingo and support the Mount Pearl hockey league. The nightly bingo ran until the bank, unhappy with the rental arrangement, put forth an ultimatum either to buy the building or stop the bingo. Ralph and his friends decided to buy the building and redo it. Soon afterwards, Ralph bought out the other gentlemen. Ralph Neal has owned the business ever since. The original manager, Jerry Stevens, opened another bar in St. John's in the 1960s, but after a few years left Newfoundland for good and moved to Oshawa. At 95 years old, he still keeps in touch with present owner Ralph Neal.[20]

PORTUGAL COVE ROAD

The original Old Colony Club was a beautiful two-storey wooden building with a winding staircase, built by Mr. B. D. "Benny" Parsons.

It opened in 1941, and featured a dance hall, cafeteria, offices, men's and lady's dressing rooms, and accommodation for manager and staff on the second floor. Fire destroyed it in 1943 around the same time as the Knights of Columbus Hostel fire. Four staff members died, and many St. John's residents suspected espionage, because the Old Colony Club was a popular place for the troops to go during World War II.[21]

Parsons rebuilt the club and had his grand opening on New Year's Eve 1943. The Colony Club did not have a liquor licence at that time, so if you were holding a private party, you brought your own liquor. Many patrons got their 40-ouncers from the American army base at Fort Pepperell, and on Saturday nights quite a few tables sported these large bottles of liquor. In 1950 it became the first licenced club in Newfoundland. Sam Soper bought out Parsons and became the new owner/operator.

Patrons at the Old Colony held close relationships, and one patron described it as "one big happy family." It was no sweat to get a date if you were going to the Old Colony Club. Social etiquette of the time dictated that a man would go with his girlfriend or his wife and have the first and last dance with her. In between, he left her alone to socialize with her female friends and the men went table-hopping.

Bands playing there included Chris Andrews and Leo Michael, Joe Murphy, the Princess Orchestra, and Micky Duggan's band. These four- to eight-piece bands played for 8 to 10 dollars a night, and packed in as many as 300 people. The cover charge of one to two dollars per person was pretty big money in those days. Then on top of that, patrons ordering their coke and ice would often get hungry and order steaks and sandwiches.

The Old Colony held a formal dance on New Year's Eve with everyone dressing up in their finery. You had to be a member if you wanted a ticket for the big New Year's Eve celebration, and people lined up and waited for ages to get in. While they were waiting, they drank outside in the parking lot, their car bars well stocked with three or four bottles of rum to keep out the cold. Once in, patrons danced the night away, reluctant to stop. Often, to keep the orchestra playing, everyone would sit on the floor after the last number until the band played again.

In the mid-1960s, Sam Soper worked the bar of the Old Colony, a stern but nice gentleman. If men came in after work and their wives

phoned looking for them, Sam would never lie. When the bar closed at
8 p.m., Sam told the men to go home to their wives. Primarily a dinner
club, the Old Colony's bar kept regular hours from Monday to Friday, but
stayed open later for parties or weddings. One gentleman that came into
the club could throw his voice without moving his lips and would constantly play pranks on the other patrons by calling out their names and
sending them off on wild goose chases. The patrons enjoyed good times
gathered around the piano with real estate agent Tom Byrnes on the keys
and Dave Barrett singing.

Sam Soper lived in an apartment over the Old Colony while his
brother and sister owned Neyle Soper's hardware store on Water Street,
now the home of Rocket Bakery.

Paul Johnson bought the club in 1985 but sold it in 2004. The Old
Colony was torn down and a senior's home now stands in its place. It was
a loss to the city, but renovations to bring everything up to code in the old
building, wheelchair accessibility, etc., would have been far too expensive.[22]

TOPSAIL ROAD

Freddy Michael started a club on Topsail Road called the Piccadilly. The
club opened up on December 23, 1949, and stayed under Freddy's management until 1955. He claims to have had the first commercial liquor
licence at that time. Prior to that, the clubs made most of their money on
cover charge. Starting off, entertainment at the Piccadilly consisted of a
jukebox which played lots of the popular songs of the day, "Blue Tango"
being the favourite. After confederation, local bands played live music
there on the weekends. The Old Colony, the Bella Vista, and the Octagon
Pond Pavilion (on the site of McNamara Construction) were other popular spots at that time.[23] The Piccadilly shows up in the city directories
until 1974.

HAYWARD AVENUE

The Georgetown Pub opened up in 1949.[24] In those days, people used a
lot of coal to heat their houses, and they had to get rid of the ashes. In

the forties, the drivers, or ashmen, went around picking up the ashes for the city. They often rested their horses in the vacant lot across the street from what was then called the Corner Tavern. They routinely popped in for a beer, hence its nickname 'the Ashcan' or 'the Ashman's Tavern'. By the early 1960s the tavern seems to have been replaced by a real-estate company for a short while, but then turns back into a tavern in 1968, still under the name Corner Tavern.

A true "neighbourhood" pub, it was one of the last "men only" bars in St. John's. The patrons protested vehemently in 1977 when plans arose to let women into the tavern with comments like "She's gone, b'y, this is it, she's gone," "We don't want no women in and that's it period," and "I don't want women here—I come to get away from them."[25] Previously, these male hangouts afforded men time to talk among themselves, bond, and discuss everything from politics to work life and more besides. Still today, one bar owner reiterated the comments of the 1970s saying that letting women into the bars "ruined it," making them less social venues and more pick-up spots.

The Corner Tavern did finally admit women, but grudgingly. A co-owner at the time stated that with only one washroom for men, if the women came in and wanted to use it, they could take their chances. He stated that they wouldn't be doing anything to encourage women as long as the tavern made money in its present state. Management changed, however, and so did the attitudes at the Corner Tavern.[26]

New owners renamed it the Georgetown Pub in 1982. It lay vacant for a while in 1992-93 and then fired up again. It is still in business today as a bar.

BONCLODDY STREET

Another one of the old neighbourhood taverns, the Sports Tavern, located at 11-13 Boncloddy Street, started at least as early as 1951 under Alf Conners. It carried on until 2013 when it closed, much to the relief of many local residents who complained of noise, drug deals, loud music, and lack of parking around the bar. The Sports Tavern had a reputation as a rough spot. In its earlier days, the clientele consisted mostly of young men from the boarding houses on Lime Street. They came in from around the bay, enjoyed "living it up" and certainly knew how to take care of themselves. Purported to be "not as bad as the Cottage Gardens," Sports Tavern patrons stayed loyal to their neighbourhood watering hole, and tended not to set foot around the corner at the Cottage.

COCHRANE STREET

Cochrane Street had a couple of good bars—the bar at the Cochrane Hotel and, right around the corner, the Royalton owned by Freddy Michael.

The Cochrane Hotel may have started as a tavern run by Mr. Kearney in 1893 but opened as the Cochrane Hotel in 1894. In 1930, the proprietor, Mr. W.E. Stirling, formed a company with Mr. Cyril Tessier to run the hotel. The Cochrane boasted a colourful history, with Leon Trotsky and Guglielmo Marconi as guests. In the early 1970s it was a popular venue for university types. As with so many old buildings in downtown St. John's, it ultimately burned to the ground.

The Royalton, at 49 Cochrane Street, was just around the corner from the Cochrane Hotel and its bar. Known as the "Hottest spot north of Havana," "Freddy's Bar," and "Where the Elite Meet," Freddy Michael and his brother, Leo, bought the former Merchant Mariner club in 1967. After many years selling insurance, Freddy fulfilled his life-long dream of owning a bar and bought his brother out. Freddy, Micky, and Leo were all part of Leo Michael's Big Little Band, well known in St. John's during the war years, so as an entertainer at heart, Freddy revelled in the joking and general shenanigans of his new bar life.

Freddy used the main floor as the bar, rented out the second storey for private parties and weddings, and rented the third floor to residential tenants. One interesting feature left behind from the club's Merchant Mariner days was a large compass inlaid in the tile surface of the main floor.

The bar drew its patrons from a variety of sources: people from the neighbourhood, the university, and the arts community. When Freddy opened up each day at 12 p.m., he had a bunch of regulars that came religiously, developing into a sort of unofficial men's club. Dave Barrett and VOCM's Bill Squires instigated a lot of the fun. Regaling each other with jokes, they often improvised their own bit of theatre and pretence.

Cochrane Hotel building, circa 1895. *Photo courtesy of Archives and Special Collections, Queen Elizabeth II Library, Memorial University.*

One of their favourite games was to act as if they were passengers on an airplane. They arranged the bar chairs in two rows and simulated landing the aircraft and taking off by rearing back in their chairs. Freddy acted the part of the flight attendant, mincing down to jokingly offer his passengers a sort of "coffee, tea, or me" service.

When racist hooligans threatened Freddy and trashed his car, he was forced to install a door with a medieval-like peephole. After a certain hour in the evening, patrons had to knock to gain entry. Freddy would put on a little hat and open the window to check on who was there. He would let you in if he knew you were okay. Patrons of the bar loved this new innovation and felt privileged and special to be allowed into the bar. This is perhaps where some people got the impression it was a private club.

Freddy, being a former band member, liked to sing and would often get up and sing a song with whoever was playing that night. The last time Freddy ever sang in the club was on one evening when Terry Reilly and Glenn Tilley were playing. At the end of the night, they accompanied him as he sang, "When the moon hits your eye like a big pizza pie," down on one knee with his arms spread dramatically.[27]

COOKSTOWN ROAD

Janet and Paul Kelly applied for a tavern licence in 1964 and opened one of the most well-known bars in St. John's—Bridgett's Pub. Located at 29 Cookstown Road, its ambiance and live musical performances drew regular crowds. The sign outside the building, produced by one of the local beer companies, incorrectly spelled the name Bridget. The term pub or public house had not been commonly used in Newfoundland for a drinking establishment since the 1600s, but Janet and Paul adopted it to give the lounge an air of old-English tradition. The Kellys were delighted when the liquor licence arrived and it stated "lounge" and not "tavern." In those days a tavern could sell only beer and wine; whereas a lounge could sell any sort of liquor. In the 1960s, when Joseph R. Smallwood reigned as premier of the province, potential bar owners couldn't just apply for a tavern licence. They had to find a place in the neighbourhood for sale. The government of the time did not give out any new licences; you had to acquire an existing licence from someone willing to sell. Janet and Paul got their property from "Babe" Kelly (no relation), who had a bar called the Hilltop Tavern, then on LeMarchant and Cookstown Roads.

Back in the heyday of the Hilltop Tavern, bar-hoppers prior to the mid-sixties often had to have strong immune systems. Many taverns back then did not have plumbing, and Babe's place was no exception. Her patrons cleaned their glasses by "swishing" them in a tub of hot water which sat on the potbelly stove in the middle of the bar. When you needed a clean glass you just reached in and took one out. Babe had a little porthole in the door of the Hilltop that she opened, and if she didn't like you, you weren't coming in. In addition to the difficulties getting a licence, the government of the day tended to overlook sanitation misdemeanours, such as those at the Hilltop, if tavern owners stayed loyal to the party.

Government minister John Crosbie was the first to change the rule on the acquisition of tavern licences. After the amendments, you didn't have to buy an existing tavern: you could buy a new licence and open your own bar or lounge. The drinking age was 21 in the days of the Smallwood government, and bars closed by 11:30 p.m. or 12 midnight, but you could pay to get an extension of an hour or so for a special occasion like a wedding.

Because Bridgett's was in what was then known as a rough area, with a number of rowdy bars nearby, the Kellys upped their image by having the waiters and bartenders dress up in fine clothes. Staff wore grey pants with black stripping down the side, white shirts, and polished shoes. The all-male clientele at the time apparently loved it. The patrons could come in and have a drink in their work clothes after work, from 5 to 7, but afterwards, to gain admittance, they had to wear a shirt and tie. The men seemed to like getting dressed up. Another advantage to this system was that men in their best clothes were much less likely to start a fight.

When Janet Kelly came to work at Bridgett's in the early seventies, the male patrons did not want her there at first, especially when she made up little cards offering a free beer at Bridgett's and distributed them to all her feminist friends. The law didn't ban women from taverns, but society at the time considered it unladylike to go in and have a drink. Women only went out to a club or bar when accompanied by a man.

Some women did go out to buy take-out drinks. One old lady would regularly come into Bridgett's and asked the bartender to sell her a six pack to go—which wasn't really legal, but many bars did it because beer wasn't available at corner stores then as it is today.

One day, Janet suggested that an elderly female customer didn't have to do that: she could come in and sit down. One of the male patrons looked up and said, "She can't stay. We don't have any facilities here for women." The elderly woman spat right back at him: "I came for beer, not a piss." After that, Janet had two bathrooms set up: one for ladies and one for gents.

Women who ran taverns and hotels worked very hard, but were well respected. Janet Kelly's Auntie Crae ran a hotel in St. John's and only sold her customers drinks until she thought they had had enough.

Janet Kelly practised a similar "social control" at her bar, sometimes cashing a customer's cheque, but only letting them spend $20 of it. She told them to come back the next day to collect the rest. The hope was they would be sober enough the next day to bring the rest of the money back to their families.[28]

The host of a folk night for many years, the tradition continued at The Ship when Bridgett's closed in 1994. A video-rental business occupied the space for a short time, and then Peter Easton's, still in business today, opened as a pub in 1997.

CHURCHILL SQUARE

Big Ben's began selling alcohol on February 10, 1972, and still serves up drinks in Churchill Square. When the Cook family first opened Ben's, John "Bull" Cook's father had just retired and wanted to try his hand at running a bar. They opened Ben's on a shoestring budget with mother doing the books and father taking care of the inventory. Ben's was a favourite spot for both students and professors from Memorial University. One English professor actually held classes there, engaging in lively discussions much loved by the students. Nowadays, fire capacity rules limit Big Ben's to 100 people, but in the old days as many as 200 people crowded in, making it very difficult to move. Ben's, in its heyday, would sell up to 2,400 bottles of beer in a day.

Soon after Big Ben's started up, two other bars opened in the square: Milt's and the Circle Lounge. The Circle Lounge was originally called the Park Lounge, with a hotel operating out of the upstairs. The hotel part shut down, and the Circle opened up instead. The owners renovated the ground floor into a steakhouse called Milt's, which was popular on Friday nights. Both Milt's and the Circle burned down in the mid-1970s. This was bad for Ben's because the bars all lived off one another. People would go from one to the other in a night, liking the change in location so they could see different crowds.[29]

MCMURDO'S LANE

John Cook started another iconic St. John's pub in 1987, The Duke of Duckworth, and sold it to two former employees, Terry O'Rourke and Colin Dalton in 1990. Located in a small alley called McMurdo's Lane, which runs between Water Street and Duckworth Street, it is now world famous as part of the set of Newfoundland's former hit TV show Republic of Doyle. This St. John's pub occupies a building once owned by

The interior of the Duke. *Photo from author's private collection.*

a uniform manufacturer named White's Clothing Company, and before that it belonged to Clara Smallwood. The owners tell me The Duke is the most successful bar in the city.

John Cook and his family also took over the Corner Tavern (now the Georgetown Pub) at one point in its history. Cook helped open many other bars, too: Uncle Albert's, the Fogo-a-Gogo, the Sundance, Barrister's, the Cock and Bull, the Rob Roy (along with Frank Taylor), and Barkley's in Mount Pearl. [30]

SOLOMON'S LANE

A British couple from Liverpool, Peter and Sheina Parnham, opened The Ship, located on Solomon's Lane, another small alleyway running between Water and Duckworth Streets. The Parnhams arrived in Newfoundland in 1953 and bought the building in the early 1960s. Peter Parnham rented out some of the space, and his tenants started up a bar called Dirty Dick's on the main floor. These tenant/bar owners ran into a spot of trouble with the law and left town quickly. Mr. Parnham tried a second lease, but after another unhappy experience, he decided to try opening a bar of his own. The Parnhams started The Ship Inn in 1977 as a restaurant, closing every evening at 7 p.m. They quickly realized they had enough business to stay open into the night as well. Because of its location, they naturally attracted the theatre crowd and people from the nearby newspaper offices and the CBC radio building. The Parnhams took the name of an old Newfoundland tavern, The Ship, which had graced the "Lower

OPPOSITE: The Ship Inn. The original owners, the Parnham family, named their pub after one of the earliest taverns in St. John's, the Ship Tavern. Located on the north side of Water Street, east of the War Memorial, the Ship was reputed to have had some famous customers: Lord Nelson in 1781, William Bligh of Bounty fame, Captain James Cook and Sir Joseph Banks, the botanist. There is no mention of the Ship in the nineteenth century—eclipsed, perhaps, by the popularity of the London Tavern. The original Ship Inn most probably had a swinging sign showing a large sailing ship. In Michael P. Murphy's book *Pathways through Yesterday*, he states that the original ship was possibly run by a Mrs. Betty Burton, wife of a British sea Captain lost at sea during one of his frequent trips from Bristol to Newfoundland. *Photo from author's private collection.*

Path" several centuries ago, and ran the bar from 1977 to 2003. Known as patrons of the arts, they would occasionally settle bar tabs with art, or simply buy art off local artists. Well-known Newfoundland artist Gerry Squires paid his bar tab one day by painting the original sign for the pub, a sailing ship on the high seas.

One story told about Newfoundland singer-songwriter Ron Hynes occurred at The Ship. It seems that Ron was playing at the pub and a group of customers began to argue and debate quite loudly. Ron started playing louder and louder, until finally the music lover jumped up and yelled out, "Don't you realize we're trying to have a conversation here!" Hynes played at The Ship over 200 times, once in the middle of a blackout.

Still in operation but no longer part of the Parnham family, The Ship, like The Duke, has been featured in movies, TV series, music, and art.[31]

QUIDI VIDI

Many well-known bars exist outside the city centre. The Inn of Olde, in Quidi Vidi Village, has been a popular spot since it opened in 1977. Linda Hennebury and her husband bought a house and initially operated it as a store in 1965, then a pool room was added, and finally it became a pub. When patrons walk into the Inn of Olde, the breathtaking array of artefacts and memorabilia on the walls and ceiling strikes them right away. This curious old building has slanting floors where the original builder adapted the house to the shape of the cliff rocks below it.

Linda has done her share of Screech-ins as well. The Countess Mountbatten of Burma, first cousin to Prince Phillip, came to visit one day and insisted she be Screeched-in.

One day, Linda even had a horse as a patron. A lady with a horse arrived outside the Inn of Olde and Linda's husband, Bob, struck up a conversation and invited her and the horse into the bar. The horse came up to the bar—reins, saddle, and all—and stood looking at a very startled Linda. The equestrian did not order a drink, but he certainly gave whole new meaning to the term "watering hole."[32]

TORBAY

Torbay's best-known bar, Mrs. Liddy's, has an interesting story. The history of the land it occupies goes back to when Lord Amherst landed in Torbay in 1762. St. John's was occupied by the French, and Amherst had a plan to take it back. Since it was meant to be a surprise attack, and since getting from Torbay to St. John's back then wasn't an easy task on just a cow path, Amherst hired two local men, one named Gosse and another named Codner, to show him and his forces the way to St. John's. After the successful battle, he marched back to Torbay and rewarded the two men with a parcel of land each. Gosse got the parcel of land on which the Liddy's bar of today was built. About 160 years ago, a descendant of the original guide built a house here, and one of his Gosse descendants ended up marrying a Morey. Mary Morey inherited the property and eventually married into the Liddy family, becoming the famous Mrs. Liddy. In 1898 her husband, William Liddy, practised as a druggist in Torbay South. Mrs. Liddy passed away in 1970, but her picture still hangs above the pool table. When Glen Stokes bought the bar in the late 1990s, he and his wife gave it a new lease on life, running the bar downstairs and an escape-room business upstairs. Still very proud of its history, Stokes loves to recount these stories from the bar's history.

Mr. and Mrs. Liddy outside Liddy's in Torbay. It can probably lay claim to being one of the oldest bars in Newfoundland. *Photo courtesy of Glenn Stokes.*

Mrs. Liddy's had the first telephone in Torbay, but you weren't allowed to use it unless you had a couple of drinks first. There's a story about a fellow who came into the bar on a Tuesday dressed up in his Sunday finest, shirt and tie and all. And some one said, "Geez, George! What are you doing all dressed up on a Tuesday?" "Expecting an important phone call from St. John's." George replied, straightening his tie.

Another funny story concerned a certain fisherman from Petty Harbour. His son explained:

> When I was a kid, Dad used to go to Torbay to get caplin for bait, and he'd be gone for three or four days. Now we thought Torbay must be up by St. Anthony somewhere because he was gone so long. Eventually we found out he was passing the time at Liddy's, drinking. He'd get a room for the nights and spend the three days happily inebriated, warming a seat at the bar.[33]

It must have been a pleasant place to pass time as it had a giant woodstove that would take five-foot-long logs. If those walls could talk...!

Marilyn Pumphrey, wife of former radio personality and writer Ron Pumphrey, recounts the story of how her parents got together at Mrs. Liddy's. The young couple wanted to go out for a drink to get to know each other better, but it was a Sunday night and there was nowhere open in St. John's. Liddy's was the answer. When she returned home, her grandfather, a Methodist teetotaller from Northern Ireland, admonished his granddaughter, "My dear, you are going to perdition drinking on a Sunday night." Perdition or not, it seems to have worked out well for her since she married the Sunday-night boy.[34]

Mrs. Liddy's claims to be the oldest bar in Newfoundland.[35]

PORTUGAL COVE-ST. PHILIPS

With no bar in the Portugal Cove-St. Philips area in the 1950s, '60s or '70s, men went to the Legion to drink. When you fancied a drop of rum on the off hours, you visited the bootlegger. You could always get "a drop of stuff" down in the cove. The bootlegger would park on the wharf by the ferry and sell from there. He would never get out of the car, just hand the customer the keys to the trunk. A trusting soul, he let you pick out your flask of liquor and pay him through the window of the car. Sunday mornings was the most popular time for this exchange.

Other bootleggers sold from their house, a risky business and unpleasant with people knocking on your door at 2 a.m.[36]

BELL ISLAND

In the 1930s, on nearby Bell Island, residents got their supplies of alcohol from a lady named Rosie. She made her own wines of blueberry, dogberry, and dandelion and found a unique spot to hide them. Living in a house close to one of the mines, one day she discovered a way into one of the mined-out rooms from her basement. What better place to store wine? Cool, damp, and no one ever went in there. Well-known as a bootlegger, the Newfoundland Rangers continually raided her home, trying to find her stash, but she simply covered the access to the mine and the rangers never found it or the booze. The poor woman had lost her husband in a mining accident, and so with no other means of support, bootlegging kept her going. Another enterprising Bell Island woman operated a she-been out of her front parlour, and local men congregated there, especially on Sunday afternoons.

One of the local Rangers, Leo Kennedy, was a regular over on Bell Island. He would come over looking for stills and illegal alcohol but rarely found any. As word of Leo's arrival quickly travelled around the island, everyone hid their alcohol. One day, when Ed Fitzgerald's father had gone to work, word got out that Leo had arrived on the island and Ed's mother was left with the task of disposing of her husband's homebrew. When Ed's father got home from work that evening, he heard the news and asked her where she had put his beer. "In the piss pail," she replied. Horrified, he sputtered, "My God, woman, couldn't you have thought of throwing it into the water bucket?"

Some individuals bought their alcohol from foreign-going vessels docked at the local pier to load up on iron ore. Others went "fishing" for a bottle. They would go out in their small boats, pretend to fish, and then pull alongside one of the big ships asking, "Do you want to buy any fish?"

This was code for "Have you got any booze on board to sell?" When the answer was yes, the ship's crew countered with "How many fish have you got?" That let them know how many bottles you could afford to buy. They would then send down a basket with the required number of bottles and the fisherman would send the basket back up again with the correct amount of money and a few fish just for show.

One miner named Arthur brought a special "tea bottle" to work in the mines. The bottle held rum with a few tea leaves thrown on top to make it look good. At the end of the day, Arthur's bottle of tea would be empty just like everyone else's, but Arthur would be feeling much better than most. A mucker, he spent his days shovelling iron ore, and as an educated man he could recite poetry, either drunk or sober, to "bring tears to your eyes."[37]

BEYOND THE OVERPASS

If you lived in Harbour Grace you might have strolled down to the Avalon Tavern on Harvey Road in 1957. In Holyrood, you had at least two to choose from: Crawley's Tavern and Matt Davis's Tavern.

Many settlements outside of St. John's did not formally come into being until the twentieth century. Corner Brook, for example, was previously a collection of four smaller independent towns until they amalgamated in 1956. These four towns—Corner Brook East, Corner Brook West, Townsite, and Curling—all seemed to be conservative when it came to drink. In 1942 Corner Brook West's first town council inherited one tavern, and kept it down to that number. They rejected five applications for beer taverns in 1944, asserting that a beer tavern was not an asset to any town and it would only overtax the already busy police force.

Corner Brook East (Humbermouth) were just as conservative with regard to liquor establishments. In 1951, the town council held a plebiscite looking for the opinion of the townsfolk as to whether or not to allow Michael Williams, owner of the Silverdale Restaurant in Humbermouth, to operate a tavern in his restaurant. The residents turned it down. Of the 965 voters, 813 voted against it. Those looking for a drink had to visit taverns elsewhere.

William Lundrigan showed his annoyance with the Corner Brook West town council in 1952 when he wrote a letter to the editor describing the tavern history of the area and complaining about the increased number of places where one could buy alcohol. He was particularly upset with the decision of council to allow a tavern to operate in close proximity to the Jewish synagogue. At this time, the town had two taverns and several other places where beer and wine were offered for sale.

The attitude in Curling was slightly different, as taverns are recorded in the area: Boland's Tavern in 1952 and Walker's Tavern in 1951. And Corner Brook (Townsite) had a few taverns: Whelan's, Corbage's, and the Humber Road Tavern, 1949-51.

When Townsite held a vote as to whether to increase the number of taverns, the response was a resounding no. The same results came up in the plebiscite held in Corner Brook East. Lundrigan blamed "certain groups" for persistently lobbying the council—as it happens, the application came from someone within council.[38]

The Ford Tavern in Bonavista, originally owned by Robert Ford and his family, was built as a public house by Robert's father, Steven, possibly as early as the 1820s. It had rooms to rent upstairs, as many public houses of the time did. Diaries kept by merchant James Ryan of Bonavista refer to the premises as a 'gentleman's saloon' and local oral history suggests it also functioned as a brothel. *Photo from author's private collection.*

Not far from Corner Brook, Ray Wellon unofficially opened his cocktail lounge in Steady Brook in January 1951, replacing the previous club that was lost to a fire. The *Western Star* described the interior as having large red leather and chrome chairs with seating for 160 people, but explained, "Ladies admitted only with an escort." The lounge had a semicircular bar built of glass blocks with coloured lighting, and a stage for an orchestra. The nearby dining room seated 40 and the upstairs hotel had 10 rooms and two bathrooms. The expected completion date was June of 1951.[39]

After liquor restrictions eased in 1966, bars became commonplace. Anyone growing up in the 1960s and '70s in Corner Brook remembers going to Al Kawaja's on Connolly Drive and the Seaport Lounge on Main Street. On hot summer nights, it was always a treat driving out to Wellons, up the road to the Lakeland Motel in Pasadena, or Maxwell's in Deer Lake.

CHAPTER NINE

THE BREWERIES

THE COMMERCIAL BREWING INDUSTRY IN ST. JOHN'S BEGAN IN the early nineteenth century. In the *Christmas Review* of 1892, Sir Robert Pinsent stated that a Mr. Haire erected the first brewery in St. John's at Mundy's Brook in 1801. Perhaps Mr. Haire moved on or had a partner because Alexander Caine's name appears in connection with a malt-beer brewery in a letter from Governor Gambier in 1802. This letter states that it was Caine who established the malt-beer brewery on Mundy's Brook.[1]

No matter who started the brewing industry in St. John's, it certainly enjoyed immediate success. The 1857 census shows three unnamed breweries in town producing a total of 16,000 gallons (72,800L) of malt liquor.[2] But from 1869 and 1874, after an economic downturn and the resulting population change, the number of breweries reduced to just one (probably Bennett Brewing), and in 1877, there were two: C. F. Bennett & Company, and Lindberg and Backstrom. By 1895, the number increased again to three.

BENNETT BREWING

The most well-known of the local breweries, Riverhead Brewing Company, later known as Bennett Brewing, brewed beer in the city for over 125 years. Its records stretch from at least 1827 to 1962. A map of the facility discovered in the 1950s indicates it may have started as early as 1790. Located in the west end of the city, in an area known as Riverhead, this 'mixed factory' was one of the earliest manufacturing complexes in St. John's and included a brewery, a distilling plant for whisky (1860), a saw mill, a flour mill, an iron foundry, a forge, and a boat-building yard.

The Bennetts built a dam on Mullin's River, creating another small pond at the site of the former Grace Hospital near Bennett Avenue. They then successfully re-directed the river down through Victoria Park, very close to the brewery and factories. A wooden water wheel powered the complex, and the river supplied water to the brewery, which was located on what is now Sudbury Street. This Riverhead Complex, and later Bennett Brewing, contributed significantly to the local economy.

Charles Fox Bennett, operator and owner of the complex, was an interesting character. Born in Shaftsbury, Dorset, England, he involved himself heavily in local politics for many years. In 1870, at the age of seventy-seven, he was elected prime minister of Newfoundland. When he died in 1883, at age ninety-one, his confidential clerk, Edward W. Bennett (no relation), assumed control of the company, which now produced ale, porter, stout, cider, aerated water "champagne," sarsaparilla, lemonade, and raspberry nectar.[3]

Bennett Brewery in St. John's. *Courtesy of NL Collection, Provincial Resource Library.*

When the first sign of temperance reared its head in Newfoundland during the late 1800s, local breweries continued to operate but adapted to the changes in taste by marketing foreign stout, ale, and porter as medicinal beverages for those in 'delicate health.' In 1897, E. W. Bennett's Riverhead Brewery produced an "Invalid Stout." Most of the breweries also produced syrups and aerated waters, known today as soft drinks.

Despite their good intentions to supply those in need with a medicinal draught, Bennett Brewing was quickly blamed for a troubling incident on October 15, 1876. On that day, several fires broke out in St. John's, including one at the Protestant 'Free Kirk.' Some local residents questioned the quality of the firefighting and, by Sunday, insinuated that the firemen had been drinking at Bennett's brewery and were well in their cups by the second fire. One of the firemen (many of whom were Irish Catholic) purportedly yelled, "Let the bloody Protestant church burn down." But an investigation concluded that the failure to rescue the Kirk was due more to a lack of organization than a lack of zeal on the part of the firefighters.[4]

And as if troubles with public opinion were not enough, Bennett's occasionally had difficulty with their staff as well. One brewmaster, a Mr. Langston, was forced to go to the hospital due to a bad case of eczema. The doctor assured the company president that after a few days in hospital Mr. Langston would be cured. Unfortunately, Mr. Langston did not have the patience to stay under medical care. He discharged himself, found a tavern, got good and drunk, and eventually ended up in the poor asylum.[5]

Even some less-exalted staff members caused trouble. On the morning of Thursday, February 20, 1908, A. A. Lush, the manager at Bennett's, sent Hedley LeMessurier, an office boy, to deposit a large sum of money in the bank. Lush had given Hedley the company bank book, but when the young man returned promptly at 1 p.m., he was without the bank book, explaining that the bank had kept it to write the receipt. This was common practice, so Mr. Lush's suspicions were not aroused. Hedley came to work on Friday, Saturday, and Monday, but not on the following Tuesday. On Wednesday, Lush received a note from Hedley stating that he was ill and would not be at work for a few days. By Saturday, people noticed that there was no sign of Hedley anywhere, and a general search began. By Monday, March 2, Lush sent a stable boy to check on Hedley. The stable boy returned with a sobbing Mrs. LeMessurier, who said she hadn't seen her husband for a week. When Mr. Lush phoned the bank, he discovered that no deposit had been made and no bank book left behind. Hedley had made off with $459.24 (roughly $12,000 today) from the brewery. Mr. Lush immediately put detectives Cox and Byrne on the case, but Hedley had flown the coop.

The brewery received a letter from New York several weeks later. It was from Hedley, and he stated what a good time he was having and that he was heading to British Columbia under an assumed name. He enclosed the bank book with his note, returning it to its rightful owners, and after closing with "Hoping by the time you get the book, I will be dam [sic] near B. Columbia," he signed it, "Yours, Hedley."[6,7]

In 1902, the company changed hands, and John R. Bennett, the deceased Edward's younger brother, took over and changed the company

Beer jugs from Bennett Brewery. *Photo by author; items courtesy of John Wicks.*

to a limited liability venture. In 1916, the plant closed for two years due to prohibition. The manufacture of a beverage known as 'Near Beer,' beer of very low alcohol content, brought the company back to life in 1918.

With the end of prohibition in 1924, the brewery located at 258-260 Water Street West, began to brew strong beers again, including one of its most well-known brews, Bennett Dominion Ale, along with Dominion Stout, Golden Lager, and Haig Ale.

Things modernized at Bennett's during the war years, and they replaced the wooden puncheons with glass-lined tanks and bottles fitted with metal caps instead of cork stoppers. Still located on Sudbury Street, the company sported the by-line "Mfrs. [of] Ale and Stout."[8] By the 1950s Bennett's popular beers included Dominion Pale Ale, Dominion Stout, and Rainbow beer. Even though Bennett's Dominion was called an ale, it was actually a lager and bottom fermented. Canadian Breweries Ltd took over Bennett Brewing in 1962, and they, in turn, were bought out by Rothman's/Pall Mall in 1973 and renamed under Carling O'Keefe.[9]

In a brilliant stroke of marketing, the company designed The Newfoundland Song Book and distributed it from the 1950s until the 1970s by placing a songbook in each case of beer. Many people still have copies of this songbook today.

When Carling O'Keefe acquired Bennett Brewing in the 1970s, the brewery continued to operate at the same Water Street location. In 1981, it pumped out 4,500,000 gallons and employed close to one hundred people. The company manufactured Haig Ale, Black Horse, Dominion Ale, O'Keefe's Old Stock, O'Keefe's Extra Old Stock, and Old Vienna (no longer found in Newfoundland). The 1989 merger with Molson closed the plant on Water Street, and the firm consolidated operations at the Molson facility on Circular Road.[10]

LINDBERG BREWING COMPANY

The Lindberg Brewing Company also operated out of St. John's in the late nineteenth century. In 1877, John Lindberg plied two trades. He is recorded as a watchmaker on Water Street and is also listed as "Lindberg and Backstrom, Distiller &c." on Signal Hill Road, near the old St. Joseph's convent. From this Signal Hill location, the company brewed Klondike and Jubilee beer.[11]

Lindberg sold mostly imported American lagers and traditional English stouts and ales. He imported Barr, Bass, Guinness, and McEwen beers in the 1870s, including the popular "Bavarian bitter beer." By 1885, he had named his brewery Bavarian Brewery, employing on average twelve men, and by the 1890s the brewery produced 8,000-9,000 gallons a year. Mr. Lindberg was the first to manufacture Bavarian beer in this country. Determined to be cutting-edge, in 1895 he advertised the use of a new patent stopper which sealed hermetically but could still be easily removed. The local directories list a Bavarian Beer Depot (on 117 and, later, 113 Duckworth Street) from 1885 to 1908. This may have afforded a convenient outlet store for his customers to purchase beer.

Lindberg Brewery, visible in the upper right-hand side of the photo. *Photo courtesy of St. John's City Archives.*

In 1895, Lindberg dissolved his partnership with Backstrom and joined a Mr. Franklin. This duo claimed their beer had "no superior on this side of the Atlantic," taking prizes at Barcelona (1888) and Paris (1889), and again in 1891, when they won a medal for their lager at the Paris Exhibition.[12] The only producer of lager in Newfoundland, Bavarian continued to brew and sell ale, porter, and aerated waters, which included nectar, ginger ale, lemonade, soda water, champagne cider, and Kola champagne. An article on the brewery in 1885 stated:

> The brewery, when in full swing, is worthy of a visit, especially by outport people who may not have had an opportunity of seeing it before. It stands on a breezy eminence in the east end of the city and can be reached in a few minutes from any part of Water-street.[13]

In 1898, Lindberg broke with Franklin, but he is still listed on Signal Hill Road as both a watchmaker/jeweller and as a brewer of Bavarian lager. He continued to bottle Bass & Co.'s Best Ale while acting as an agent for various other types of beer.

When the temperance wave gathered strength, Lindberg introduced 'light' beers and marketed his Barr and Company Ale, Dog's Head, Guinness, and McEwen's as medicinal products.

Lindberg's Bavarian Beer at this time was supposed to have been non-alcoholic, but on testing, it turned out to contain a small percentage of alcohol. A teamster for the company, Tom Murdock, testified he could drink gallons of the stuff and it wouldn't affect him. Some local poet then wrote a song about Lindberg beer:

> When Tom Murdock is dead and in his grave
> For Bavarian Beer he will not crave
> For on his tombstone will be wrote
> Many's the gallon flowed down his throat.[14]

The 1913 St. John's Newfoundland Directory listed the location of the Lindberg brewery on Signal Hill Road. There is no further record of the brewery, and later, Lindberg shows up as a resident of Halifax, Nova Scotia.

THE NEWFOUNDLAND BREWERY

The Newfoundland Brewery started in 1893 in St. John's, with its original location near the intersection of Elizabeth Avenue and Rennie's River. Unfortunately, it burned down in 1894, and followed by the bank crash that same year, the business did not resurface until 1900 in new premises at 55 Belvedere Street.[15]

The Newfoundland Brewery began brewing aerated waters in 1904 in addition to beer and porter. During prohibition, beer sales stopped, but the brewery continued to operate, producing aerated waters and a 'near beer' beverage. After 1924, beer came back in vogue, and the company manufactured India Beer and India Pale ale. With the advent of the Second World War, the demand for beer increased again, so the plant stopped making soft drinks and concentrated on beer. The brewery changed its address from Belvedere Street to Circular Road in 1941. Managed by J. L. O'Dea, they advertised their company as "Brewers & Bottlers of Ales and Stout." Molson took over The Newfoundland Brewery in July 1962

Newfoundland Brewery, which later became Molson Brewery. *Photo courtesy of NL Collection, Provincial Resource Library.*

and is still operating at its Circular Road location today. Other beers produced included Moose Pale Ale, Old Stock, India Pale Ale, India's Holiday Bock, and Red Top Golden Amber.

The 1932 city directory recorded the former publican and liquor seller Garrett Brownrigg as a brewer living on Leslie Street. By 1934 he was operating the newly opened Bavarian Brewing Company (not to be confused with the previous Bavarian Brewery operated by John Lindberg).

This Bavarian Brewing Company brought over a German brewmaster, Hans Schneider, who lived in an apartment on the premises. He created the first two original recipes for the company: Jockey Club (known as the "champagne of beers") and Dark Munich. The company added a soft drink operation in 1937 and developed two ten-cent 'near-beer' lagers. The aerated waters ended in 1940, no doubt because beer sales rose with the influx of foreign (Canadian and American) troops. Under the new management of Albert E. Hickman, the company produced Jockey Club, Red Label, and Black Label beers until 1949. The Bavarian Brewing Company also manufactured Bulldog, Silver Doctor, Irish Style Porter, and Three Star Lager.

After several other mergers and changes of ownership, John Labatt of London, Ontario, bought the Bavarian Brewing Company in October 1962. Under his stewardship, several new brands appeared: Labatt's Blue, Labatt's 50, and Labatt's Special Lite. Labatt continued to produce two Newfoundland favourites, Blue Star (an award winner at the 1954 international beer-making competition in Munich, Germany) and Jockey Club.

The iconic stubbie with its distinctive logo. *Photo by author from private collection.*

Many people in Newfoundland today still remember the Blue Star jingle:

Blue Star, Blue Star,
The finest in the land
You can drink a toast
To Newfoundland
With a Blue Star in your hand.

The commercial ends with a rousing "Up she comes!" This old commercial shows a group of men in a tavern drinking Blue Star.[16]

OTHER BREWERIES

Smaller breweries also plied their trade in the city. In the 1930s *Who's Who in and from Newfoundland,* The American Aerated Water Company on Barter's Hill in St. John's, Proprietor George Janes, manufactured American Ale, Dublin Stout, and other high-grade carbonated beverages in addition to syrups and vinegars.

A. J. and George W. Kavanaugh's brewery operated on Military Road in the 1890s. From 1936 into the 1940s, the brewery brewed beverages at 18 Water Street West.[17]

The Union Aerated Waters Co., possibly also known as Pike's Brewery, where proprietor William Arthur Pike manufactured syrups, vinegars, aerated waters and sold or manufactured Lindbergh [sic] ale.[18]

The Atlantic Brewing Company began in Stephenville in 1968, but only lasted for about a year, closing out in 1969. They produced two beers: Atlantic Lager and Atlantic Draft. When Bison Petroleum and Minerals Ltd. bought the Brewery in 1970 and renamed it Bison Brewery, they introduced a beer called Bison Brew. This was to be short lived as well, and Labatt Brewery bought the brewer in 1974. They had no more success than the previous owners, and the brewery closed for the last time in 1981.[19]

Today in St. John's and beyond the overpass, breweries are popping up all over the place. One of the biggest in the local brewery scene would be Quidi Vidi Brewery. Two engineers in the offshore oil industry, David Rees and David Fong, founded the Quidi Vidi Brewery in 1996. Quidi

Vidi makes seven core brands and various seasonal beers, producing a wide selection of craft beers. They brew specialty ales and lagers with colourful names like Honey Brown, 1892, Mummer's Brew and Eric's Cream Ale. The company renovated a vacant building, on the shore of the small fishing village of Quidi Vidi, that had formerly been used as a fish plant back in the Second World War, and as Village Seafoods in the 1970s. It was here they started their brewing plant, advertising it as 100 percent Newfoundland owned and operated, as it still is today.

YellowBelly Brewery is located in a designated historic structure that survived the great fire of 1892, and archaeological evidence dates the site to before the fire of 1846. Some claim the basement dates to 1725. While it may not be quite that old, when archaeologist Steve Mills did a dig on the premises several years ago, he found of evidence of eating, drinking, and leisure activity dating from the seventeenth to the mid-nineteenth century. No doubt they brewed beer in the area, as Yellowbelly Brook, a good supply of fresh water, ran nearby. YellowBelly Brewery's present location was a place of great commercial activity in the early centuries of the city's history. Articles found in the vicinity include plates, cups, mugs, a spigot, tobacco pipes, stoneware bottles, glassware, and bottles, even an eighteenth-century champagne bottle—all the paraphernalia of a public house.

Craig Flynn opened YellowBelly Brewery on Water Street in 2008. Together with his brewmaster Liam Mckenna, they made YellowBelly into a full brew pub. YellowBelly crafts four regular beers and one cider as well as a seasonal beer. They brew 1,000 litres at a time, brewing four to five times a week.

Storm Brewery has also been around for a long while. It started as Freshwater Brewing Company in Carbonear, in 1995, and then moved to Mount Pearl where it became known as Storm Brewery. Its products are available at several bars in downtown St. John's. Storm Brewery prides itself on bringing back the stubby, a 341 ml bottle. Traditionally, in Newfoundland, beer was bottled in a variety of ways from stoneware jugs to corked bottles, to metal capped bottles. We went from long bottles, to short stubbies and back to long again. The majority of the local beer bottles are shorter than most others in North America. Nowadays Newfoundland Brewereries still bottle beer in a bottle known as the bob-21. This was an interim bottle to be used in the changeover from stubbies to long-necks. We have not yet made the change. This was mostly because there were so many of those bottles around and it was pure economics, better to use what they had, rather than buy all new. Storm Brewery introduced the 341ml Canadian-industry standard, long-neck bottle to the Newfoundland beer industry. Storm also bottles beer in 650ml bottles.

The craft beer market takes up only a small percentage of the brewing industry here in Newfoundland, but it continues to expand. All over the island, craft breweries are gaining popularity with new ones opening all the time. Small breweries are becoming tourist destinations across Canada. Craft beer is attractive to many because of its distinctive tastes and the fact that its brewers use hops, and few or no preservatives.[20] Some well-known newcomers include Port Rexton Brewing Company located in, of course, Port Rexton; Bootleg Brew Company in Corner Brook; Scud Runner Brewery in Gander; Dildo Brewing Company in Dildo; and the Split Rock Brewery in Twillingate, just to name a few.

ALCHOHOL-RELATED CRIMES AND COURT CASES

In the earlier centuries, getting caught as a criminal could bring nasty consequences, but in many cases there seems to have been a tendency towards leniency. The court cases posted in the local newspapers shed light on the justice system with regard to alcohol abuse in the nineteenth century.

From various newspapers, 1831 to 1872[1]:

Monday, 12 April. Patrick White, keeper of a Sailor's boarding house, Water St., fined $25.00 for selling liquor without license. His second offence.

Edward Power, 18 King's Road fisherman fined $1.00 for being drunk and disorderly.

Thomas Stamp, age 25, a sailor of the *Lady Bird* fined $2.00 for being drunk and disorderly. James Neary, Age 22, Labourer, Marsh Hill; Michael Brown, Age 23, Labourer, Carter's Hill; Richard Raftis, Age 27, Attorney; Patrick Grace, Age 22, Shoemaker; Michael Wall, Age 19, Sailor of the "Phoca"; Edward Lawlor, Age 24, Cooper. All found drunk on public streets and admonished by the Magistrate, no fines were enforced.

John Brennan was seen before Justice Peters on charges of drunkenness and assaulting police; James McDonald, drunk but had his case dismissed. Maurice Hickey disorderly conduct; Michael Connors, Jr., the same. Thomas Brennan, drunk; John Hammond, James Moran, John Harris, John Burk, Cornelius Kennedy all drunk; Michael Dormady, St. John's charged with repeated drunkenness.

Police Court, *Evening Telegram*, Monday, May 12, 1879:

Drunk on the streets: "David Duncan, 24, seaman of the S.S. *Esquimeaux*, was the first on the docket. He was found drunk on the street, and (in accordance with the rules by which the Peace Preservation Society is governed) escorted to the lock-up. David claimed to be a descendant of the unfortunate Scottish King Duncan; but owing to the treachery of Macbeth and several other important occurrences, the family became so far reduced as to make it necessary for him to go to sea. [...] Evil communication corrupted David's good manners and he fell through the seductive influence of the intoxicating cup, and hence his appearance in court this morning. But his worship being a compassionate, as well as a just, judge, the Duncan was allowed another opportunity to retrieve the lost fortunes of his family."[2]

Police Court, *Evening Telegram*, Monday, May 15, 1879:

Drunk and Disorderly: "James Johnston, 30, seaman, didn't know how to behave himself, and consequently he was handed over to the police by Mr. Monroe; but as the *Esquimeaux*, the ship to which he belonged, was ready for the whale fishery this forenoon, and "Jemmy" being a crack shot with the harpoon, he was allowed to go north."[3]

Drunk: "Thomas Stand, 23, seaman of the same ship, took to drink and fell into the hands of the "peace-makers" yesterday; but his worship did not care to jeopardize the success of the voyage by detaining him, and he too was permitted to go to the regions of eternal snow."[4]

Police Court, *Evening Telegram*, Monday, September 19, 1882:

Drunk and Disorderly: St. John's was a busy place for the Constabulary on the Monday night of September 18th. They arrested seven drunks, and on the Sunday before that, 13 drunks who they put in four small cells due to drunkenness and disorderly conduct. One of the 13, a man named Neagle from River Head in the west end of St. John's, assaulted an officer when taken into custody. He was put in a cell with the 'Indomitable' Andrew Kearney who, annoyed at Neagle's prattling, meted out his own punishment in the form of a black eye and a nose bleed. These fellows must have caught the good Judge Prowse on a really bad day and they received an unusually stiff sentence. His Honour was not amused and brought down a heavy sentence for the perpetrator—twenty days for the assault in the cell while the other man got fifty days for striking a constable.[5]

Police Court, *Evening Telegram*, Monday, May 23, 1879:

Drunk and Insulting Females on the Streets: "John Baird, 28, seaman of the S.S. *Arctic*, was the most contemptible character brought into court for moral adjustment for some time past. Having imbibed rather freely yesterday he so far forgot all sense of honour and manliness as to insult a female on the public street. But he was soon made to realize the fact that such conduct is not tolerated in the metropolis of Newfoundland. For a moment an indescribable expression flitted across the usually placid features of his worship [Judge Renouf], and then the just but awful sentence was pronounced, $5 or 15 days in the penitentiary. Serves him right!"[6]

Illegal liquor sales: Mrs. Catherine Callahan, Barne's Lane, fined $25.00 for selling intoxicating liquor without a license.[7]

Police Court, *Evening Telegram*, Monday, May 15, 1879:

Using Abusive Language: Catherine Lacey, of Moreton's Lane, was charged with wielding a formidable two-edged weapon called a tongue so dexterously as to inflict a severe wound on the 'fair reputation' of Mary Martin;

but as the latter did not appear to prosecute, Catherine received a little wholesome advice and then withdrew, giving an ominous shake or two of the head as she passed out.[8]

Police Report: Michael Power, Poet, Pokeham Path (Hamilton Avenue), complained of assault commenced upon him by John Ryan, Barman to Mr. Thomas Farrel, Water St. The judge dismissed the complaint and he recommended the poet take the pledge and write a book of poems instead of repeating his fugitive pieces in public houses.[9]

More serious crimes than drinking and brawling sometimes transpired in the taverns of St. John's. Tavern owner Francis Canning was hanged for the murder of barmaid Mary Nugent at his tavern on 190 New Gower Street, just east of Casey Street. A kind man and described as genial, he took to drink and became violent when intoxicated. An apparently motiveless crime, Canning shot Mary from behind but she managed to survive long enough to accuse him of the deed. The hanging took place on July 29, 1899.[10]

The 1879 St. John's arrest record shows: 280 drunk and 151 disorderly, a total of 431. For smaller outports near St. Johns: 12 drunk and nine disorderly for a total of 21. Foreign Sailors: 27 drunk 26 disorderly for a total of 62. Counting a small number from further flung outports the total for Newfoundland stood at 527.[11]

Twillingate Sun, February 19, 1887:

"An amusing event happened in connection with this temperance movement. Mr. Courtney had a puncheon of rum come by the S.S. Plover. It was left in the Company's store on the wharf, possibly by the Magistrate's orders. Some smart fellows or fellow marked carefully its location in the store and either for mischief or the sake of a cheap and large drink (the latter is most likely) they, or he, no doubt in the dead of night, for no clue has yet been found, bored up through the floor, through the puncheon, and thus the whole of the liquor escaped. It is evident by the strong smell and appearance of the ground a large quantity was spilt. There is in Little Bay a Sergeant and two Constables, but in spite of such a strong police force, the guilty party has not been discovered."[12]

Alcohol permeated all classes and even the legal system, and some offenders did not escape unscathed. In 1898, scandal hit the local newspaper, the *Evening Telegram*. A writer to the paper described the steamer, *Fiona*, which transported the circuit court to the island's outports, as "little better than a floating brothel" with the legal gentlemen drunk in their berths and unable to land or 'stagger ashore when court opened'. The esteemed gentlemen of the court sued the author of the letter and the editor of the paper with libel and 30 days in jail followed.[13]

Petty crime could sometimes be amusing. Hughie Finnegan, a well-known tin whistle player, decided to erect his own beer tent for the Regatta. He had a permit to set up this beer tent and he did so on what was then the left-hand side of the Church of England fence. He stored his forty to fifty drum beer barrels at the back of the tent, all ready for the big day. He had it up, however, very much before the day of the Regatta and kept it up for a good time after the Regatta. Last going off they had to get an order of council to get him to take the tent down. Most residents were not complaining, however, and it was a popular spot to go. Hughie would play his whistle and if you gave him five dollars for a drink there was no change given back. You received beer in lieu of change. As time went on, it got pretty bad with no toilet facilities, and people would drink and pass out, after which they would get up and drink themselves into a stupor again. After about a month the law finally shut him down.[14]

18TH-CENTURY TAVERN OWNERS IN ST. JOHN'S

Proprietor, Business Type (Name of tavern), Address, Years of operation

Angell, Edward, Public house (Britannia), corner of Water & Springdale St., Unknown date in the 1700-1807

Beck, Thomas, Public house, Beck's Cv., Water St., 1777-1845/1810-45

Best, William, Public house (Bunch of Grapes), Bulley's Farm, south of present-day LeMarchant Rd., Unknown date in 1700-1807

Bolan, John, Publican, Unknown, 1796-1797-1798

Brophy, John, Publican, Between the Engine House & King's Beach, 1794-95/1797-98

Cahill, Michael, Publican, Between the Engine House & King's Beach, 1794-95

Collier, George, Publican, On Thomas Babbs' property between Nobles Cv. & the Engine House, 1794-95

Cannon, Edward, Publican, James Brooks property between Nobles Cv. & the Engine House, Unknown date in 1700s

Codey, Mark, Public house, Unknown, 1797-98

Darcy, George, Publican, Between Engine House & King's Beach, 1794-95

Delaney, Daniel, Publican/public house, 1796-1797/1797-98

Dooling, Robert, Public house (Red Cow), West of Hunter's Cv. (Bottom of Prescott St), Unknown date in 1700-1807

Doyle, Edmund, Publican/public house (Blue Ball), Bulley's property between Nobles Cv. & the Engine House, 1794-95/1797-98/1807

Doyle, Patrick, Public house (The Globe), Unknown location, Unknown date in 1700s

Driscoll, Daniel, Public house (Bird-in-Hand), East of Hunter's Cv., Unknown date in 1700/1807

Flood, John, Publican, On Geo. Hutching's property between R. H. Roope's Cv. & Jn. Noble's Cv., 1794-95/1797-98

Fitzgerald, John, Public house (Jolly Fisherman), West of Hunter's Cv., Unknown date in 1700s/1807

Flannery, James, Publican, Unknown location, 1796-1797

Flannery, Pat, Publican, Jn Tucker property between Noble's Cv. & the Engine House, 1794-95/1797-98

Hanlen, Michael, Public house (Shoulder of Mutton), West of Hunter's Cv., 1797-98/1807

Hanlon, Michael, Public house, Unknown location, 1797-98

Harrahan, Phil, Public house, Unknown location, 1797-98

Hayse, James, Public house (The Ship), Water St. E. corner of Haymarket Square, Unknown date in 1700/1760-70/1807

Little, Michael, Public house (London Tavern), On the corner of York & Wood St., Unknown date in 1700s/1797-98/1804/1807/1810-1832

Lynch, John, Publican, On Dewes & Coke's property between the Engine House & King's Beach, 1794-95

Lyons, Peter, Publican, On Wm Burke's property between King's Beach & the old Garrison, 1794-95/1797-98

McDonald, Patrick, Public house, Unknown Location, 1797-98

McCarthy, Wm, Public house, Unknown location, 1797-98

McCarthy, Wm, Publican/public house (Hope), Unknown location between Riverhead & Bulley's Farm, 1796-97/1807

McNamara, Augustus, Publican, On Jn Renelle's property between Noble's Cv. & the Engine House, 1794-95/1796-97/1797-98

Mara, Michael, Public house (Sun), East of Hunter's Cv., Unknown date 1700s/1797-9/1807

Maher, James, Public house, Unknown location, 1797-97

Martin, Sarah, Public house, Unknown location, 1797-98

Molloy, Edward, Publican, On N. Parker's property between the Engine House & King's Beach, 1794-95

Murphy, Thomas, Public house (Three Crowns), East of Hudson's Cv. (Bottom of Prescott St.), 1797-98/1807

Nevean, John, Public house, Unknown location, 1797-98

Pendergrast, Wm, Publican, On Wm. Pendergrass' property between Noble's Cv. & the Engine House, 1794-95

Penney, John, Publican, Unknown Location, 1796-97

Perchard, Richard, Public house (Royal Oak), Faced Hunter's Cv., Unknown date 1700s/1807

Perry, John, Publican, On H. Radfoul's property between Roope's Cv. & Jn. Noble's Cv., 1794-95

Phealan, James, Public house (London Tavern), On the corner of York & Wood St., Unknown date in 1700s/1797-98/1804/1807/1810-1832

Potts, Wm, Publican, On Dan Donovan's property between Noble's Cv. & the Engine House, 1794-95

Power, David, Publican, On Michael Ellis' property between King's Beach & the Old Garrison, 1794-95/1797-98

Power, William, Public house (Angel), Between Bulley's Farm & present day Job's Cv., 1797-98/1807

Power, John, Publican, On Tim Fogarty's property between Noble's Cv. & the Engine House, 1794-95/1796-97/1797-98

Prendergast, Wm, Publican/public house, Water St., 1796-97/1797-98

Quirk, Cornelius, Public house (London Tavern), On the corner of York & Wood St., Unknown date in 1700s/1797-98/1804/1807/1810-1832

Redmond, Patrick, Public house (Ship Assistance), On W. Kersey's property between Noble's Cv. & the Engine House, Unknown date in 1700s/1794-95/1796-97/1797-98/1807

St. John, Andrew S. Public house, Unknown location, 1797-98

Saul, John, Publican, On Sam Henley's property between the Engine House & King's Beach, 1794-95

Shepherd, George, Public house, Unknown location, 1797-98

Steele, Samuel, Public house (London Tavern), On the corner of York & Wood St., Unknown date in 1700s/1797-98/1804/1807/1810-1832/1917

Welsh, Michael, Public house, Unknown Location, 1796 - 97/1797-98

Welsh, Wm, Public house, From Hudson's Cv. to the easternmost part of St. John's, 1797-98/1807

Welsh, William, Public house (Swan), On Jn. Livingstone's property between the Engine House & King's Beach, 1794-95/1807

Widdicomb, John, Publican (The Rose & Crown), On G. Williams' property between Roope's Cv. & Noble's Cv., 1794-95/1796-97/1797-98/1807

Woolcocks, S, Publican, On Jas. Kavanagh's property between the Engine House & King's Beach, 1794-95

ST. JOHN'S ALCOHOL-RELATED BUSINESSES FROM THE 19TH-CENTURY UNTIL PROHIBITION

Because the records are so imprecise, some of these people may be duplicates or close relatives. Surname spellings vary across the historical records. Where several different spellings occurred, alternates appear in brackets. Street numbers changed constantly, and some premises moved as well. Until 1943, Water Street was divided into East and West at Springdale Street.

Proprietor, Business Type (Name of Business), Address, Years of operation
Unknown owner, The Crown & Anchor Tavern, Duckworth St., 1828
Allen, T. J. Liquors wholesale & retail, 22–26 Upper Water St. W, 1908–09
Allan, Thomas W. Groceries & Liquors/Importer of Wines, Spirits, Teas, & Sugars, Water St., 1864–65
Anderson, George. Listed under Liquors & listed as a tavern, 258 Water St., 1864–65/1870–71/1877–84
Anderson, John. Wines & Liquors, 258 Water St., 1877
Angell, Edward. Public house (Britannia), West corner of Water & Springdale St., Unknown date in the 1700–1807
Arrol, Catherine. Public house, Unknown, 1836
Baine, Johnston & Co. Wines & Liquors, 205 Water St. E, 1890

Baird, D & J./from 1890 on James C. Baird, Grocers/Wines, Spirits, Liqueurs, Ale & Porter/wholesalers of liquor, 217 Water St. E/181 Water St./ 18 Water St. W/in 1908, the Baird Building, 1864–65/1870–71/1877/1890/ 1894–97/1904/1908–09/1915

Barrett, Robert. Liquors, 376 Water St., 1864–65

Banon, Mrs. J. Liquors, 142 New Gower St., 1870–71

Barron, Pierce. Tavern, 142 New Gower St., 1870–71

Barron, Mrs. Wines & spirits, 136 Water St., 1877

Barry, Edward. Public house, Water St., 1836

Beer, Thomas. Liquor dealer, Quidi Vidi, 1864–65/1870–71

Beck, Thomas. Public house, Beck's Cv./Water St., 1777–1845/1836

Bennett, C. F. Foundry/brewery/distillery/importer, 385 Water St./252 Water St. W, 1864–65/1870–71

Bennett & Co., E. W. Riverhead Brewery/Lager Beer Brewer, Water St. W/ Riverhead/258–260 Water St., 1880–81/1890/1894–97/1898/1904

Blundon, John. Liquors, 248 Water St., 1864–65

Blundon, Mrs. Anastasia. Boarding house, 248 Water St., 1870–71

Blundon, Mrs. A. (widow of John), Tavern, 250 Water St., 1870–71

Boan, Elizabeth. Public house, King's Rd., 1836

Boden & Seymour, Wines & liquors, 247 Water St., 1864–65

Bolger (Bulger), James. Liquor dealer, 116 Water St., 1885–86

Bowring Brothers. Wholesale wines & liquors, 277 Water. St. E, 1890

Bray, Edward. Public house, Water St., 1810–45

Brennan, Edward (Brannin). Public House/liquors/tavern/wines & spirits, 286 Water St./282 Water St./190 Water St., 1836/1864–65/1870–71/1871/1877

Brennan, James. Groceries & liquors, 190 Water St., 1880–81/1885–86

Brennan, Mary. Liquors, 58 Water St. W, 1864–65

Brennan, Thomas. Public house, Water St., 1836

Brien, Pierce. Beer saloon, 394 Water St., 1898/1904

Brine, Robert. Public house (Butchery), Pringle's Farm (near present–day Pringle Pl.), 1807

Brine, James. Public house, Water St., 1836

British American House. Liquor dealers, 376 Water St., 1913

Brophy, Stephen. Wines & spirits, Limekiln Hill, 1877

Brophy, Mrs. E. Liquor dealer, 8 Duckworth St., 1885–86

Brownrigg/Browndrick, Mrs. Mary (widow of J). Boardinghouse/Tavern, 122 Water St./126 Water St./124 Water St., 1864–65,/1870–71

Brownrigg, Garrett, Sr. Wines & liquors/licensed publican, Water St. E/102 Water St. E, 1885–86/1894–97/1898/1904/1908–09/1913/1915

Brownrigg, Henry. Wines & liquors, 408 Water St. W/108 Water St. E/408 Water St. W, 1898/1904/1908–09

Bryan, Patrick. Public house, Riverhead, 1836

Buckley, William. Public house, King's Rd., 1836

Burke, John. Liquors, 326 Water St., 1864–65

Butler, Thomas. Public house, Water St., 1836

Byrne, Patrick. Public house, Duckworth St., 1836

Byrne (Byne), Richard. Liquors wholesale & retail, 362 Water St., 1904/1908–09/1913/1915

Byrnes, William. Liquors & sea captain, 88 Water St., 1864–65

Cahill, Joseph. Groceries/wines & spirits, 269 Water St. W/167 Water St. W, 1864–65/1877

Cahill, John. Farmer/a tavern for all weathers, 269 Water. St. W, Unknown date in 1700s, 1797–98/1870–71/1897–98/1907

Callanan, Michael. Storekeeper, 122 Duckworth St., 1864–65

Callaghan, M. Liquors, 46 Gower St., 1870–71

Callanan, Michael. Tavern, 45 Gower St., 1870–71

Canning, Francis. Wines & liquors/saloon keeper, 190 New Gower St. (Theatre Hill), 1898

Canning, Mrs. Hannah. Liquors (wholesale & retail), 374 Water St. W, 1908–09

Cantwell, James. Liquors/grocer/tavern, 374 Water St./363 Water St., 1864–65/1870–71/1871/1877

Cantwell, John. Groceries & liquors, 250 Water St./252 & 376 Water St./252 Water St., 1864–65/1880–81/1870–71/1871/1877/1885–86/1890

Carrigan, Walter. Liquors/tavern, 128 Duckworth St /130 Duckworth St., 1864–65/1870–71/1871

Carrigan, Miss Alice. Saloon, 166 Duckworth St., 1890

Carter, John. Groceries & liquor/tavern/retail wines & spirits, 30 New Gower St./32 New Gower St., 1864–65/1870–71/1871/1877/1880–81/1897

Carter, Edward F. Wines & liquors, 30 New Gower St., 1885–86/1890/1894–97, 1898, 1904

Cash, James. Liquors/grocer/boarding house, 188 Water St., 1864–65

Cash, Mrs. Margaret (widow of James). Tavern, 188 Water St./184 Water St., 1870–71/1871/1877

Cashin, Michael. Liquors, 110 Water St., 1864–65

Chadder, Capt. James. Liquors wholesale & retail, 53 Harvey Rd., 1908–09

Chafe, William B. Liquor dealer/Temperance saloon/beer shop, 374 Water/390 Water St., 1880–81/1885–86/1894–97/1898/1904

Chafe, Emmanuel. Liquors, Goulds, 1894–97

Chafe, Jacob. Liquors wholesale & retail, 134 Water St. E, 1904/1908–09

Charles, Thomas. Wines & liquors, Water St. E/136 Water St. E/208 Duckworth St., 1898/1904/1908–09

Clarke, John F. Liquors wholesale & retail (Devonshire Inn), 112 Water St./110 Water St., 1904/1908–09/1913/1915

Coady, John. Public house, 272 Water St. E/274 Water St. E, 1836/1890/1894–1897/1898/1904/1908–09/1913

Coady, T & J. Liquors, 124 Water St., 1885–86

Coady, Thos. Wines & liquors, 272 Water St., 1894–1897/1898/1904/1915

Colford, Richard. Liquors wholesale & retail/beer depot, 127 New Gower St., 1904

Collier, Henry G. Liquor dealers, 69 Queen's Rd., 1913

Collins, Henry G. Way office/dealer in groceries & Temperance beer, 237 Water St. W., 1890

Collins, Jas J. Wines & liquors/licensed publican (American House), Water St./Water St./250 Water St. E, 1894–97/1898/1904/1908–09

Collis, H. C./Henry G. Beer depot/beer saloon/grocery, beer shop/liquor dealer, 69 Queen's Rd., 1898/1904/1908/1913

Comerford, Mathew. Public house, Water St., 1836

Comerford, Mike. Public house, Water St., 1836

Comerford, Richard. Public house, Water St., 1836

Condon, James. Public house, Water St., 1836

Connors, John. Public House, Water St., 1836

Connors, Timothy/Connors, Mary (widow of Tim), Wines & liquors, 374 Water St./376 Water St. W, 1885–86/1894–97/1898/1904/1908–09/1915

Conolly, Lawrence. Wines & spirits, 82 Military Rd., 1877/1880–81

Cooney, Mrs./Cooney, Michael J. Liquors/tavern/wines & spirits, 42 Water St., 1870–71/1877

Corbett/Corbit, William/Mary. Liquors/wines & liquors/cooperage, Cookstown Rd./6 Le Marchant Rd./2 Le Marchant Rd., 1877/1885–86/1890/1894–97/1898/1908–09/1915

Cormack, Patrick. Public house, Water St., 1836

Costigan, Michael. Storekeep/tavern, 152 New Gower St., 1870–71/1871

Cox, James. Liquor, 166 Water St., 1797/1870–71/1871

Cox, Wm. Liquor, Duckworth St., 1894–1897

Crane, J. Wines & liquors/groceries & liquors, Water St. (corner of Job's Lane), 1877/1880

Crawford, Mathew. Public house, Water St., 1836

Crotty, Miss Mary Ann. Liquors wholesale & retail/publican, 64 Water St./64 Cochrane, 1904/1908–09/1913/1915

Crotty, William/Mrs. Crotty. Liquors/fisherman/wines & spirits, 3 Signal Hill
    Rd. near Temperance St./1 Signal Hill Rd./8 Signal Hill Rd., 1864–65/1870–71/
    1877/1885–86/1890/1898

Croake, Marten. Carpenter & dealer/tavern, 60 Water St. W, 1870–71/1871/1880–81

Croke, E. Liquors, Water St. W, 1885–86

Cuddihy, Thomas. Liquors/tavern/wines & spirits, 72 Duckworth St.,
    1864–65/1870–71/1877

Cullen, James. Public house, Water St., 1836

Cullan (Cullen), William. Groceries/provisions/wines & liquors/ship chandlery,
    348 Water St./345 & 348 Water St., 1864–65/1870–71/1877/1880–81

Dady, Martin. Public house, Water St., 1836

Daily, Nate. Public house, Duckworth St., 1836

Darmarell, Thomas. Public house, Water St., 1836

Darsie, Walter. Liquors, 288 Water St., 1880/1885–86/1890

Delgado, A.A. New York Lager Beer Depot, 422 Water St., 1885–86

Dempsey, Pat & Bow, Mike. Public house, Duckworth St., 1810–45

Davies, John. Wines & spirits/liquors, 124 Water St., 1877/1880–81

Deady, Thomas. Wines & liquors/shop, 163 Water St., 1877

Deneff/Denieff, J. P. Liquors, 269 Water St. W, 1885–86

Devine, James. Wines & liquors, 317 Water St., 1870–71/1877

Deveine (Devine, Divine), Mrs. James (widow). Liquors, 249 Water St., 1885–86

Devine, James/Devine, Mrs. Joanna. Groceries & liquors/wines & liquors, 170
    Water St., 1880–81/1890

Dillon, Walter, Public house, Water St., 1836

Doherty, Francis. Public house, King's Beach, 1836

Donovan, John. Liquors, King's Bridge Rd., 1864–65

Donovan T. (see O'Donovan). Liquors, 168 Duckworth St., 1870–71

Donovan, John. Wines & spirits, 168 Duckworth St., 1877

Donovan, Catherine (widow of Timothy). Liquors, Duckworth St., 1894–97/1898

Donovan, Tim. Public house, Water St., 1836

Dooley, Dennis. Butcher/seller of liquors, 108 Water St., 1836/1864–65/1871

Dooley, James. Ship carpenter/tavern, 74 Water St., 1864–65/1871

Dooling, Robert. Public house (Red Cow), West of Hunter's Cv. (Bottom of
    Prescott St.), Unknown date in 1700s/1807

Dooling, J./Doolan, John. Liquors/liquor store/wines & spirits, 160 Water St.,
    1870–71/1871/1877/1880–81

Dougherty, B. Liquors, 4 New Gower St., 1870–71

Doogan, Henry. Tavern, 114 Water St., 1870–71

Dooney, Maurice. Liquors, 314 Water St., 1864–65

Downey, John. Publican, Unknown location, 1810–1814/1894

Doyle, Thomas. Public house, Water St., 1836

Doyle, Edmund. Publican/public house (Blue Ball), Geo. Bulley's property between Nobles Cv. & the Engine House/Between Bulley's Farm & present day Job's Cv., 1794–95/1797–98/1807

Driscoll, Daniel. Public house (Bird–in–Hand), East of Hunter's Cv., Unknown date in 1700s–1807

Duggan, Henry. Grocer/liquors/tavern/wines & spirits, 161 Duckworth St./114 Water St./99 Water St., 1864–65/1870–71/1871/1877/1880–81

Duggan, Bridget. Wines & spirits/groceries & liquors, 206 Water St./106 Water St./202 Water St., 1877/1880–81/1885–86/1890/1894–97/1898/1904/1908–09

Dunn, Miss E./Miss Kate. Liquors wholesale & retail (Dunnsmere Hotel), Topsail Rd. (halfway between St. John's & Topsail), 1904

Dunn, John T./Dwyer, John. Groceries & liquors, 43 Garrison Hill/Duckworth St., 1864–65/1885–86

Dwyer, Thomas S. Liquors/assayer of weights & measures/money–order office/post office, 426 Water St. 1864–65/1870–71

Eagan, Don. Licensed publican, Water St., 1836

Eagan, John. Liquors, King's Bridge Rd., 1864–65/1870–71

Eagan, John & Francis Kenney. Public house, Water St./363 Water St., 1836/1864–65

Earle, Henry. Liquors/Proprietor of Prince of Wales Hotel. 171 Water St., 1864–65/1870–71

Edwards, Thomas. Liquors wholesale & retail, 12 Queen's Rd, 1904

Ellis & Co. Ltd. Liquors wholesale & retail, 203A Water St., 1908–09/1913/1915

Elmsley, George & Shaw. Grocers & liquor wholesalers/general importers/wines & spirits, 305 Water St./193–195 Water St., 1864–65/1870–71/1877/1880–81

Elward, Michael. Liquors/boot & shoemaker, 404 Water St., 1864–65/1870–71

English, William. Public house, Water St., 1836

Ennis, Miss Julie. Liquors wholesale & retail, 29 Water St., 1908–09

Farrell, James/Farrell, B. Groceries & liquors/liquors/public house, 10 Queen St., 1864–65/1870–71/1871

Farrell, Maurice. Public house, Water St., 1836

Farrell Michael. Groceries & liquors/wines & liquors/snuff & candle manufacturer, 161 Duckworth St., 1864–65/1870–71/1871

Farrell, Thomas. Groceries & liquors/liquors/tavern, 190 Water St., 1864–65/1870–71/1871

Farrell, Wm. J., Captain/Mrs. Catherine Farrell. Liquor dealers/publican, 55 Harvey Rd./51 Harvey Rd., 1913/1915

Feehan, John/Feehan, Michael/Feehan, Mary J. (widow of Michael).
Liquors/tavern/wines & spirits/saloon/wines & liquors, 58 Water St. W,
1870–71/1871/1877/1880–81/1885–86/1890/1894–97/1898/1904

Feehan, Patrick. Grocer/groceries & liquors, 128 Water St. W, 1870–71/1880–81

Feehan, Mary (widow of Patrick). Saloon, 72 Water St. W, 1890

Fitzgibbon, Thomas. Wines & liquors, 380 Water St., 1890/1894–97

Fitzgerald, John. Public house (Jolly Fisherman), West of Hunter's Cv., unknown
date in 1700s–1807

Fitzgerald, James. Liquors & groceries/tavern, 138 New Gower St., 1870–71/1871

Fitzgerald, Annie. Wines & liquors, 374 Water St., 1898

Fitzgerald, Maurice. Public house, King's Rd., 1836

Flanery (Flannery) James. Liquors/tavern/wines & spirits, 226 Water St.,
1864–65/1870–71/1877

Fling, Wm. Public house, Near Fort William, 1836

Flinn, Edmund. Public house, Water St., 1836

Flynn, Andrew D./Mary J. (widow of Andrew). Liquors wholesale & retail, 52–54
Water St. W, 1908–09/1913

Flynn, John. Liquors wholesale & retail, Address not given, 1904

Finn, William. Liquors, 172 Water St. W, 1885–86

Flinn, Maurice/Flynn, Mrs. Alice/Flynn, Miss Mary. Liquors/tavern/wines &
spirits/groceries & liquors, 372 Water St./374 Water St., 1864–65/1871/1877/
1880–81/1885–86/1890/1894–97/1898/1904

Flinn, William. Public house/liquors/china, glass, & earthenware products, Water
St./160 Water St., 1836/1864–65

Flinn, William. Public house, Near Fort William, 1836

Foley, Mike. Public house, Beach, 1836

Foley, Wm. Public house, Duckworth St., 1836

Foran, John W. Liquors/wines & spirits/confectionary & liquors/wines & liquors,
159 Duckworth St/103 Water St. E/105 Water St. E, 1870–71/1877/1880–81/1890

Ford, John/Ford, E/Ford, Mrs./Ford, Robert. Liquors, Southside near dock/
Southside E/Walkham's Bridge, 1864–65/1870–71/1877/1880–81/1885–86/1894–97

Furlong, Lawrence. Liquors/tavern, 43 Queen's Rd., 1864–65/1870–71/1871

Furlong, Patrick. Public house/liquors/grocer, Water St./306 Water St.,
1836/1864–65/1870–71/1871

Galway, Nicholas. Liquors/cooper, 4 Pokeham Path, 1864–65/1870–71/1871

Gaule, Richard. Liquors, Topsail Rd., 1894–97

Gibbons, Francis (widow of John). Saloon, 267 Water St. W, 1890

Gillian, (Gillion) Wm./Gillian, Louisa (widow Wm.). Wines & liquors/liquors,
South Side E/53 South Side Rd., 1894–97/1898/1904/1908–09/1913

Glasco, Mary, (widow of Lawrence), Liquors wholesale & retail, 21 Water St. W, 1908–09

Glasco, Peter. Public house, King's Rd., 1836

Golloway/Golway, William/Golway, Ellen [Galway] (see Fitzgibbon, Thomas), Liquors/groceries & liquors/wines & spirits, 380 Water St./378 Water St., 1864–65/1870–71/1877/1880–81/1885–86

Goss, David A./Goss, Anastasia/Goss, Mrs. A. Wines & liquors/liquors/ liquor dealer, 74 New Gower St./74A New Gower St./74 New Gower St., 1898/1904/1907–08/1913/1915

Grace, Pierce. Public house, Water St., 1836

Goudie, Wm. H. Wines & liquors & proprietor of Bavarian Beer Depot/liquors, 113 Duckworth St./113 Duckworth St., 1898, 1904

Grant, Thomas. Liquors, Harvey Rd., 1864–65

Gready, Jeremiah. Public house, King's Beach, 1836

Gregory, John, Jr. Public house, Water St., 1836

Grey, Michael. Public House, Water St., 1836

Habberlin, Stephen. Liquors/tailor, 254 Water St., 1864–65/1870–71/1871

Hamlin, Hugh. Public house, Prince's St., 1836

Hammon, A. Liquors, 100 Military Rd., 1870–71

Hammond, Mrs. Wines & spirits, 28 Military Rd., 1877

Hanlen, Michael. Public house (Shoulder of Mutton), West of Hunter's Cv., 1797–98/1807

Hanlon, James. Liquors, 428 Water St., 1864–65

Harding, Michael. Public house, Riverhead, 1836

Harr, Thomas. Liquors, 28 New Gower St., 1870–71

Hawe (Haw), Thomas/James. Groceries & liquors/wines & spirits/ liquor dealers, 28 New Gower St./28 New Duckworth [sic] St., 1864–65/1877/1894–97/1890/1898/1904/1908–09/1913/1915

Hayes, Thomas. Public house, Water St., 1836

Hayse, James. Public house (The Ship), Water St. E, 1807

Hayward, George J./Hayward H. E./Hayward & Company. Commission merchant, importer/ship owner, commission & wine merchant/wines & liquors/wholesale/liquor dealer, 253 Water St./255 Water St./253 Water St. E/ 73 Water St. E, 1864–65/1870–71/1871/1880–81/1892/1894–97/1898/1904/ 1908–09/1913/1915

Heaney, Richard. Public house (Struggler), Between River Head & Bulley's Farm, 1807

Hearn, John. Saloon/wines & liquors/liquors, 326 Water St. E/128 Duckworth St./124 Duckworth St., 1890/1892/1894–97/1898/1904/1908–09/1913/1915

Hearn, P & T/Hearn & Co. Auctioneers & commission merchants, wholesale
dealers in wines & spirits/liquors, Stabb's Wharf, 139 Water St./Hunter's Cv.,
1864–65/1870–71/1871

Henderson, W. J. Liquors, 129 Water St., 1870–71

Hennessey, Mary. Public house (Royal Standard), Between Riverhead & Bulley's
Farm, 1807

Hennessy, Dan. Public house, Duckworth St., 1836

Hennessy/Hennesay, James. Wines & spirits/liquors, 130 Duckworth St./128
Duckworth St., 1877/1885–86

Hobson, B./Hobson, Mrs. Ellen (widow of Chas. [sic]). Spirits/wines & liquors,
388 Water St. E/388 Water St. E, 1880–81/1885–86 /1890/1894–97

Hogan, Patrick/Hogan, D.M. Groceries, wines & spirits, provisions/wines &
spirits/liquors, 197 Water St./314 Water St./312 Water St., 1864–65/1870–71/
1871/1877/1880–81/1885–86/1890/1894–1897

Ivory, Richard. Groceries/liquors/wines & spirits, 94 Prescott St.,
1864–65/1885–86/1870–71/1877/1890

Jardine, Robert. Brewer/foreman at Bennett's Distillery/distiller/brewer, 252
Water St. W/South Side/53 Patrick St., 1870–71/1871/1885–86

Jocelyn, John. Farmer/wines & spirits, Cottage Farm, Groves Rd./Quidi Vidi/
Queen's Bridge (Quidi Vidi), 1864–65/1870–71/1877

Joncas, Archibald/Mr. T Bulger's daughter married A. Joncas & kept the saloon.
Wines & liquors, 116 Water St., 1890

Keating, Thomas. Wines & spirits/liquors/wines & liquors, 134 Water St./
132 Water St./After 1892 corner of Prescott & Water, 1877/1880–81/1885–86/
1890/1892/1894–97/1898

Kean, Charles. Wines & spirits, 300 Water St., 1877

Kearney, John J./Army & Navy Depot/Mary E. Kearney. Liquors/wines &
liquors/liquors, 119 Duckworth St./119 Duckworth St. (corner of Cochrane &
Duckworth), 1885–86/1890/1894–97/1898/1904/1908–09

Keefe, James. Liquors, 328 Water St., 1864–65

Kelly, William. Groceries & liquors, 148 Water St., 1864–65

Kelly, Michael. Liquors/tailor/liquors, 146 Water St./148 Gower St., 1864–65/1870–71

Kelly, John. Liquors. 358 Water St. W/Junction Waterford Bridge & Topsail Rd./
Cross Roads, 1885–86/1890/1904/1908–09/1913/1915

Keough, George J. Provisions, grocery & wine merchant/wines & liquors, 362 &
364 Water St./2 Queen & 362 Water St., 1890/1894–97/1898

Kennedy, James S. Wines & liquors, 124 Water St./Water St., 1890/1894–97

Kennedy, Nick. Public house, Water St., 1836

Kennedy & Co. Groceries/wines merchants, 207 Water St. E, 1885 –1890

Kenny, John. Liquors, 47 Duckworth St., 1864–65

Kent, James. Liquors, 192 Water St., 1864–65

Kent, Michael/Miss Mary Corbett. Liquors wholesale & retail, 1 Freshwater Rd., 1904/1913

Kielly, Edward J. Liquors wholesale & retail, 72 Prescott St., 1904/1908–09

Kielly, Mrs. Sarah. Liquors wholesale & retail, 380 Water St., 1904/1908–09/1913/1915

King, Dominick. Publican,/public house (White Hart), On Geo Gaden's property between the Engine House & King's Beach/Between Bulley's Farm & present day Job's Cv., 1794–95/1797–98/1807

Lacy, James. Public house, King's Beach, 1836

Laing, (Laimy) Michael. Liquors/boardinghouse & liquors, 184 Water St., 1864–65/1870–71

Langley, Henry. Public house, Water St., 1836

Lannigan, Edward. Public house, Court House Lane, 1836

Laracy/Larracy, James. Groceries & liquor/tavern/wines & spirits/groceries & liquors, 324 Water St./328 Water St./324 Water St./328 Water. St., 1870–71/1871/1877/1880–81

Lash J. & G (George & Jeffrey)/Lash, M. G./Lash, Mortimer. Bakers & confectioners, sellers of cigars/wines & liquors/wines, spirits, champagne, ales & porters/selling retail & wholesale/billiard saloon at 303, 303 Water St. E/305 Water St. E/303 Water St. E, 1864–65/1870–71/1871/1877/ 1880–81/1885–86/1890/1908–09/1913.

Lawlor, Edward. Public house, Water St., 1836

Lawlor, James/Lawlor, Mrs. Johanna (widow of James). Groceries & liquors, 176 Water St., 1864–65/1870–71/1871

Leary, Mike. Public house, Water St., 1836

Leary, James/John/Mrs. Margaret. Liquors, 32 Gower St., 1885–86/1870–71, 1877, 1890/1894–1897

Leamy, Thomas (from Blackhead). Wines & spirits, 363 Water St., 1877

LeDrew, William. Liquors, Kellegrews [sic], 1894–97

Leitch, Mrs. B. Liquors, 49 Duckworth St., 1864–65

Leo, Miss/Mrs. Mary (widow of Michael). Groceries & liquors/liquors/wines & spirits, 53 Duckworth St., 1864–65/1870–71/1871/1877/1885–86/1890/1894–97

Liddy, Mrs. Ellen. Groceries & liquors/liquors, groceries & provisions, 163 Water St./274 Gower St., 1864–65/1870–71

Liddy, William. Liquors, Torbay South, 1894–97

Lindberg, John /Lindberg & Franklin. Watchmaker & jeweler/manufacturing jeweler & watchmaker & proprietor Bavarian Brewery/lager beer brewer, 171 Water St./117 Duckworth St./Signal Hill Rd., 1870–71/1890/1894–97/1898.

Linegar, Mrs. Wines & spirits, 122 Duckworth St., 1877

Little, Graham. Public house, Between Bulley's Farm & present day Job's Cv., 1807

Little, Michael/Quirk, Cornelius/Phealan, James/Steele, Samuel. Public house (London Tavern), Corner of York & Wood St., Unknown date in 1700s/ 1797–98/1804/1807/1810–1832/1917–?

Lonergan, Nicholas /Lunergan (Lannergan), Mrs. Helen (Ellen) (widow of Nicholas)/Lunergan, Miss Mary. Liquors/saloon/wines & liquors/liquors, 124 Duckworth St./126 Duckworth St./122 Duckworth St., 1864–65/1871/ 1885–86/1890/1894–97/1898/1904

Long, James (Janus). Liquors, 126 Duckworth St., 1864–65.

Loughnan (Loughman), Charles. Grocer & provision dealer/liquors/grocer, 92–96 Water St./96 Water St., 1864–65/1870–71/1871

Louis, Samuel. Public house, Water St., 1836

Maan, Patrick. Tavern, 367 Water St., 1871

Macdonald, Hugh. Liquors & boarding house, 396 Water St., 1864–65

MacKay/Mackay, Wm. Liquors/wines & spirits/liquor/liquor dealer, 175 Water St. W/275 Water St. W, 1870–71/1877

Macnamara, Angus. Public house, (Agincourt), Between Bulley's Farm & present day Job's Cv., 1807

McArdell, James. Unknown/liquors/tavern, Cove Rd./312 Water St./318 Water St., 1864–65/1870–71/1871

McCarthy, William. Liquors/tavern, 438 Water St., 1864–65/1870–71/1871

McCarthy, John. Fisherman/liquors/tavern, Boards at 438 Water St./128 Water St./428 Water St., 1864–65/1870–71/1871

McCarthy, John. Wines & spirits, 144 Water St., 1877

McCarthy, Timothy. Avalon Saloon, 228 Water St., 1877

McCarty, Pat. Public house, Near Fort William, 1836

McCarty, Patrick. Public house, Duckworth St., 1836

Maccasy, Lawrence/Maccassey, Lawrence. Public house/groceries & liquors, Water St./362 Water St., 1836/1864–65

McCourt, Philip. Draper/wines & spirits, 39 New Gower/282 Water St., 1864–65/1877

McGrath, T. Wines & spirits, George's Town, 1877

McGrath, Timothy. Avalon Saloon/liquors/wines & liquors, 228 Water St./376 Water St., 1880–81/1885–86/1890/1894–97

McGrath, Maurice. Public house, Water St., 1836

McGrath, Mrs. (Brigit) (widow of John) formerly Mrs. Farrell. Wines & spirits/ liquors/wines & liquors, 10 Queen St., 1877/1885–86/1890/1894–97/1898

McGuire, Jack. Public house, Water St., 1836

McKay, Edward. Wines & liquors, 380 Water St., 1898

McKay, George/McKay, Eliza (widow of George). Liquors & Skittle Alley/
wines & liquors/liquors, 434 Water St. E/269 Water St. E/269 1/2 Water St.,
1885–86/1894–97/1898/1904

McKay, James (Brigit). Liquors/wines & spirits, Prescott St./239 Water St.,
1885/1870–71/1877

McKay, James/McKay, Mrs. J. Liquors/Arcade Saloon/saloon, 343 Water St./344
Water St./341 Water St. E/318 Water St. E, 1880–81/1885–86/1890/1894–97/1898

McKay, Wm./William J./McKay, Mrs. Minnie. Wines & liquors/liquors, Water
St. E/156 Water St., 1894–97/1898/1904/1908–09/1913/1915

McKay (Mackey). Tavern, Prescott St., 1871

McLarty, Ann. Public house, Water St., 1836

McNally, Lawrence. Public house, Duckworth St., 1836

McNamara, Thomas. Public house, Water St., 1836

McNeil, Thomas H. Liquor dealer, 168 Water St., 1913

McPherson, Walter. Public house, Maggotty Cv., 1836

Miller & Co. Temperance beers/botanic beer/birch beer/hop beer/ginger beer/
unfermented wines, Ordnance Yard, 1885–86

Maher, Bridget. Liquors wholesale & retail, 28 Waldegrave St., 1904

Maher, Thomas. Public house, Water St., 1836

Maher, Edward. Clothier & liquor seller/liquors/liquor store/wines & spirits/
groceries & liquors, 198 Water St., 1864–65/1870–71/1871/1877/1880–81

Maher, Patrick. Public house, Water St., 1836

Malone, Maurice. Liquors/wines & liquors, 410 Water St.,
1885–86/1890/1894–97/1898/1904

Manning, Michael. Liquors/tavern, 330 Water St., 1864–65/1870–71/1871

Mara, Michael. Public house (Sun), East of Hunter's Cv., Unknown date
1700s/1797–97/1807

Marnell, James. Public house, Water St., 1836

Matthews, B. Public house (Golden Lion), Foot of Holloway St., 1818

Maynard, F. Wines & liquors, 51 Harvey Rd., 1898

Meehan, Edward. Commission merchant & importer/wholesale alcohol/
liquors/general importer, Meehan's Wharf near 153 Water St./151 Water St.,
1864–65/1870–71/1871

Meehan, Patrick. Wines & spirits, 388 Water St., 1877

Meehan, Mrs. Wines & spirits, 3 Rennie's Mill Rd., 1877

Meehan, Ann. Liquors, Military Rd., 1885–86

Meehan, John. Liquors wholesale & retail, 53A Duckworth St., 1904/1908–09/
1913/1915

Meehan, John. Saloon, 91 Military Rd., 1890

Melvin, Jas. W. Wines, spirits & cigars, Water St., 1897

Mitchell, Bryan. Grocers, wines & liquors, 99 Water St. E., 1890

Moore/Moores, Solomon. Wines & spirits/publican/wines & liquors, 252 Water St./260 Water St., 1877/1880–81/1885–86/1890

Moore, Philip F. Wines & liquors, Duckworth St., 1894–97

Morey & Co. Groceries & liquors/wines & liquors wholesale, 173 Water St. E, 1880–81/1885–86/1890

Molloy, James A. Liquor dealers, 296½ Water St. W, 1913/1915

M'Rae, D. W. Liquors, 304 Water St., 1885–86

Morey, M. (Morey & Co.). Groceries & liquors, 173 Water St., 1880–81/1885–86

Morrisey, Mathew. Public house, Garrison Hill, 1836

Morrissey, Mrs. Walter. Beer, Allendale Rd, 1894–97

Morris, Simon. Public house, Water St., 1836

Morse, Mike. Public house, Water St., 1836

Mudge, Tim. Public house, Water St., 1836

Mullally, Peter. Liquors, 192 Water St. W, 1880–81

Mullins, William. Brewer, 232 Water St. W, 1885–86

Mullowney, Mrs. E. Groceries & liquors/liquors, 249 Water St./241 Water St, 1864–65/1880–81

Mullowney, John. Groceries & spirits, Unknown location, 1864–65

Mullowney, Patrick. Public house, Water St., 1836

Mulloy, Mike. Public House, Water St., 1836

Murphy, Dennis. Public house (Wheatsheaf), East of Hunter's Cv., 1807

Murphy, Lawrence. Public house, Gower St., 1836

Murphy & Kenny. Public house, Water St., 1836

Murphy, Michael. Tavern, 341 Water St. W, 1871

Murphy, Patrick. Groceries & liquors/liquors/tavern, 392 Water St., 1864–65/1870–71/1871/1877/1880–81

Murphy, Richard. Groceries & liquors/grocer/wines & spirits, 168 Water St. W/170 Water St. (Present day 562–564 Water St.), 1864–65/1870–71/1871/1877/1880–81

Murphy, John. Groceries & liquors, 70 Water St., 1880–81

Murphy, John. Public house (Duke of York), Duckworth St., East of Cochrane St., 1807

Murphy, Michael. Public house (Dove), Between Riverhead & Bulley's Farm, 1807

Murphy, Thomas. Public house, Unknown location, 1794–95

Murphy, Thomas. Public house (Three Crowns), East of Hudson's Cv. (Bottom of Prescott St.), 1797–98, 1807

Murine, Patrick. Public house (Flower Pot), Between Riverhead & Bulley's Farm, 1807

Murphy, Thomas. Groceries & liquors/liquors/general grocer, 57 Duckworth St./55 Duckworth, 1864–65/1870–71/1871

Nangle, Frank/Naugle, Frank P./Nagle, Francis P. Wines & liquors/liquors/liquor dealer, 172 Duckworth St., 1898/1904/1908–09/1913

Neal, Arthur. Public house, Water St., 1836

Nelson, Andrew. Wines & liquors, 228 Water St., 1890

Newfoundland Brewery. Lager beer brewer, Circular Rd., 1898

Norbury, Charles. Brewer, 272 Water St. W, 1885–86/1890

Nowlan, Denis. Public house, Water St., 1836

Nowlan, Edmund. Public House, Water St., 1836

Nowlan, Michael/Mrs. J. Nolan (widow of Michael), Grocer, provisions dealer & wholesale liquor sales/liquors/tavern, 95–97 Water St./312 Water St./316 Water St., 1864–65./1870–71/1871

Nugent, E. Sr. Liquors. Kellegrews, 1894–97

O'Brien, Maurice. Liquors, 88 King's Rd., 1864–65.

O'Brine, Timothy. Liquors, Freshwater Rd., 1864–65

O'Bryne, Mrs. Bridgit/B. O'Brien/B. O'Brien (widow of John) Groceries & liquors/liquors/tavern, 116 Water St./166 [sic] Water St., 1864–65./1870–71/1871

O'Connor, Michael, Groceries & liquors, 63 Duckworth St., 1864–65

O'Connor, Timothy. Wines & Liquors, 374 Water St., 1890

O'Connor, William. Liquors, 97 Gower St., 1870–71

O'Donnell, Thomas/James. Groceries & liquors/grocer/wines & spirits/groceries & liquors, 290 Water St., 1864–65/1870–71/1871/1877/1880–81/1885–86

O'Donnovan [O'Donavan], Timothy/Catherine (widow of Timothy). Liquors/saloon, 168 Duckworth St., 1885–86/1890

O'Dwyer, John. Liquors/tavern, 166 Duckworth St., 1870–71/1871/1877/1885–86

O'Keefe, Andrew. Liquors, Harvey Rd., 1864–65/1870–71

Oldridge/Oldrige, Henry/Oldridge, Ann (widow of Henry)/Oldridge, Susan. Liquors & boarding house (The Devonshire Inn)/tavern/boarding & lodging/liquors/wines & spirits, 120 Water St. E/170 Water St. E/Water St. E/114 Water St. E, 1864–65/1870–71/1871/1880–81/1885–86/1890/1894–97/1898

O'Mara, John. Liquors/general merchant/groceries & liquors, 99 Water St., 1864–65.

O'Mara, Thomas. Groceries & liquors/liquors, 170 Water St./370 Water St., 1864–65/1870–71

O'Meara, Thomas. Tavern, 368 Water St., 1871

O'Neill, Daniel. Liquors, King's Bridge Rd., 1864–65

O'Neill, Thomas. Stonemason/liquors sold wholesale/tavern/wines & spirits/ liquors & groceries/liquors/wines & liquors, 140 Water St./170 Water St., 1864–65/1870–71/1871/1877/1880–81/1885–86/1890/1894–97/1904/1913/1915

O'Reilly, J.J. & G./George. Liquors/groceries, wines & liquors, 198 Water St., 1885–86/1890

O'Reilly, John J./O'Reilly Patrick J.F., Importer of provisions, groceries, wines & liquors, wholesale & retail/wines & liquors, 290 Water St. & 43/45 King's Rd./290a Water St., 1890/1894–97/1898/1908–09/1915

O'Reilly, Albert. W. & Robert. Saloon/wines & spirits/liquors, 170 Water St. W/2 Patrick St., 1890/1894–97/1898/1904/1908–09

O'Reilly, Patrick J. Wines & liquors/liquors, 29 Gower St./124 Water St. E, 1898/1904/1908–09/1913/1915

Parker, Robert. Public house, King's Beach, 1836

Parker, Thomas. Public house, Garrison Hill, 1836

Parker, Wm. Public house, Duckworth St., 1836

Partridge, John. Public house, Upper Path [Duckworth St.], 1804/1806

Parsons, Roberts (High Constable). Public house (West India Coffee House [East India Coffee House]), Location unlisted, 1807

Pennicuick, James G. Groceries & liquors, 100 Military Rd., 1864–65

Perchard, Richard. Public house (Royal Oak), Faced Hunter's Cv., Unknown date 1700s/1807

Phelan, Denis. Saloon on the "beach"/Wines, spirits & cigars, Duckworth St., 1897

Phealan, Thomas. Public house, Water St., 1836

Phelan, Timothy/Phelan, Margarette (widow Timothy)/Phelan, John T./ Phelan, Nora/Phelan, Miss Hannah. Groceries & liquors/liquors/wines & spirits/liquors/liquor dealer, 338 Water St./161 & 338 Water/336 Water St. W, 1864–65/1870–71/1877/1880–81/1885–86/1890/1894–97/1904/1908–09/1913/1915

Phelan, James. Wines & spirits, 164 Water St., 1877/1885–86

Phelan, James. Groceries & liquors, 172 Water St., 1880–81/1885–86

Phelan, Mrs. J./Phelan, Miss Minnie. Wines & liquors, 174 Duckworth St., 1898/1904/1908–09

Pine, Patrick. Public house, Water St., 1836

Polk, George. Public house, Water St., 1836

Pool, Charles R. Wines & liquors, 190 Water St. (next door to Court House)/193 Water St., 1890/1894–97/1898/1904

Power, Andrew. Public house, Magotty Cv., 1836

Power (Pour), Charles. Public house (The Plough), Top of what is now Temperance St. at Brine's bridge, also known as Pour's (Power's) Bridge, 1807

Power, M.A. Wines & spirits, 128 Water St., 1877

Power, Edward. Public house, Water St., 1836

Power, Edward. Wines & spirits, 371 New Gower St., 1877

Power, Edward/Power, Mrs. Honora. Liquors/wines & liquors, 421 Water St./408 Water St., 1885–86/1890/1894–97

Power, William. Public house (Angel), Between Bulley's Farm & present day Job's Cv., 1797–98/1807

Power, James. Liquors & boarding house, 260 Water St., 1864–65

Power James. Liquors, 430 Water St., McAlpine's, 1870–71

Power, James. Groceries & liquors/trader & shopkeeper/wines & liquors/liquors, Unlisted location/190 New Gower St., 1864–65/1870–71/1877/1885–86/1890/1894–97

Power, John. Liquors, wholesale, 335 Water St., 1864–65/1870–71

Power, James. Brewer, Plank Rd., 1871

Power, Michael/Mogue Power. Liquors/tavern/wines & spirits/liquors/liquor saloon, 42 Cochrane St., 1864–65/1870–71/1871/1877/1885–86/1890/1894–97/ 1898/1904/1908–09/1913/1915

Power, Patrick. Public house, Water St., 1836

Power, Mrs. P.L. Liquors, 2 Beck's Cv., 1864–65/1870–71

Power, Philip. Liquors & groceries, 368 Water St., 1864–65

Power, Philip. Liquors/cooper & grocer, liquors, 70 Water St. W, 1864–65/ 1870–71

Power, William. Public house (Angel), Water St., 1836

Power, William. Brewer, 136 Pokeham Path, 1885–86

Prendergast (Pendergast), Mary. Public house, Water St., 1836

Prendergast (Pendergast), Mike. Public house, Water St., 1836

Prendergast (Pendergast), Wm. Wines & spirits, 192 New Gower St., 1877

Quinn, John. Public house, Water St., 1836

Quinn, Thomas D. Public house, Water St., 1836

Raftis, Coleman/Mrs. C. Coleman. Fisherman/liquors/tavern/wines & spirits, 323 Water St. W, 1864–65/1870–71/1877

Rankin, Chas. Groceries & liquors, 365 Water St., 1880–81

Rankin, Alex D./Rankin C. Groceries & liquors/wines & liquors/liquors, 228 Water St., 1870–71/1871/1877/1885–86/1894–97/1880–81/1890/1898/1904/1913/1915

Rankin, C. B. Liquor dealer, 263 Water St., 1885–86

Rankin & McMillan. Provisions, groceries, wines & liquors, wholesaler, 121&125 Water St., 1864–65

Rawlins, John. Groceries & liquors, 213 Gower St., 1864–65

Rawlins, Mrs. Ellen (widow of Edward). Groceries & liquors, 108 Military Rd., 1864–65/1871

Reardon, Dennis V./Reardon, Mrs. (widow Dennis). Groceries & liquors/
  wholesaler/liquors/tavern, 136 Water St./131 Water St., 1864–65/1870–71
Redmond, Patrick. Public house (Ship Assistance), West of Hunter's Cv./
  On W. Kersey's property between Noble's Cv. & the Engine House,
  1794–95/1796–97/1797–98/1807
Rice, Michael. Grocer/liquors, Court house, Limekiln Hill, 1864–65/1870–71
Rodgers, Joseph. Beer shop, Waldegrave St., 1904
Rourke, William. Beer & cigars, 274 Gower St., 1904
Rourke, Mike. Public house, Water St., 1836
Rutledge, Peter. Wines & liquors/liquors, Quidi Vide Lake Rd./Quidividi [sic],
  1890/1894–97
Ryan, John. Tavern, 204 Water St., 1871
Ryan, Michael. Tavern, 322 Duckworth St., 1871
Ryan, J. D. Liquors/wines liquors/liquors, 249 Water St./281 Water St. E/279
  Water St. E/281 Water St. E, 1885–86/1890/1894–97/1898/1890/1904/1908–09
Ryan, Stephen. Public house, Water St., 1836
Scanlon, John. Public house, Water St., 1836
Scanlon, Mike. Public house, Water St., 1836
Scanlan, Ellen. Liquors, Rear 164 Water St., 1864–65/1870–71
Scott, William. Groceries & liquors/liquors/grocer, 318 Water St./320 Water St.,
  1864–65/1870–71
Shea, Edward. Tavern, 120 Water St., 1871
Shea, Miss Elizabeth. Tavern, 44 Cochrane St., 1871
Shea, Patrick J. Wines & liquors (Terra Nova Saloon)/wines & liquors, 314 Water
  St./334 Water St./314 Water St., 1894–97/1898/1904/1908–09/1913/1915
Seymour, Wm. Liquors wholesale & retail, 59 New Gower St., 1904
Shelby, J. Liquors, Water St. E, 1880–81
Shortall, Mrs. Peter J. (widow) (Bridgit T.). Liquors wholesale & retail, 392 Water
  St. W, 1908–09/1913/1915
Sheean [sic]/Sheehan, John. Wines & spirits, Water St. W, 1877
Simms, Henry. Beer saloon, 118 New Gower St., 1898/1904
Sinnott, Edward F. Wines & liquors/liquors/liquor dealer, 200 Water St.,
  1898/1904/1908–09/1913/1915
Skinner, Mary (widow of Patrick). Saloon, 60 Water St. W, 1890
Smith, Dennis. Liquors/fisherman, 78 Water St. W/80 Water St. W, 1864–65/
  1870–71
Stott, James/Stott, David. Groceries & wines/grocer, tea, wine & spirit merchant/
  wines & liquors, 125 Water St. E/123–125 Water St. W, 1880–81/1885–86/1890/
  1894–97/1908–09/1913/1915

Strang, John/Strang & House/Strang, Mrs. John C./Strong, John C. Groceries &
wines/liquors/wines & liquors/liquors (Caledonian House), 134 Water St./
138 Water St./136 Water St./Acadia Bldg. 343 Water St./331 Water St./
329–331 Water St./327–329 Water St., 1880–81/1885–86/1890/1894–97/1898/
1904/1908–09/1913/1915
Strang, Robert. Liquors wholesale & retail/liquor dealers, 193 Water St. E,
1908–09/1913
Sullivan, Daniel. Tavern, 390 Water St., 1871
Sullivan, Denis. Public house, Duckworth St., 1836
Tarahan, Patrick. Public house, Water St., 1836
Thomas, Charles. Liquor dealer, Water St., 1898/1904
Tobin, Bridgit. Wines & liquors, 335 Water St./392 Water St./331 Water St.,
1898/1904/1908–09
Tobin, James J. Wines & liquors/liquors (wholesale)/liquor dealer (Regina
Bar Room), 178 Duckworth St./176 Duckworth St., 1898/1904/1908–09/
1913/1915
Tobin, John C./Tobin, Bridget (widow of John C). Wines & liquors, 392 Water
St./331 Water St./335 Water St., 1890/1894–1897/1898/1904/1908
Tobin, John. Liquors, 336 Water St., 1885–86
Tobin, John. Boarding house, 5 Beck's Cv., 1870–71
Tobin, M. Liquors & groceries, 172 Water St., 1880–81
Tobin, Michael. Wines & spirits/liquors, 337 Water St./335 Water St., 1877/
1885–86/1894–97
Tobin, Michael/Mrs. Mary Tobin. Wines & liquors/liquors, 74 Prescott St., 1898/
1904/1908–09
Tobin, Michael/M & J Tobin. Importer of general groceries, provisions, wines,
liquors, etc., 335 & 385 Water St., 1890
Torpey, Mrs./Torphey, Dennis. Wines & spirits/liquors & groceries, Mill Lane,
1877/1880–81
Thorpe, J. Liquors, 378 Water St., 1885–86
Tracy, James. Public house, Water St., 1836
Trasy, James. Public house, Near Fort William, 1836
Trelligan, James J. Liquors wholesale & retail, 318 Water St. W, 1904/1908–09/
1913
Trelligan, Richard/Trelligan, Francis/Trelegan, Mrs. F/Trelegan, John. Grocer/
liquors/wines & spirits/groceries & liquors/liquors/saloon (Trelegan's Social
Saloon), 12 Queen St., 1864–65/1870–71/1877/1880–81/1885–86/1890/1894–97/
1898/1904/1908–09/1913/1915
Trilegan, Richard. Public house, Water St., 1836

Thorburn, James. Liquor dealer, 170 Water St. W, 1885–86

Thorburn, William. Distiller/wines & spirits, Lazy Bank Rd./362 Water St., 1864–65/1870–71/1877/1885–86

Tynan, John. Groceries & liquors, 310 Water St., 1864–65

Travis, Mary. Tavern (King's Place Tavern), King's Beach [near present–day war memorial], 1832

Tritle, Miss Mary. Tavern, 76 Water St., 1871

Villeneuve, A. Liquors, 274 Water St., 1885–86/1877

Vinnicombe, Nicholas J. Liquors wholesale & retail, 122 Duckworth St., 1908–09/ 1913/1915

Wadden, Ellen. Liquors/tavern/wines & spirits, 410 Water St., 1870–71/1871/1877/ 1880–81

Wadland, H. Liquors, 49 Duckworth St., 1870–71

Wall, Thomas. Liquors wholesale & retail, 410 Water St. W, 1908–09/1913/1915

Walsh, Mrs. Ellen. Wines & liquors, 72 Prescott St., 1898

Walsh/Welsh, Mrs. Ann (widow of H.). Tavern/liquors/wines & spirits, 386 Water St., 1871/1877/1880–81

Walsh, Mrs. James. Wines & liquors, 94 Prescott St., 1894–97

Walsh, John. Public house, Duckworth St., 1836

Walsh, John/Kate (widow of John). Liquors/wines & liquors, 51 Harvey Rd., 1885–86/1890/1894–97

Walsh, Margaret. Public house (Sailor), West of Hunter's Cv., 1807

Walsh, Mary. Wines & liquors, 96 Prescott St., 1894–97

Walsh, Mary. Public house, Water St., 1836

Walsh, Mrs. Mary. Wines & spirits, F.W. Fort Townsend, 1877

Walsh, Patrick. Public house, Water St., 1836

Walsh, Patrick. Public House (Union Flag), East of Hudson's Cv., 1807/1810

Walsh, William P./Patrick /Mrs. Mary (widow of Patrick). Liquors & groceries, wholesaler/liquors/tavern, 232 Water St., 1864–65/1870–71

Walsh, Richard. Groceries, flour dealer, wines & liquors, wholesale spirit & provision dealer (Newfoundland Tavern), 107 Water St., 1864–65

Walsh, Thomas. Groceries & spirits Unlisted location, 1864–65

Walsh, William. Tavern, 180 Water St. W, 1871

Walsh, William P. Provisions & groceries, 145 Water St., 1870–71

Walsh, William/Walsh, Mrs. Mary. Groceries & liquors/liquors/tavern/wines & spirits, 96 Prescott St., 1864–65/1870–71/1871/1877/1890/1894–97

Walsh, William. Liquors, Harvey Rd., 1870–71

Walsh, Wm. Wines & spirits, 92 Military Rd., 1877

Walsh, William. Liquor dealer, 113 Military Rd., 1885–86

Walsh, William. Wines & spirits, Patrick St., 1877

Walsh, William L. Liquors/tavern/wines & spirits, 119 Duckworth St., 1870–71/ 1871/1877

Walsh, Walter. Liquors & groceries, Unlisted location, 1864–65

Wells, Thomas. Public house, Water St., 1836

Welsh, Wm. Public house, From Hudson's Cv. to the easternmost part of St. John's, 1797–98/1807

Welsh, William. Public House (Swan), On Jn. Livingstone's property between the Engine House & King's Beach/Between Bulley's Farm & present–day Job's cv., 1794–95/1807

Whelan, Mrs. Bridget. Wines & liquors, 388 Water St., 1898

Whelan, James/Mrs. Mary Whalen (widow of John). Liquors/tavern, 274 Water St., 1864–65/1870–71 /1871

White, Margaret (widow of Patrick). Tavern, 402 Water St., 1871

Widdicomb, John. Publican (The Rose & Crown), On G. Williams' property between Roope's Cv. & Noble's Cv. west end of St. John's, Pye Corner [Waldegrave St. area], 1794–95 /1796–97/1797–98/1807

Wiely, Robert. Public house, Water St., 1836

Williams, John. Public house (Nelson), Between Riverhead [west end of St. John's, railway station area] & Bulley's Farm, 1807

Young, Ellen (widow of William). Liquors/tavern, 106 Water St., 1864–65/1870–71

19TH-CENTURY ALCOHOL-RELATED ESTABLISHMENTS OUTSIDE ST. JOHN'S

Many Newfoundland communities, such as Gander and Corner Brook, did not exist in the nineteenth century.

Proprietor, Type of Business, Location, Years
Allen, William, Publican, Topsail, 1904
Arshell, John S., Liquors, Water St. E, Carbonear, 1864–65
Ashford, William, Liquors, Catalina, S.W. Arm, 1864–65
Barry, John, Liquors, Water St. near Bannerman, Harbour Grace, 1864–65
Beer, Albert, Beer and confectionary, Channel, 1904
Best, George, Liquors, Water St. W, Carbonear, 1864–65/1870–71
Best, James, Tavern, Carbonear, 1870-71
Brown, Patrick, Liquors, Water St. E, Carbonear
Brown, Samuel, Liquors, Kings Cove, 1904
Brown, William, Liquors, Water St. W, Carbonear, 1864–65/ 1870–71
Buck, John Sr., Publican, Conception Harbour, 1894–97/1898
Butler, P. , Wines and liquors, Water St. near Cochrane/26 Cochrane, Harbour Grace, 1864–65/1870–71
Byrne, John, Liquors, Water St. near LeMarchant, Harbour Grace, 1864–65
Callahan, Groceries and liquors, 89 Water St., Harbour Grace, 1870–71
Callahan, James, Liquors, 202 Water St., Harbour Grace, 1870-71
Callanan, James, Saloon, 202 Water St., Harbour Grace, 1870-71/1877

Callanan, John, Tavern, 89 Water St., Harbour Grace, 1870–71

Casey, Mary, Liquors, Water St. E, Carbonear, 1864–65

Chafe, Emanual, Liquors, Gould's Section, 1894–97

Coady, John, Wines and spirits, Water St., 1877

Colbert, Philip, Wines and spirits, Water St., 1877

Connell, Maurice, Tavern, 74 Water St., Harbour Grace, 1870–71

Connolly, George, Publican, Greenspond, 1864-65

Cornell, Morris, Liquors, Water St. and corner of Cochrane, Harbour Grace, 1864–65

Curtis, Gerald, Publican, Salmonier, 1898

Daly, James, Publican, Brigus, 1864–65

Day, William, Liquors, Catalina, S.W. Arm, 1864–65

Dermody, John, Tavern, Brigus, 1870–71

Dooling, Catherine, Liquors, 80 Water St. near Cochrane, Harour Grace, 1864–65/1870–71

Dormady, John, Publican, Brigus, 1864–65

Ezekiel, Patrick, Liquors, Harbour Main, 1894–97

Ezekiel, Samuel, Liquors, Salmon Cove, 1894–97

Fagan, Michael, Publican, Riverhead/St. Mary's Bay-Placentia district, 1898

Fanning, John, Liquors, Water St. E, Carbonear, 1864–65

Farrell, Margaret, Liquors, Water St. near Cochrane, Harbour Grace, 1864–65

Farrell, Michael, Groceries and liquors, 104 Water St., Harbour Grace, 1870–71

Fitzgerald, John, Groceries and liquors, 18 Cochrane St., Harbour Grace, 1870–71

Fitzgerald, Owen, Publican, Bay Roberts, 1864–65

Flannery, John, Publican, Topsail, 1904

Flannery, Matthew, Publican, Topsail, 1898

Foley, Edward, Liquors, Water St. near Victoria, 1864–65

Foley, Mary (widow of Edmund), Saloon, 216 Water St., Harbour Grace, 1870–71

Ford, Robert, Publican, Bonavista/Walkham's Bridge, 1894–97/1898

Garnier, Ernest, Liquors, St. George's Bay, 1894–97

Gaule, Richard, Liquors, Topsail Rd., 1894–97

Gladney, Patrick, Liquors, Windsor Lake, 1904

Gould, Michael, Liquors, Water St. W, Carbonear, 1864–65

Harmon, John, Publican, Riverhead/Harbour Main, 1898

Harmon, John, Publican, Conception Harbour, 1904

Harrison, John, Liquors, Conception Harbour, 1894-97

Hearn, Richard, Liquors, Colliers, 1898

Hennessey, John, Liquors, Holyrood, 1894–97

Hogan, Thomas, Liquors, Water St. E, Carbonear, 1864–65

Horace, Patrick, Liquors, Conception Harbour, 1894–97

Keefe, John, Liquors, Water St. near Victoria, 1864–65

Keefe, John, Liquors, Water St. near LeMarchant, Harbour Grace, 1864–65

Keefe, Mary, Liquors, 224 Water St., Harbour Grace, 1870-71

Kenealy, Johanna, Liquors, Water St. E, Carbonear, 1864–65

Keough, James, Liquors, Water St. W, Carbonear, 1864–65

LeDrew, Abram, Publican, Kelligrews, 1904

LeDrew, William, Liquors, Kelligrews, 1894–97

Lee, Edward, Liquors, Riverhead, St. Mary's, 1898

Leroux, Walter, Liquors, Sandy Point, 1894–97

Lewis, James Jr./Anastasia, Liquors, Holyrood, 1894–97/1904

Lewis, Philip Sr., Liquors, Holyrood, 1894–97/1898/1904

Liddy, William, Liquors, Torbay South, 1894–97

Lynch, Thomas, Wines and liquors, Water St. near Bannerman, Harbour Grace, 1864-65

McCarthy, Richard, Liquors, Carbonear, 1870–71

McGee, Patrick, Publican, Avondale, 1904

McGrath, Mrs. J., Liquors, King's Cove, Bonavista, 1898

McGrath, Tobias, Publican, Salmonier, 1898

Moran, John, Liquors, Water St. E, Carbonear, 1864–65

Mulcahy, Bartholomew, Liquors, Water St. near Cochrane, Harbour Grace, 1864–65

Murphy, Edward, Liquors, Catalina, N.E. Arm, 1864–65

Neville, R., Liquors, Topsail, 1898

Nolan, John, Publican, St. Mary's, 1898

Norman, John, Liquors, Catalina, S.W. Arm, 1864–65

Nugent, E. Sr., Liquors, Kelligrews, 1894–97

O'Brien, Michael, Liquors, Holyrood, 1894–97

O'Brien, Patrick Sr., Publican, Holyrood North Arm, 1904

O'Brien, William, Saloon keeper, Petrie's Crossing, 1904

O'Neill, John Sr., Liquors, Holyrood, 1894–97

O'Neill, Margaret, Liquors, Water St. near Bannerman, Harbour Grace, 1864–65

O'Rourke, Lawrence F., Liquors, Holyrood, Harbour Main, 1894–97/1898/1904

Parsons, Ebenezer, Wines and spirits, 92 Water St., Harbour Grace, 1864–65/ 1870–71/1877

Peters, William, Trader and liquor dealer, Ragged Harbour, 1864–65

Power, Matthew, Liquors, Water St. W, Carbonear, 1864–65/1870–71

Quirk, Richard, Liquors, Fortune Harbor, 1904

Roach, Patrick, Hotel keeper and publican, Manuals, 1898

Routledge, P., Liquors, Quidi Vidi, 1894–97

Scanlon, Patrick, Wines and liquors, Water St. near Noad, 1864-65

Shea, John, Wines and spirits, Carbonear Rd. , 1877

Shea, Dennis, Tavern, 164 Water St./Main St. Harbour Grace, 1870–71/1877

Shea, Dennis, Liquors, Water St. near Bannerman, Harbour Grace, 1864–65

Squires, George, Publican, Long Pond, 1864–65

Sweeny, Patrick, Liquors, Water St. W, Carbonear, 1864–65

Thompson, William, Tavern, 186 Water St., Harbour Grace, 1870–71

Thompson/Thomson, William, Liquors, Water St. near Bannerman, Harbour Grace, 1864–65

Toussaint, William, Wines and liquors, Water St. near Bannerman, Harbour Grace, 1864–65

Vass, Edward, Liquors, Water St. near Cochrane/32 Cochrane, Harbour Grace, 1864–65/1870–71

Walsh, Garret, Liquors, Holyrood, 1894–97

Walsh, James, Saloon, Brigus, 1870–71

Walsh, Mark, Wines and spirits, Water St., 1877

Walsh, Mark, Liquors, Water St. near Cochrane, Harbour Grace, 1864–65

Walsh, Michael, Publican, Holyrood, 1904

Walsh, Patrick, Liquors, St. Mary's, 1898

Walsh, Patrick Sr., Publican, Open Hall/Bonavista, 1898/1904

Walsh, Philip, Hotel keeper and publican, Kelligrews, 1898

Walsh, Philip, Publican and farmer, Kelligrews, 1904

Walsh, Philip, Liquors, Water St. near Cochrane, Harbour Grace, 1864–65

Walsh, Richard, Liquors, Holyrood, 1894–97

Walsh, William, Liquors, 76 Water St., Harbour Grace, 1864–65/ 1870–71

Woodford, Richard, Liquors, Woodford, 1904

APPENDIX E

MID 20TH-CENTURY DRINKING ESTABLISHMENTS OUTSIDE ST. JOHN'S

From the 1951 proceedings of the House of Assembly:

Name of Business, Municipality, Proprietor
Archibald's Hotel, Harbour Grace, Licensed to Rose Archibald
Ash's Tavern, Harbour Grace, Licensed to J. M. Ash
Popular Tavern, Curling, Licensed to J. Basha
Wheeler's, Curling, Licensed to Mrs. M. Wheeler
Miller's, Curling, Licensed to Mrs. G. Miller
Bradbury's Tavern, Bay Roberts, Licensed to E. J. Bradbury
Noseworthy's, Bay Roberts, Licensed to A. Noseworthy
Whalen's, Corner Brook, Licensed to J. W. Whalen
McCarthy's, Corner Brook, Licensed to Mrs. M. McCarthy
Corbage's, Corner Brook, Licensed to Mrs. M. Corbage
Byrne's Tavern, Donavan's, Licensed to G. Byrne
Cahill's, Placentia, Licensed to Mrs. M. Cahill
Cranford's, New Harbour, Licensed to A. B. Cranford
Curran's, Gambo, Licensed to Thomas Curran
Bennett's, Holyrood, Licensed to Mrs. Hilda Davis
Butterpot Inn, Holyrood, Licensed to J. J. Hickey
Gander Tavern, Gander, Licensed to Gander Tavern Inc.
Geehan's, Topsail, Licensed to Mrs. M. Geehan
Hutching's Tavern, Whitbourne, Licensed to Aaron Hutchings

Hutching's, Bell Island, Licensed to Max Hutchings
Middleton Inn, Bell Island, Licensed to E. Parsons
Kelly's, Avondale, Licensed to Mrs. T. Kelly
Lundrigan's, Colinet, Licensed to A. Lundrigen
Beachview Hotel, Stephenville Crossing, Licensed to Mrs. M. McFatridge
McLean's, Mackinsons, Licensed to J. A. McLean
Cabot Hotel, Brigus, Licensed to John Marshall
Murrin's, Spaniard's Bay, Licensed to L. Murrin
Cuban Tavern, Deer Lake, Licensed to John Noah
The Caribou Tavern, Deer Lake, Licensed to Albert Boulos
O'Toole's, Conception Harbour, Licensed to R. O'Toole
Bar 50, Whitbourne, Licensed to Mrs. E. Peckford
Piercey's, Kelligrews, Licensed to A. Piercey
Power's, Dunville, Licensed to Gerald Power
Power's Tavern, Salmonier, Licensed to Jack Power
Argyll Hotel, Botwood, Licensed to Mrs. A Ryall
Vail's, St. Mary's, Licensed to Mrs. E. M. Vail
Veteran's Inn, Torbay, Licensed to Messrs. Cole & LeMessurier
Walsh's, Goulds, Licensed to Mrs. P. Walsh
William's Tavern, Bay Bulls, Licensed to Mary Williams
Collin's Tavern, Chamberlains, Licensed to James Collins
Parson's Tavern, Seal Cove, Licensed to R. Parsons
Junction Tavern, Notre Dame Junction, Licensed to Messrs. Woolfrey & Moore
Albert's Tavern, Harbour Main, Licensed to Mrs. A. Furey
The Oasis, Grand Falls, Licensed to James Constable
Green's Tavern, Bishop's Falls, Gordon Green

From the 1956 Conception Bay telephone directory:

Name of Business, Municipality
Furey's, Holyrood
Crawley's, Holyrood
Albert's, Harbour Main
Fewer's Tavern, Avondale North
James' Tavern, Brigus
Herbert Bowering, Tavern, Bay Roberts
The Bayview "Conception Bay's Tavern," Birch Hills
Kozy-Glo Tavern, Spaniard's Bay
The Avalon Tavern, Harbour Grace

From the 1957 Western Newfoundland Telephone Directory:

Name of Business, Street, Municipality
Basha's Tavern, 103 BRd.way, Corner Brook
Esquire Tavern , Herald Avenue, Corner Brook
Tourist Tavern , Main St., Corner Brook
Bonn[le] Tavern , BRd.way, Corner Brook
Port Tavern , Humber Rd., Corner Brook
Al's Tourist lounge , Ball Diversion, Corner Brook
Wellon's Nite Club, Riverside Drive, Corner Brook
Westmount Club, BRd.way, Corner Brook
Terra Nova Tavern Ltd, North Main St., Deer Lake
Dhoon Lodge, Black Duck
Beachview Hotel, Stephenville Crossing
The Red Rose Club, Main St., Stephenville
Corral Club & Restaurant, Main St., Stephenville

From the 1961 Bonavista & Central Newfoundland Telephone Directory:

Name of Business, Municipality
Big Dipper Bar, Gander
Cabot Club, Clarenville

NOTES

CHAPTER ONE

1 Anonymous folksong, "Ye Mariners All," lyrics from version by Fairport Convention, http://lyrics.wikia.com/wiki/Fairport_Convention:Ye_Mariners_All.

2 Roy Adkins, *Nelson's Trafalgar* (Toronto: Viking Press, 2005),

3 Joseph R. Smallwood and Robert D. W. Pitt, eds., *Encyclopedia of Newfoundland and Labrador Vol. 1* (St. John's: Newfoundland Book Publishers, 1981), s.v. "Breweries."

4 Shannon Ryan, *A History of Newfoundland in the North Atlantic to 1818* (St. John's: Flanker, 2012), 106.

5 Joshua Tavenor, "Imports to Newfoundland in the Late Seventeenth and Early Eighteenth Centuries," *Newfoundland and Labrador Studies* 26, no.1 (2011): 78.

6 Edward Wynne, "Letter to George Calvert". Correspondence from August 17, 1622, Heritage Newfoundland and Labrador, accessed March 2020. https://www.heritage.nf.ca/.

7 Nicholas Hoskins, "Letter to W.P.,". Correspondence from August 18, 1622, Heritage Newfoundland and Labrador, accessed March 2020. https://www.heritage.nf.ca/.

8 Edward Wynne, "Letter to George Calvert."

9 Peter E. Pope, "The Historical Anthropology of Demand for Alcohol in Seventeenth-Century Newfoundland," *Acadiensis* 19, no.1 (1989): 75. https://journals.lib.unb.ca/index.php/Acadiensis/index

10 Stephen F. Mills, "Made Right Here: Archaeological and Historical Data from the 17th Century Tippling House to the 1930's Beer Shop in Newfoundland" (paper presented at the 47th Annual Meeting of the Canadian Archaeological Association, St. John's, NL, May 2, 2015.)

11 Max Reid, "Rum and the Navy," in *Tempered by Rum: Rum in the History of the Maritime Provinces*, eds. James H. Morrison and James Moreira (Nova Scotia: Pottersfield, 1988), 32.

12 Ibid, 33.

13 Ibid, 16.

14 *The Colonial Office 194 Series*, October 1812, C.O. 194 V.52, 150-151.

15 Frederick H. Smith, *Caribbean Rum: A Social and Economic History* (Gainesville: University Press of Florida, 2005), 26.

16 Bernard Tobin, Survey Card, MUNFLA. 91-343, Memorial University of Newfoundland Folklore Archives, St. John's, NL, collected in Kilbride, 1988.

17 G. M. Story, W. J. Kirwin, and J. D. A. Widdowson, *Dictionary of Newfoundland English* (Toronto: University of Toronto Press, 1990) s.v. "throttles."

18 Paul O'Neill, *The Oldest City*, Rev. ed. (Portugal Cove-St. Philips: Boulder, 2002), 230.

19 Frederick William Hackwood, *Inns, Ales and Drinking Customs of Old England* (New York: Sturgis and Walton, 1909), 100.

20 A. M. Lysaght, *Joseph Banks in Newfoundland and Labrador, 1766: His Diary, Manuscripts and Collections,* accessed March 2020. https://books.google.ca/.

21 Jean M. Murray, *The Newfoundland Journal of Aaron Thomas, Able Seaman in H.M.S. Boston: A Journal Written During a Voyage from England to Newfoundland and from Newfoundland to England in the Years 1794 and 1795* (London: Longmans, 1968), 60-61.

22 Ibid, 77.

23 Philippa Glanville and Sophie Lee, ed. *The Art of Drinking* (London: V&A Publications, 2007), 12.

24 Tobias Venner, *A Treatise Wherein the Right Way and Best Manner of Living for Attaining to a Long and Healthful Life is Clearly Demonstrated* (London: 1650), accessed via MUN library search, date unknown. https://search.proquest.com/.

25 Peter E. Pope, "Outport Economics: Culture and Agriculture," 161-162. https://journals.lib.unb.ca/index.php/NFLDS/index.

CHAPTER TWO

1   Masefield, John, "Captain Stratton's Fancy" http://www.famouspoetsandpoems. com/poets/john_masefield/poems.

2   Sir William Vaughan, *Naturall and artificial directions for health: derived from the bestphilosophers, as well moderne, as ancient. By William Vaughan, Master of Artes, and student in the civill law,* Series: *Early English Books Online,* images 45-46, accessed via MUN library search, March 2020. https://search.proquest. com/legacyredirect/eebo.

3   Maria Godoy, "Lust, Lies And Empire: The Fishy Tale Behind Eating Fish On Friday," April 6, 2012. *National Public Radio,* Washington, DC, accessed March 2020. https://www.npr.org/sections/thesalt/.

4   Peter E. Pope, "The Historical Anthropology," 86.

5   Peter E. Pope, "Fish to Wine: The Historical Anthropology of Demand for Alcohol in Seventeenth-Century Newfoundland," *Histoire Sociale,* 27,(54) (November 1994) 267, https://hssh.journals.yorku.ca/index.php/hssh.

6   Grant Head, *Eighteenth Century Newfoundland* (Toronto: McClelland and Stewart, 1976), 101.

7   "History of Port," *Taylor Fladgate,* accessed March 20, 2020, https://www. taylor.pt/us/what-is-port-wine/history-of-port.

8   Harris Munden Mosdell, *When Was That? A Chronological Dictionary of Important Events In Newfoundland Down to and Including the Year 1922* (St. John's: Robinson-Blackmore, 1974), 144.

9   D. W. Prowse, *A History of Newfoundland,* 1895 (Portugal Cove-St. Philips: Boulder, 2002), 450.

10 Robert Barakat, *Report of an Archaeological Excavation at the Newman Wine Vaults, St. John's, Newfoundland* (St. John's: Memorial University, 1973).

11 Hunt, Roope and Company Ltd., *The Story and Origin of Hunt, Roope & Company, London and Oporto, Newman, Hunt & Company, London, Newman & Company, Newfoundland* (London: Hunt, Roope and Company, 1951), 9.

12 Suzanne Robicheau, "The Port of St. John's," *Saltscapes* 11, no.1 (2010).

13 C. R. Fay, *Life and Labour in Newfoundland* (Toronto: University of Toronto Press, 1956), accessed March 2020, https://books.google.ca/.

14 Implementing Order no. 1247-A/95 of 17th October 1995—[which] Suspends Port Wine export in bulk. http://bdjur.almedina.net/index.php

15 James H. Morrison and James Moreira, eds, *Tempered by Rum: Rum in the History of the Maritime Provinces* (Nova Scotia: Pottersfield, 1988), 12.

16 Jack S. Blocker, David M. Fahey, and Ian M. Tyrrell, *Alcohol and Temperance in Modern History*, Vol 2, (Santa Barbara, Calif.: ABC-CLIO, 2003), s.v. Rum.

17 Prowse, *History of Newfoundland*, 198.

18 Joshua Tavenor, "Imports to Newfoundland in the Late Seventeenth and Early Eighteenth Centuries," *Newfoundland and Labrador Studies* 26, no. 1 (2011): 78.

19 Stephen F. Mills, "Made Right Here," 7-8.

20 Peter E. Pope, *Fish into Wine: The Newfoundland Plantation in the Seventeenth Century* (Chapel Hill: U of North Carolina Press, 2004), 404.

21 John Josselyn, *An Account of Two Voyages to New-England: Made During the Years 1638, 1663* (Boston: William Veazie, 1865), accessed March 2020, https://archive.org/details/accountoftwovoyaoojoss/page/n8.

22 "America and West Indies: March 1714," in *Calendar of State Papers Colonial, America and West Indies: Volume 27, 1712-1714*, ed. Cecil Headlam (London, 1926), 302-325. *British History Online*, http://www.british-history.ac.uk/cal-state-papers/colonial/america-west-indies/vol27.

23 Grant Head, *Eighteenth Century Newfoundland*, 102, 117, 119-121, 151-153,159, 169, 234; Smallwood and Pitt, ed., *Encyclopedia*, s.v. "Liquor, Beer and Wine," 311; Joshua Tavenor, "Imports to Newfoundland in the Late Seventeenth and Early Eighteenth Centuries," 79.

24 Wayne Curtis, *And a Bottle of Rum: A History of the New World in Ten Cocktails* (New York: Three Rivers Press, 2006), 98.

25 Hugh Barty-King, and Anton Massel, *Rum: Yesterday and Today* (London: William Heineman Ltd., 1983), 161.

26 Peter E. Pope, "Fish into Wine," 268.

27 Curtis, *Bottle of Rum*, 110.

28 Frederick W. Rowe, *A History of Newfoundland and Labrador* (Toronto: McGraw-Hill Ryerson Ltd., 1980), 252.

29 Prowse, *History of Newfoundland*, 198.

30 Curtis, *Bottle of Rum*, 32.

31 Smallwood and Pitt, eds., *Encyclopedia*, s.v. "Liquor, Beer and Wine."

32 Newfoundland Colonial Blue books; Journal of the House of Assembly.

33 1845 list of provisions. Unpublished interpretive manual, Commissariat Provincial Historic Site.

34 Cheryl Krasnick Warsh, "John Barleycorn Must Die," in *Drink in Canada: Historical Essays*, edited by Cheryl Krasnick Warsh (Montreal: McGill-Queen's UP, 1993), 11.

CHAPTER THREE

1 Andre Picard, "Why People Don't Drink: It's None of Your Business," *Globe and Mail*, December 18, 2017. https://www.theglobeandmail.com/opinion/.

2 "Heavy Drinking 2018," Statistics Canada, accessed March 2020. https://www150.statcan.gc.ca/n1/pub/82-625-x/2019001/article/00007-eng.htm.

3 Frank Clarke, *A Most Wholesome Liquor: A Study of Beer and Brewing in 18th-century England and Her Colonies* (Williamsburg, Virginia: Colonial Williamsburg Foundation Library Research Report Series, 2000). https://www.colonialwilliamsburg.org/learn/research-and-education/.

4 Tom Standage, *A History of the World in 6 Glasses* (New York: Walker & Co., 2005), 55-56.

5 Jane O'Hara-May, *The Elizabethan Dyetary of Health* (Kansas: Coronado Press, 1977), 211.

6 Ian S. Hornsey, *A History of Beer and Brewing* (Cambridge: The Royal Society of Chemistry, 2003), 295.

7 C. Anne Wilson, *Food and Drink in Britain* (London: Constable, 1973), 337.

8 Ibid, 333.

9 Ibid, 330, 335, 337.

10 Hornsey, *A History of Beer and Brewing*, 324.

11 Frank Clarke, *A Most Wholesome Liquor.*

12 Head, *Eighteenth Century Newfoundland*, 8.

13 Sir Walter Raleigh, Lord Treasurer Burleigh, Cardinal Sermonetta, and Mr. Walsingham, *Instructions for Youth, Gentlemen and Noblemen* (London: Randal Minshull, 1722), 36-37, Gale. accessed January 27, 2019. Accessed via MUN library search, date unknown. https://www.gale.com/.

14 Sandy Newton, "Tales of our Tippling Houses," *Enjoy!* Winter (2004): 8.

15 Prowse, *History of Newfoundland,* 261.

16 John Mannion, "Irish Migration and Settlement in Newfoundland: The Formative Phase, 1697-1732," *Newfoundland and Labrador Studies* 17, no. 2 (2001): 288.

17 Ibid, 288-289.

18 Ibid, 262.

19 Ibid, 262.

20 Head, *Eighteenth Century Newfoundland*, 147.

21 Ibid, 149.

22 Murray, *The Newfoundland Journal of Aaron Thomas*, 187.

23 R. B. McCrae, *Lost Amid the Fogs: Sketches of Life in Newfoundland, England's Ancient Colony* (London, 1869), accessed March 2020. http://collections.mun.ca/.

24 Blocker, *Alcohol and Temperance*, s.v. Gin.

25 James Moreira, "Rum in the Atlantic Provinces," in *The Tradition of Rum* (Nova Scotia: Pottersfield, 1988), 22.

26 O'Neill, *The Oldest City*, 32.

27 Smallwood and Pitt, eds., *Encyclopedia*, s.v. "Liquor, Beer and Wine."

28 Nicholas K. Johnson, "World War I, Part 2: The British Rum Ration," *Points: The Blog of the Alcohol and Drugs History Society*, accessed March 2020. https://pointsadhsblog.wordpress.com/2014/05/29/world-war-i-part-2-the-british-rum-ration/.

29 C. S. M. Weston, "To Rum," *The Veteran*, December (1927): 68.

30 O'Neill, *The Oldest City*, 255.

31 Stephen F. Mills, "Made Right Here."

32 O'Neill, *The Oldest City*, 117-118.

33 Prowse, *History of Newfoundland*, 375.

34 Frederick W. Rowe, *A History of Newfoundland and Labrador* (Toronto: McGraw-Hill Ryerson Ltd., 1980), 254-5.

35 Rowe, *A History of Newfoundland and Labrador*, 253.

36 "N.L. and St. John's both lead country in most bars per capita: StatsCan," *Western Star*, August 17, 2017.

37 McCrae, *Lost Amid the Fogs*.

38 Ibid, 254.

39 Philip Toque, "When I was a Boy," *Evening Telegram*, February 15, 1897, 3.

40 P.J. Wakeham, "The Day Our Hens Got Drunk." *New-Land Magazine*. (3) 1963, 46-48.

41 Smallwood and Pitt, eds., *Encyclopedia*, s.v. "Liquor, Beer and Wine."

42 Rev. William Marshall, *William Marshall Diary 1839-1842*, http://collections.mun.ca/.

43 Mosdell, *When Was That?* 141.

44 McCrae, *Lost Amid the Fogs*, 191.

45 Rev. L.A. Anspach, *History of Newfoundland* (London: Printed for the author and sold by T. and J. Allman, 1819), 473.

46 Jack S. Blocker, David M. Fahey, Ian M. Tyrrell, *Alcohol and Temperance in Modern History, Vol 2*, s.v. "St. Patrick's Day."

47 "Festival of St. Patrick," *The Newfoundlander*, March 26, 1829, 2-3.

48 Ibid.

49 Jack Fitzgerald, *Peculiar Facts and Tales of Newfoundland* (St. John's: Creative, 2014), 105.

50 Owen Hiscock, *The Way It Was* (St. John's: Jesperson, 1990), 67-68.
51 Toque, Philip, "When I was a Boy," *Evening Telegram*, February 15, 1897, 3.
52 Paul O'Neill, "The Temperance Wars," *Canadian Collector* 20, no. 2 (1985): 66.

CHAPTER FOUR

1 Prowse, *History of Newfoundland*, 154.
2 Peter E. Pope, "Historical Archaeology," 85.
3 Karen Harvey, "Barbarity in a Teacup? Punch, Domesticity and Gender in the Eighteenth Century," *Journal of Design History* 21, no. 3 (2008): 205-221. https://academic.oup.com/jdh.
4 William Taverner, "Remarks on the Present State of the English Settlements in Newfoundland." Received by the Board of Trade 19 March 1713/14, NAC, MG 11, CO 194/5, ff. 91-96. http://www2.swgc.mun.ca/nfld_history/CO194/CO%20194-5-91-96-Taverner-on-English-Settlements-in-Nfld.htm.
5 Stephen F. Mills, "Made Right Here."
6 "America and West Indies: March 1714", in *Calendar of State Papers Colonial, America and West Indies: Volume 27, 1712-1714*, ed. Cecil Headlam (London, 1926), 302-325, *British History Online* http://www.british-history.ac.uk/cal-state-papers/colonial/america-west-indies/vol27/pp302-325.
7 "America and West Indies: March 1716, 1-14," in *Calendar of State Papers Colonial, America and West Indies: Volume 29, 1716-1717*, ed. Cecil Headlam (London: His Majesty's Stationery Office, 1930), 28-49. *British History Online*, accessed February 2, 2019, http://www.british-history.ac.uk/cal-state-papers/colonial/america-west-indies/vol29/pp28-49.
8 D'Alberti Papers, vol. 06, 1797 Correspondence, incoming and outgoing, between the Colonial Office and the Governor's Office in Newfoundland. http://collections.mun.ca/.
9 *The Colonial Office 194 Series*, CO 194 v.39, Aug. 13, 1797, 113v-114, http://www2.swgc.mun.ca/nfld_history/CO194/CO194-39.htm.
10 Ibid, 115-116; D'Alberti Papers.
11 Bannister, Jerry, "The Fishing Admirals in Eighteenth-Century Newfoundland," *Newfoundland Studies* 17, no. 2 (2001): 172.
12 Ibid, 173.
13 O'Neill, *The Oldest City*, 19.
14 Bannister, "The Fishing Admirals in Eighteenth-Century Newfoundland," 173.
15 Lounsbury, *The British Fishery*, 254.
16 Rowe, *A History of Newfoundland and Labrador*, 254.

17 *The Colonial Office 194 Series*, C.O. 194 V.37, 44-45, October 17, 1787, http://www2.swgc.mun.ca/nfld_history/co194/index.htm.

18 Letter from Capt. Caleb Wade to the Lords of Trade, CO 194/5 March 16, 1715, 306-315, http://www2.swgc.mun.ca/nfld_history/co194/co194-5.htm.

19 America and West Indies: April 1680", in British History online, April 5, 1339, https://www.british-history.ac.uk/cal-state-papers/colonial/america-west-indies/vol10/pp507-521.

20 Smallwood and Pitt, ed., *Encyclopedia*, s.v. "Liquor, Beer and Wine," 311.

21 Marian Frances White, *The Untold Story* (St. John's: Marian Frances White, 1997), 5.

22 Prowse, *History of Newfoundland*, 30.

23 Susan Hillier, Alison M. Quinn, and David B. Quinn, *Newfoundland from Fishery to Colony* (New York: Arno Press and H. Bye, 1979), 162.

24 W.G. Gosling, *Labrador: Its Discovery, Exploration, and Development* (London: Alston Rivers, 1910), 353-54.

25 Margot Duley, *Where Once Our Mothers Stood We Stand* (Charlottetown: Gynergy Books, 1993), 15.

26 Prowse, *History of Newfoundland*, 356.

27 D'Alberti Papers, vol. 08, 1798 (Correspondence, incoming and outgoing, between the Colonial Office and the Governor's Office in Newfoundland), http://collections.mun.ca/.

28 Ibid, 127.

29 J. W. Withers, "Dirty, Diseased and Dangerous—And Always Exciting: St. John's in 1807" in *The Book of Newfoundland*, ed. Joseph R. Smallwood, vol 5. (St. John's: Newfoundland Book Publishers, 1937), 58.

CHAPTER FIVE

1 E. Doyle Wells, *All Quiet: From the Diaries of Thomas E. Wells* (St. John's: DRC, 2011), 36.

2 Maudie Whelan, "The Newspaper Press in Nineteenth-Century Newfoundland: Politics, Religion and Personal Journalism," (PhD diss., Memorial University of Newfoundland, 2002), 121.

3 White, *The Untold Story*, 5.

4 J. Beete Jukes, *Jukes' Excursions: Being a revised edition of Joseph Beete Jukes' "Excursions In and About Newfoundland During the Years 1939 and 1840"*, eds. Robert Cuff and Derek Wilton (Harry Cuff Publications Limited, 1993), 107.

5 Whelan, "The Newspaper Press," 110-111.

6 Newman Wine Vaults, Documents obtained from the vaults, St. John's, NL, May, 2018.

7 Whelan, "The Newspaper Press," 111-112.

8 "The Grand Temperance Parade," *The Newfoundlander,* January 12, 1843.

9 Edward Wix, *Six Months of a Newfoundland Missionary's Journal: from February to August 1835,* 2nd edition (London: Smith, Elder and Co., 1836) 145.

10 Rowe, *A History of Newfoundland and Labrador,* 256.

11 Addison Bown, "Politics in Newfoundland," (address given by Mr. T. Addison Bown, vice-chairman of the Newfoundland Board of Commissioners of Public Utilities, on the occasion of a dinner tendered by the Board to the Executive of the Atlantic Provinces Trucking Association in the Battery Motel, St. John's, on Thursday night, October 15th, 1970).

12 Larry Dohey, "Let Me Treat You to a Drink," *Archival Moments,* http://archivalmoments.ca/category/archival-moments/.

13 Whelan, "The Newspaper Press," 103.

14 Don Morris, "Organized Abstinence Groups in Newfoundland for 150 Years," *Sunday Express,* Christmas 1987, 2. Advertisement in the Weekly Herald, Harbour Grace August 15, 1849.

15 Letter to the Editor. *Weekly Herald,* March 8. 1854. "From a Friend of Temperance" quoted in Maudie Whelan, "The Newspaper Press in Nineteenth-Century Newfoundland: Politics, Religion and Personal Journalism" PhD diss., (Memorial University of Newfoundland, 2002).

16 Ibid, 135.

17 Ibid, 119.

18 Gosling, *Labrador,* 353-54.

19 Pat Doyle, "St. John's Temperance Society Decides to Throw in the Towel," *Evening Telegram,* February 10, 1986.

20 *Jubilee Volume of the St. John's Total Abstinence and Benefit Society 1858-1908,* (Chronicle Print, 1908), 13.

21 Lady, *The Whole Duty of a Woman: Or, An Infallible Guide to the Fair Sex,* (Eighteenth-Century Collections Online 1701). Accessed via MUN library search, date unknown. https://www.gale.com/.

22 *The Newfoundlander,* Tuesday, August 28, 1828.

23 Jack Fitzgerald, *Rum-Runners and Mobsters* (St. John's: Creative, 2017), 116-117.

24 Consolidated Statutes of Newfoundland, "Licenses, etc. of Intoxicating Liquors", 1892, 932.

25 Mosdell, *When Was that?* 76.

26 D. W. Prowse, "Address of Judge Prowse," *Evening Telegram,* December 31, 1879.

27 White, *The Untold Story,* 5; Duley, *Where Once Our Mothers Stood,* 16, 17.

28 Duley, *Where Once Our Mothers Stood*, 16-17.
29 Ibid, 16.

CHAPTER SIX

1 Rev. E. Hunt, "The Prohibition-Plebiscite era, 1917-1924," *Evening Telegram*, March 28, 1962.
2 Mosdell, *When Was that?* 76.
3 "As We See It," *St. John's Daily Star*, November 26, 1915.
4 Leo Moakler, "Screech and Prohibition," *Newfoundland Ancestor* 7.3 (1991): 105.
5 Hunt, 'The Prohibition-Plebiscite era, 1917-1924.'
6 The Prohibition Act, Passed June 5th, 1915, paragraph 20; Smallwood and Pitt, ed., The *Encyclopedia of Newfoundland and Labrador, Vol. 3*, s.v. "Liquor, beer and wine."
7 Inflation Calculator, Bank of Canada, https://www.bankofcanada.ca/rates/related/inflation-calculator/.
8 Provincial Archives of Newfoundland and Labrador, (PANL), Box 39, GN2/5, 271-B, letter explaining the status of port wine, October 24, 1919.
9 Provincial Archives of Newfoundland and Labrador, (PANL), Box 39, GN2/5, special file: 271-B, letter explaining how whisky could be imported in bond, October 29, 1919.
10 Provincial Archives of Newfoundland and Labrador, (PANL), Box 39, GN2/5, 271-C, letters from the Newfoundland Constabulary, June 23 and 24, 1920.
11 Rev. E. Hunt, "The Prohibition Racket," *Newscene*, Jan. 23, 1970, 8.
12 Moakler, "Screech and Prohibition," *Newfoundland Ancestor* 7(3), 1991, 105.
13 Phillip, "The Big Drought," *St. John's Woman*, November 1963, 17-18.
14 Rev. E. Hunt, "Prohibition's cure was worse than disease," *Evening Telegram*, March 29, 1962.
15 Bonnie Woodworth, "The rum-running revival," *Atlantic Insight* February (1983): 47.
16 Provincial Archives of Newfoundland and Labrador, (PANL), Box 39, GN2/5, special file: 271-F, constabulary diary entry by Constable John Byrne, September 13, 1920.
17 Provincial Archives of Newfoundland and Labrador, (PANL), Box 39, GN2/5, special file: 271-G, letter on the analysis of Brown's Bronchial Elixer, January 17, 1921.
18 Provincial Archives of Newfoundland and Labrador, (PANL), Box 39, GN2/5, 271-F, letters and reports from Head Constable Byrnes, March 2, 3, and 11, 1919.

19 Ibid.
20 "Hard Up", *Newfoundland Magazine* July vol 1(1) 1917: 35.
21 Hunt, 'The Prohibition-Plebiscite era, 1917-1924.'
22 Provincial Archives of Newfoundland and Labrador, (PANL), Box 39, GN2/5, special file: 271-C, letter March 3, 1917 from Dr. H. Rendell to the Colonial Secretary.
23 Daily Star, July 24, 1917.
24 "The Prohibition Act", *Evening Telegram* (St. John's Newfoundland) July 21, 1917
25 Provincial Archives of Newfoundland and Labrador, (PANL), Box 39, GN 2/5, special file: 271-C, February 1, 1917.
26 Provincial Archives of Newfoundland and Labrador, (PANL), Box 39, GN2/5, special file: 271-G letter from Governor Harris to the Colonial Secretary May 25, 1921.
27 Leo Moakler, "Screech and Prohibition," *Newfoundland Ancestor* 7.3 (1991): 104.
28 Provincial Archives of Newfoundland and Labrador, (PANL), Box 39, GN2/5, special file: 271-E, letter to John R. Bennett from the Minister of Justice recommending that fines be repaid, July 2, 1919.
29 Provincial Archives of Newfoundland and Labrador, (PANL), Box 39, GN2/5, special file: 271-E, letter from Minister of Justice W. R. Warren to the Governor C. Alexander Harris, February 21, 1920.
30 Provincial Archives of Newfoundland and Labrador, (PANL), Box 39, GN2/5, special file: 271-E, letter from the Constabulary Department, June, 23, 1920.
31 "The Police Court", *Evening Telegram,* (St. John's, NL), January 5, 1921.
32 Provincial Archives of Newfoundland and Labrador, (PANL), Box 39, GN2/5, special file: 271-E, confirmation of the distribution of fines collected under the Prohibition Acts, Minutes of Council July 27th, 1920.
33 Fitzgerald, *Rum-Runners & Mobsters*, 4.
34 Ibid, 13.
35 Smallwood and Pitt, ed., The Encyclopedia of Newfoundland and Labrador, Vol. 3, s.v. "Liquor, Beer and Wine."

CHAPTER SEVEN

1 Rev. E. Hunt, "The Prohibition-Plebiscite era, 1917-1924," *Evening Telegram,* March 28, 1962; Acts of the Honourable Commission of Government of Newfoundland 1924 (St. John's Newfoundland: David R. Thistle, King's printer, 1924) section 23 (a,e,f,g,) 53,54.

2   Fitzgerald, *Rum-Runners and Mobsters*, 143.

3   Edward P. McCarthy, "Liquor on the Rocks: A Personal Account of the Monarchy Wreck," *Downhomer*, September 2003, 63-64.

4   Newfoundland Constabulary Police Diary, January 12, 1932, (St. John's, NL: Royal Newfoundland Constabulary. Detective Staff, 1932).

5   Acts of the Honourable Commission of Government of Newfoundland, 1935 section 14 (1. a), 18.

6   Mills, "Made Right Here."

7   Ibid.

8   Ibid.

9   Provincial Archives of Newfoundland and Labrador, (PANL), Box 240, GN 13/1/B, Records of the Department of Justice and Defense, December 15, 1937.

10 Provincial Archives of Newfoundland and Labrador, (PANL), Box 417, GN 13/1/B, Records of the Department of Justice and Defense, May 11, 1938.

11 J. R. Smallwood, ed., *Newfoundland 1941 Handbook, Gazetteer and Almanac* (St. John's: Long Bros, 1941) 263.

12 Smallwood, ed., *Newfoundland 1941 Handbook*, 263; J.R. Smallwood, ed., *Newfoundland 1940 Handbook, Gazetteer and Almanac* (St. John's: Long Bros., 1940), 237.

13 Gary F. Browne, *To Serve and Protect* (St. John's: DRC, 2008), 133.

14 Ray Guy, "There's a Divinity that Shapes Our Ends," *Newfoundland Quarterly* 83, no. 3 (Winter 1988): 16.

15 Patrons of Fiddler's Pub in discussion with the author, July 2017.

16 Provincial Archives of Newfoundland, St. John's Newfoundland, Letter from Mrs. Mary O'Reilly to "Mayor, Councillors and Gentlemen," Box 134, GN 13/1/B, Records of the Department of Justice and Defense, 1940-43.

17 Ibid.

18 Smallwood and Pitt, ed., *Encyclopedia*, s.v. "Liquor, Beer and Wine."

19 Julia Bishop, "The Song Complex of 'The Moonshine Can': An Integrated Approach to the Study of Words and Music in Traditional Song," PhD diss., (Memorial University of Newfoundland, 1992), 64.

20 John Vivien, "Project Homebrew: Report on Homebrew in Western Nfld," (unpublished manuscript, St. John's, NL: John Vivien, 1974), 5.

21 Bonnie Woodworth, "The Rum-Running Revival," *Atlantic Insight,* February 1983, 47.

22 Dermot Walsh, "Alcoholism and the Irish." in *Beliefs, Behaviors, & Alcoholic Beverages: A Cross -Cultural Survey*, ed. Mac Marshall, (Ann Arbor: University of Michigan Press, 1979) 394-404; Starr, Dr. Barry, "Alcoholism May Be Rooted in Your DNA" https://www.kqed.org/futureofyou/101587/

alcoholism-may-be-rooted-in-your-dna; Dermot Walsh, M.B., B.CH., (N.U.I.), Alcoholism and the Irish, Alcohol and Alcoholism, Volume 7, Issue 2, Spring 1972, pages 40-47. https://academic.oup.com/alcalc.

23 Newfoundland and Labrador Liquor Corporation, *2017-2018 Annual Report*, https://www.assembly.nl.ca/business/electronicdocuments/ NLCAnnualReport2017-18.pdf.

CHAPTER EIGHT

1 Bryan Hennessey, "Rare Bars," *Current*, December 2006, 8.

2 Alex Bill, "Resolution # 3: find a new drinking spot," *The Muse*, January 11, 2007, 11.

3 P. K. Devine, *Ye Olde St. John's 1750-1936*, (St. John's: Newfoundland Directories), 113, http://collections.mun.ca/.

4 Don Maher (owner of The Black Sheep) in discussion with the author, September 2016.

5 "El Tico Lounge Opens in St. John's," *The Daily News,* December 23, 1963, 9.

6 Ibid, 8.

7 Ibid, 8.

8 Paul Kenney and Sim Wentzell, *On the Beat: A Pictorial and Oral History of the Royal Newfoundland Constabulary*, (St. John's: Harry Cuff, 1990), 16.

9 Mike Power in discussion with the author, Oct 2017.

10 Advertisement, Mar. 8, 1965, *Evening Telegram*.

11 E*vening Telegram*, April 16, 1938.

12 "The Muse Pub Crawl," *The Muse*, Friday, September 11, 1981, http:// collections.mun.ca, 9.

13 Thomas Dunne, interviewed by author, Mount Pearl, Newfoundland, May 2017.

14 Adams, Fred, *Potpourri of Old St. John's*, (St. John's: Creative Publishers, 1991), 10.

15 *The Crow's Nest*, A short account of The Seagoing Officers Club Issued on the occasion of the Tenth Anniversary, 1952, 3.

16 Ibid.

17 Narvaez, Peter, "On Rovers and Ron, reflections," *The Muse*, October 15, 1982, http://collections.mun.ca, 12.

18 Provincial Archives of Newfoundland and Labrador, (PANL), Box 134 GN 13/1/B, MG 868, Mrs. Rowe's expenses at the Station Inn, Provincial Archives of Newfoundland and Labrador.

19 Michael Power in discussion with the author, October 2015.

20 Ralph Neal (Old Mill) in discussion with the author, October 2018.

21 Julie Harris, *Colony Club Restaurant, 64 Portugal Cove Road, St. John's, Newfoundland*, (Ottawa, Ontario: Historic Sites and Monuments Board of Canada, 1987), 373-382.

22 Bill O'Keefe, "Pre confederation Taverns," (unpublished research paper, 1977), MUNFLA ms #77-021; Larry O'Keefe in discussion with the author, November 2017; Harris, *Colony Club Restaurant*, 373-382.

23 Ralph Neal (proprietor of the Old Mill in Mount Pearl) in discussion with the author, October 2018.

24 Bryan Hennessey, "Rare Bars."

25 "We Don't Want No Women In and That's It, Period," *Winnipeg Free Press*, January 13, 1977, 4.

26 Elizabeth Haines, "Women are drinking at St. John's Corner Tavern," *Atlantic Insight*, July 1979, 43.

27 Janet Michael in discussion with author, January 2019.

28 Janet Kelly in discussion with author, August 2016.

29 John (Bull) Cook in discussion with author, September 2015.

30 Ibid.

31 Katie Parnham in discussion with author, April 2017.

32 Linda Hennebury in discussion with author, June 2017.

33 Glenn Stokes in discussion with author, June 2017.

34 Ron and Marilyn Pumphrey in discussion with author, June 2016.

35 Glenn Stokes in discussion with author, June 2017.

36 William Clarence Tucker in discussion with author, February 2015.

37 Ed Fitzgerald (Bell Island) in discussion with the author, August 2017.

38 William Lundrigan, "Says Weakness Shown by C.B. West Council," Letter to the Editor, *Western Star*, October 31, 1952, 2.

39 *Western Star*, January 1951.

CHAPTER NINE

1 Sir Robert Pinsent, "St. John's, Newfoundland, A.D. 1800-4." *Christmas Review*, 1892, 2-4.

2 Smallwood and Pitt, ed., *Encyclopedia*, s.v. "Distilleries."

3 Smallwood and Pitt, ed., *Encyclopedia*, s.v. "Breweries."

4 O'Neill, *The Oldest City*, 573.

5 E. H. Hodder, "Saga of Defunct Bennett Brewery Intertwined with Island's History," *Sunday Telegram*, April 15, 1990.

6 Ibid.

7 Robin McGrath, "The Case of the Missing Brewery Boy," *Newfoundland Quarterly*, 91, no. 1 (Spring 1997): 44-45.

8 *Newfoundland Purchasers' Guide* (St. John's: Trade Review Office, 1895.)

9 Blocker, Fahey, Tyrrell, *Alcohol and Temperance in Modern History*, Vol 1, s.v. "O'Keefe Brewery."

10 Allen Winn Sneath, *Brewed in Canada* (Toronto, Dundern Press, 2001), 399.

11 O'Neill, *The Oldest City*, 698.

12 Bassler, *Vikings to U-Boats*, 116-117; *Newfoundland Purchasers' Guide* (1895), 10.

13 *Newfoundland Purchasers' Guide* (1895), 10-11.

14 Fred Adams, *Potpourri of Old St. John's*, (St. John's: Creative, 1991), 8-9.

15 Smallwood and Pitt, ed., *Encyclopedia*, s.v. "Breweries."

16 Harry Bruce, "Down East, drinking beer is like hearing bell buoys at dawn," *Saturday Night*, June, 1975, 86.

17 Smallwood and Pitt, ed., *Encyclopedia*, s.v. "Breweries."

18 Hibbs, *Who's Who*, 228.

19 "Atlantic Brewery", Heritage Newfoundland and Labrador, Stephenville Integrated High School, 1998, https://www.heritage.nf.ca/; Newfoundlandbeer.org/, archive, August 20, 2012. https://newfoundlandbeer.org/category/atlantic-brewery/.

20 Justin Fong (Quidi Vidi Brewer) in discussion with the author, May 2017; Glover, "Brewing Company Reviving Traditional Ale," 8.

APPENDIX A

1 Mildred Howard, *Vital Statistics and Items from Newspapers of Newfoundland, 1831 to 1872*, 164.

2 "Police Court," *Evening Telegram*, May 12, 1879, 1.

3 "Police Court," *Evening Telegram*, May 15, 1879, 1.

4 Ibid.

5 "Police Court," *Evening Telegram*, September 19, 1882, 1, quoted in Larry Dohey, "That 'chaw' trying to make a big fellow of himself...in the lock up," Archival Moments.

6 "Police Court," *Evening Telegram*, May 23, 1879, 1.

7 Howard, *Vital Statistics*, 163.

8 "Police Court" *Evening Telegram*, May 15, 1879, 1.

9 Howard, *Vital Statistics*, 163.

10 O'Neill, *The Oldest City*, 436.

11 Prowse, "Address of Judge Prowse."

12 *Twillingate Sun*, Feb. 19 1887, 3.

13 O'Neill, *The Oldest City*, 137-138.

14 Jennifer Walsh, "Reminiscences of Life in St. John's," unpublished manuscript, MUNFLA. 81-422, Memorial University of Newfoundland Folklore Archives, St. John's Newfoundland, 30.

APPENDIX B/C/D

Information compiled from city directories including McAlpine's, Polk's, and others. See Bibliography under Almanacs and Directories for complete list.

BIBLIOGRAPHY

ACADEMIC AND STUDENT PAPERS

Andrews, Debbie. "Alcohol Consumption, Temperance, the Law and the St. John's Court of 1895 and 1915." Paper submitted for Memorial University, History 4231, 1992.

Barakat, Robert. "Report of an Archaeological Excavation at the Newman Wine Vaults." Memorial University, St. John's NL, 1973.

Bartlett, William G. "Prohibition in Newfoundland, 1916-1924." (unpublished manuscript,1971.)

Bishop, Julia. "The Song Complex of 'The Moonshine Can': An Integrated Approach to the Study of Words and Music in Traditional Song." PhD dissertation, Memorial University of Newfoundland, 1992.

Bown, Addison. "Politics in Newfoundland." Address given by Mr. T. Addison Bown, vice-chairman of the Newfoundland Board of Commissioners of Public Utilities, on the occasion of a dinner tendered by the Board to the Executive of the Atlantic Provinces Trucking Association in the Battery Motel, St. John's, on Thursday night, October 15th, 1970.

Harvey, Katherine. "A Complete History of the Newman Building." Heritage Foundation of Newfoundland and Labrador. 20??.

Mills, Stephen F. "Made Right Here: Archaeological and Historical Data from the 17th century Tippling House to the 1930's Beer Shop in Newfoundland." Paper presented at the 47th Annual Meeting of the Canadian Archaeological Association, St. John's, NL, May 2nd, 2015.

O'Keefe, Bill. "Pre-Confederation Taverns". (unpublished research paper, Memorial University of Newfoundland Folklore and Language Archives, ms # 77-021, MUNFLA F2688, Memorial University of Newfoundland Folklore and Language Archives, St. John's, Newfoundland, 1977.)

Roberts, Sheilah. "An Ethnography of the Belmont Bar: with special attention given to its 'lady' customers." (unpublished manuscript, Memorial University of Newfoundland Folklore and Language Archives, ms # 96-741, Memorial University of Newfoundland, 1979.)

Tobin, Bernard. Survey Card, MUNFLA. 91-343, Memorial University of Newfoundland Folklore and Language Archives, St. John's, Newfoundland, collected in Kilbride, 1988.

Vivien, John. "Project Homebrew: Report on Homebrew in Western Nfld." (unpublished research paper, Memorial University of Newfoundland Folklore and Language Archives, St. John's Newfoundland, 1974.)

Walsh, Jennifer. "Reminiscences of Life in St. John's," (unpublished manuscript, Memorial University of Newfoundland Folklore and Language Archives, 81-422. Memorial University of Newfoundland, St. John's, 1981.)

Whelan, Maudie. "The Newspaper Press in Nineteenth-century Newfoundland: Politics, Religion and personal Journalism." PhD dissertation, Memorial University of Newfoundland, 2002.

Whiteway, Louise. "Towards an Art of Architecture in Newfoundland." Memorial University of Newfoundland, Department of Education, St. John's, NL, 1958.

ARCHIVAL MATERIALS

D'Alberti Papers, Vol. 06, 1797. Correspondence, incoming and outgoing, between the Colonial Office and the Governor's Office in Newfoundland. http://lib-lespaul.library.mun.ca/cdm/ref/collection/cns_colonia/id/9455

D'Alberti Papers, Vol. 07,08,11, 12, 21, 22, 25, 1798. Correspondence, incoming and outgoing, between the Colonial Office and the Governor's Office in Newfoundland http://collections.mun.ca/cdm/compoundobject/collection/cns_colonia/id/9722/rec/1

"Edward Wynne to George Calvert." Correspondence from 17 August, 1622. https://www.heritage.nf.ca/articles/exploration/edward-wynne-letter-17-august-1622.php.

"Nicholas Hoskins to W.P." Correspondence from 18 August, 1622. https://www.heritage.nf.ca/articles/exploration/nicholas-hoskins-letter-1622.php.

Newfoundland Constabulary Police Diary. St. John's, NL: Royal Newfoundland Constabulary. Detective Staff, Centre for Newfoundland Studies, Memorial University of Newfoundland, 1932.

Provincial Archives of Newfoundland, St. John's Newfoundland. Box 240, GN 13/1/B. Records of the Department of Justice and Defense 1937.

Provincial Archives of Newfoundland, St. John's Newfoundland. Box 417, GN 13/1/B. Records of the Department of Justice and Defense, 1968.

Provincial Archives of Newfoundland, St. John's Newfoundland. Box 134, GN 13/1/B. Letter from Mrs. Mary O'Reilly to "Mayor, Councillors and Gentlemen."

Provincial Archives of Newfoundland and Labrador. Box 134 GN 13/1/B, MG 868. Mrs. Rowe's expenses at the Station Inn.

Provincial Archives of Newfoundland and Labrador. Box 39, GN2/5. 271-B. Letter explaining the status of port wine, October 24, 1919.

Provincial Archives of Newfoundland and Labrador. Box 39, GN2/5, special file: 271-B. Letter explaining how whisky could be imported in bond. October 29, 1919.

Provincial Archives of Newfoundland and Labrador. Box 39, GN2/5, 271-C. Letters from the Newfoundland Constabulary, June 23 and 24, 1920.

Provincial Archives of Newfoundland and Labrador. Box 39, GN2/5, special file: 271-F. Constabulary diary entry by Constable John Byrne, September 13, 1920.

Provincial Archives of Newfoundland and Labrador. Box 39, GN2/5, special file: 271-F. Letter on the analysis of Brown's Bronchial Elixer, January 17, 1921.

Provincial Archives of Newfoundland and Labrador. Box 39, GN2/5, 271-F. Letters and reports from Head Constable Byrnes, March 2, 3, and 11, 1919.

Provincial Archives of Newfoundland and Labrador. Box 39, GN2/5, special file: 271-C. Letter March 3, 1917 from Dr. H. Rendell to the Colonial Secretary.

Provincial Archives of Newfoundland and Labrador. Box 39, GN 2/5, special file: 271-C, February 1, 1917.

Provincial Archives of Newfoundland and Labrador. Box 39, GN2/5, special file: 271-G. Letter from Governor Harris to the Colonial Secretary May 25, 1921.

Provincial Archives of Newfoundland and Labrador. Box 39, GN2/5, special file: 271-E. Letter to John R Bennett from the Minister of Justice recommending that fines be repaid, July 2, 1919.

Provincial Archives of Newfoundland and Labrador. Box 39, GN2/5, special file: 271: E. Letter from Minister of Justice W. R. Warren to the Governor C. Alexander Harris, February 21, 1920.

Provincial Archives of Newfoundland and Labrador. Box 39, GN2/5, special file: 271-E. Letter from the Constabulary Department, June, 23, 1920.

Provincial Archives of Newfoundland and Labrador. Box 39, GN2/5, special
file: 271-E. Confirmation of the distribution of fines collected under the
Prohibition Acts, Minutes of Council July 27th, 1920.

Provincial Archives of Newfoundland and Labrador. MG 547. Bennett Brewing
Company Fonds.

THE COLONIAL OFFICE 194 SERIES

CO 194 Vol. 52, 150-151. October 1812. Memorial of the Merchants and House
Keepers of St. John's: Concerning duties laid on spirits imported into the
Island; requesting the exemption of all articles used directly or indirectly in
the fishery from duties. http://collections.mun.ca/cdm/compoundobject/
collection/cns_colonia/id/38290/rec/53

CO 194 Vol. 5, 91-96. March 19, 1714. Taverner, William. "Remarks on the Present
State of the English Settlements in Newfoundland…" http://collections.mun.
ca/cdm/compoundobject/collection/cns_colonia/id/60375/rec/5

CO 194 Vol. 39. Aug. 13, 1797, 113v-114. http://collections.mun.ca/cdm/
compoundobject/collection/cns_colonia/id/27438/rec/40

CO 194 Vol. 39, Aug. 13, 1797, 115-116. http://collections.mun.ca/cdm/
compoundobject/collection/cns_colonia/id/27438/rec/40

CO 194 Vol. 37, 44-45, October 17, 1787. Concern expressed over the reduction in
the number of public houses http://collections.mun.ca/cdm/compoundobject/
collection/cns_colonia/id/25701/rec/38

CO 194 Vol. 5 306-315 March 16, 1715. Letter from Capt. Caleb Wade to the
Lords of Trade. http://collections.mun.ca/cdm/compoundobject/collection/
cns_colonia/id/60375/rec/5

CO 194 Vol. 3, Jan. 1706, 370-371 and Jan. 28, 376-377. http://collections.mun.ca/
cdm/compoundobject/collection/cns_colonia/id/50579/rec/3

"America and West Indies: April 1680." In British History online, April
5, 1639. https://www.british-history.ac.uk/cal-state-papers/colonial/
america-west-indies/vol10/pp507-521

"America and West Indies: March 1714." In Calendar of State Papers Colonial,
America and West Indies: Volume 27, 1712-1714, ed. Cecil Headlam. London,
1926. British History Online. http://www.british-history.ac.uk/cal-state-
papers/colonial/america-west-indies/vol27. 302-325.

"America and West Indies: March 1716, 1-14." In Calendar of State Papers
Colonial, America and West Indies: Volume 29, 1716-1717, ed. Cecil Headlam.
London: His Majesty's Stationery Office, 1930. British History Online. http://

www.british-history.ac.uk/cal-state-papers/colonial/america-west-indies/
vol29/pp28-49.

Rev. William Marshall, *William Marshall Diary 1839-1842*. http://collections.mun.
ca/PDFs/archives/WilliamMarshallDiary18391842.pdf.

Shortis, "A unique industry may be killed by recent prohibition act." Shortis
Papers, vol. 02, pt. 02. http://collections.mun.ca/u?/cns_period,31066

BOOKS

Adams, Fred. *Potpourri of Old St. John's*. St. John's: Creative Publishers, 1991.

Adkins, Roy. *Nelson's Trafalgar*. Toronto: Viking Press, 2005.

Anspach, Rev. L.A. *History of Newfoundland*. London: Printed for the author and
sold by T. and J. Allman, 1819.

Andrieux, Jean-Pierre. *Prohibition and St. Pierre: When distillers and rum runners
made France's colony off Newfoundland a principal centre for the liquor trade.*
Lincoln: W. F. Rannie, 1983.

Barty-King, Hugh and Anton Massel. *Rum: Yesterday and Today.* London:
William Heineman Ltd., 1983.

Bassler, Gerhard. *Vikings to U-Boats: the German experience in Newfoundland and
Labrador*. Montreal, McGill-Queen's University Press, ProQuest elibrary, Web.

Bicentennial History Committee of St. David's Presbyterian Church, St. John's,
Newfoundland. *The Dissenting church of Christ at St. John's 1775-1975: A history
of St. David's Presbyterian Church*. St. John's: St. David's Presbyterian Church,
1975?

Blocker, Jack S., David M. Fahey, and Ian M. Tyrrell. *Alcohol and Temperance in
Modern History, Vol 2*. Santa Barbara: ABC-CLIO, 2003.

Browne, Gary F. *To Serve and Protect*. St. John's: DRC Publishing, 2008.

Cell, Gillian. *English Enterprise in Newfoundland 1577-1660*. Toronto: University
of Toronto Press, 2017.

Chappell, Lieut. Edward. *Voyage of His Majesty's Ship Rosamund to Newfoundland*.
London: printed for J. Mawman, 1818.

Childs, David. *Invading America: The English Assault on the New World 1497-1630*.
Barnsley: Seaforth Publishing, 2012.

Curtis, Wayne. *And a bottle of rum: A History of the New World in Ten Cocktails*.
Crown Publishers, 2006.

De la Chaume, Henri., Robin McGrath and James M. F. McGrath. *Hammered by
the Waves: A Young Frenchman's Sojourn in Newfoundland in 1882-83*. St. John's:
Creative Publishers, 2010.

Devine, P.K. *Ye Olde St. John's 1750-1936*. St. John's: Newfoundland Directories.

Doyle Wells, E. *All Quiet: from the diaries of Thomas E. Wells*. St. John's: DRC Publishing, 2011.

Duley, Margot I. *Where Once Our Mothers Stood We Stand*. Edited by Roberta Buchanan. Charlottetown: Gynergy Books, 1993.

Fay, C.R. *Life and Labour in Newfoundland*. Toronto: University of Toronto Press, 1956.

Fitzgerald, Jack. *Peculiar Facts and Tales of Newfoundland*. St. John's: Creative Publishers, 2014.

Fitzgerald, Jack. *Rum-Runners &Mobsters: Prohibition's 100th Anniversary in Newfoundland*. St. John's: Creative Publishers, 2017.

Gosling, W. G. *Labrador: Its Discovery, Exploration, and Development*. London: Alston Rivers, Ltd. 1910.

Glanville, Philippa and Sophie Lee, eds. *The Art of Drinking*, s.v. Alcohol as Medicine. London: V&A Publications, 2007.

Hackwood, Frederick William. *Inns, Ales and Drinking Customs of Old England*. New York: Sturgis and Walton, 1909.

Handcock, Gordon W. *So longe as there comes noe women: origins of English settlement in Newfoundland*. St. John's: Breakwater Books, 1989.

Harris, Julie. *Colony Club Restaurant, 64 Portugal Cove Road, St. John's, Newfoundland*. Ottawa: Historic Sites and Monuments Board of Canada, 1987.

Head, Grant. *Eighteenth Century Newfoundland*. Toronto: McClelland and Stewart, 1976.

Hibbs, R. ed. *Who's Who in and from Newfoundland, 1930*. 2nd ed., R. Hibbs, 1927.

High, Steven C. *Occupied St John's: a social history of a city at war, 1939-1945*. Montreal: McGill-Queen's University Press, 2010.

Hillier, Susan, Alison M. Quinn, and David B. Quinn. *Newfoundland from Fishery to Colony. Northwest Passage Searches*. New York: Arno Press and H. Bye, Inc., 1979.

Hiscock, Owen. *The Way It Was*. St. John's: Jesperson Press Ltd, 1990.

Hornsey, Ian S. *A History of Beer and Brewing*. Cambridge: The Royal Society of Chemistry, 2003.

Howard, Mildred. *Vital statistics and items from the Newfoundlander of St. John's Newfoundland from 1834 to 1854*. St. John's: 1980.

———. *Vital statistics and items from the Newfoundlander of St. John's Newfoundland from 1854 to 1870*. St. John's: 1980.

———. *Vital statistics and items from Newspapers of Newfoundland 1831-1872*. St. John's: 1983.

——. *Royal Gazette and Newfoundland Advertiser: Vital statistics and items from 1810 to 1845.* Sydney: 1986.

Hunt, Roope and Company Ltd. *The Story and Origin of Hunt, Roope & Company, London and Oporto, Newman, Hunt & Company, London, Newman & Company, Newfoundland.* London: Hunt, Roope and Company Ltd., 1951.

Josselyn, John. *An account of two voyages to New-England: made during the years 1638, 1663.* Boston: William Veazie, 1865.

Jubilee Volume of the St. John's Total Abstinence and Benefit Society 1858-1908. Chronicle Print, 1908.

Jukes, J. Beete, Robert Cuff and Derek Wilton. *Jukes' Excursions: Being a revised edition of Joseph Beete Jukes' "Excursions In and About Newfoundland During the Years 1939 and 1840".* St. John's: Harry Cuff Publications Limited, 1993.

Keate, Lieut. Stuart. *The Crow's Nest: A Short Account of the Seagoing Officers Club.* Issued on the occasion of the tenth anniversary, 1952.

Kenney, Paul and Sim Wentzell. *On the Beat: A Pictorial and Oral History of the Royal Newfoundland Constabulary.* St. John's: Harry Cuff Publications Limited, 1990.

Krasnick Warsh, Cheryl ed., *Drink in Canada: "John Barleycorn Must Die": An Introduction to the Social History of Alcohol.* Montreal; Kingston; London; Buffalo: MQUP, 1993.

Lady. *The Whole Duty of a Woman: Or, An Infallible Guide to the Fair Sex.* Eighteenth Century Collections Online 1701, Gale Institution.

Lounsbury, Ralph Greenlee. *The British Fishery at Newfoundland 1634-1763.* New Haven: Yale University. 1934.

Lysaght, A. M. *Joseph Banks in Newfoundland and Labrador, 1766. His Diary, Manuscripts and Collections.* University of California Press, 1971

Marshall, Mac. *Beliefs, Behaviors, & Alcoholic Beverages: a cross-cultural survey.* Ann Arbor: University of Michigan Press, 1979.

Martin, Wendy. *Once upon a mine: story of pre-Confederation mines on the Island of Newfoundland.* Montreal: The Canadian Institute of Mining and Metallurgy, 1983.

McCrae, R. B. *Lost amid the fogs: sketches of life in Newfoundland, England's ancient colony.* London, 1869.

McGovern, Patrick E. *Uncorking the Past: The Quest for Wine, Beer, and Other Alcoholic Beverages.* Berkeley: University of California Press, 2009

McGrath, Robin. *Salt Fish & Shmattes: A History of the Jews in Newfoundland and Labrador from 1770.* St. John's: Creative Publishers, 2006.

Moreira, James. "Rum in the Atlantic Provinces." In *The Tradition of Rum.* Nova Scotia: Pottersfield Press, 1988.

Morrison, James H. and James Moreira, eds. *Tempered by Rum: Rum in the History of the Maritime Provinces.* Nova Scotia: Pottersfield Press, 1988.

Mosdell, Harris Munden. *When was that? a chronological dictionary of important events In Newfoundland down to and including the year 1922.* St. John's: Robinson-Blackmore Printing and Publishing, 1974.

Moyles, R. G. *"Complaints is many and various, but the odd Divil likes it: Nineteenth Century Views of Newfoundland"* Toronto; New York: Peter Martin Associates, 1975.

Murphy, Michael P. *Pathways through Yesterday.* St. John's: Town Crier Pub. Co., 1976.

Murray, Jean M. *The Newfoundland Journal of Aaron Thomas, Able Seaman in H.M.S. Boston: A journal written during a voyage from England to Newfoundland and from Newfoundland to England in the years 1794 and 1795.* London: Longmans, 1968.

O'Flaherty, Patrick. *Come Near at Your Peril: A Visitor's Guide to the Island of Newfoundland.* St. John's: Breakwater Books, 1992.

O'Hara-May, Jane. *The Elizabethan Dyetary of Health.* Kansas: Coronado Press, 1977.

O'Neill, Paul. *The Oldest City*, Rev. ed. Portugal Cove-St. Philips: Boulder Publications Ltd., 2002.

Patrick, Clarence H. *Alcohol, Culture, and Society.* California: AMS Press, 1952.

Pitt, David G. *Windows of Agates: The Life and Times of Gower Street United (formerly Methodist) Church in St. John's Newfoundland: 1815-1990.* St. John's: Jesperson Press, 1990.

Pope, Peter E. *Fish into Wine: The Newfoundland Plantation in the Seventeenth Century.* The University of North Carolina Press, 2004.

Prowse, D. W. *History of Newfoundland.* Portugal Cove-St. Philips: Boulder Publications Ltd., 2002.

Raleigh, Sir Walter, Lord Treasurer Burleigh, Cardinal Sermonetta, and Mr. Walsingham, *Instructions for youth, gentlemen and noblemen,* (London: printed for Randal Minshull at his House in Ship Yard near the Ship Tavern, Temple-Bar, 1722), Eighteenth Century Collections Online. Gale. Memorial University of Newfoundland, January 27, 2019, 36-37.

Reid, Max. "Rum and the Navy," in *Tempered by Rum: Rum in the History of the Maritime Provinces.* Edited by James H. Morrison and James Moreira. Nova Scotia: Pottersfield Press, 1988.

Rowe, Frederick W. *A History of Newfoundland and Labrador.* Toronto: McGraw-Hill Ryerson Ltd., 1980.

Ryan, Shannon. *A History of Newfoundland in the North Atlantic to 1818.* St. John's: Flanker Press, 2012.

Smallwood, J. R., ed. *Newfoundland 1940 Handbook, Gazetteer and Almanac.* St. John's: Long Bros. Printers, 1940.

Smallwood, J.R., ed. *Newfoundland 1941: Handbook, Gazetteer and Almanac.* St. John's: Long Bros. Printers, 1941.

Smith, Frederick H. *Caribbean Rum: a social and economic history.* Gainsville: University Press of Florida, 2005.

Standage, Tom. *A History of the World in 6 Glasses.* New York: Walker & Co., 2005.

Van Muyden, Madame. *A Foreign View of England in the Reigns of George I & George II: The letters of Monsieur Cesar De Saussure to his family.* London: John Murray, Albemarle St., 1902. https://archive.org/details/foreignviewofengoosausuoft/page/156.

Varriano, John. *Wine: A Cultural History.* London: Reaktion Books ltd., 2010.

Vaughan, Sir William. *Naturall and artificial directions for health: derived from the best philosophers, as well moderne, as ancient. By William Vaughan, Master of Artes, and student in the civill law.* Series: Early English Books online.

Vaughan, William. *The Newlanders cure.* London: Imprinted by N.O. for F. Constable, 1630.

Venner, Tobias. *A treatise wherein the right way and best manner of living for attaining to a long and healthful life is clearly demonstrate.* London: 1650.

White, Jack. *Streets of St. John's.* St. John's: Creative Publishers, 1989.

White, Marian Frances. *The Untold Story.* St. John's: Marian Frances White, 1997.

Wilson, C. Anne. *Food and Drink in Britain.* London: Constable, 1973.

Wilson, William. *Newfoundland and its missionaries: In two parts.* Cambridge: Dakin & Metcalf, 1866.

Winn Sneath, Allen. *Brewed in Canada.* Toronto: Dundern Press, 2001.

Wix, Edward. *Six Months of a Newfoundland Missionary's Journal: from February to August 1835*, 2nd ed. London: Smith, Elder and Co., 1836.

GOVERNMENT DOCUMENTS

Consolidated Statutes of Newfoundland. St. John's: Queen's Printer, 1871, 1898; Robinson and Co., 1916, 1917.

Statutes of Newfoundland: Acts of the General Assembly of Newfoundland. St. John's: J. W. Withers, King's Printer, 1892, 1919, 1920.

Acts of the Honourable Commission of Government of Newfoundland 1924. St. John's: David R. Thistle, King's Printer, 1924, 1935.

Trade Review office ed. *Newfoundland Purchasers' Guide containing the names of the Principal Business Firms.* St. John's: Trade Review Office, 1895.

Newfoundland Colonial Blue books. St. John's: 1822, 1826, 1836, 1841, 1843, 1856, 1861, 1866.

JOURNALS

Bannister, Jerry. "The Fishing Admirals in Eighteenth-Century Newfoundland." *Newfoundland Studies* 17 no. 2 (2001): 166-219.

Gallop, Edward S. "Port Wine and Cod-fish." *Canadian Geographical Journal* 5 no.1, (1932): 26-37.

Glavin, Ellen. "The Newfoundland Ancestry of Maurice and Charles Prendergast." *Newfoundland Studies* 10, no. 1 (1994): 82-103.

Greenaway, C. R. "Rum Heaven." *Canadian Geographic Journal* November, 11, no. 5 (1935): 218-227.

Harvey, Karen. "Barbarity in a Teacup? Punch, Domesticity and Gender in the Eighteenth Century." *Journal of Design History* 21, no. 3 (2008): 205-221.

LeBlanc, Julie M. A. "Newfoundland Born and Brewed: The Place, People, and Products of Quidi Vidi Brewery." *Culture & Tradition* 29, (2007): 124-136.

Mannion, John. "Irish Migration and Settlement in Newfoundland: The Formative Phase, 1697-1732." *Newfoundland and Labrador Studies* 17, no. 2 (2001):257-293.

Pope, Peter E. "Outport Economics: Culture and Agriculture." *Newfoundland and Labrador Studies* 19 no. 1, 153-186.

——. "The Historical Anthropology of demand for alcohol in seventeenth-Century Newfoundland." *Histoire Sociale* 27, no. 54 (November, 1994) 261-278.

——. "The Historical Anthropology of demand for alcohol in seventeenth-Century Newfoundland," *Acadiensis* 19, no. 1 (1989): 72-90.

——. "Adventures in the Sack Trade: London Merchants in the Canada and Newfoundland Trades, 1627-1648. *The Northern Mariner* 6, no. 1, (January 1996): 1-19.

Szed, John F. "Gossip, Drinking, and Social Control: Consensus and Communication in a Newfoundland Parish." *Ethnology* 5, no. 4, (October 1966): 434-441.

Tavenor, Joshua. "Imports to Newfoundland in the Late Seventeenth and Early Eighteenth Centuries." *Newfoundland and Labrador Studies* 26, no. 1 (2011): 75-85.

MAGAZINES

—— "Hard Up." *Newfoundland Magazine,* 1917.

—— "We don't want no women in and that's it, period." *Winnipeg Free Press,* January 13, 1977.

Bambrick, Richard. "Some of them days." *Downhomer*, Vol. 12(7), 1999.

Bruce, Harry. "Down East, drinking beer is like hearing bell buoys at dawn." *Saturday Night*, June, 1975.

Coish, Calvin. "Newfoundland Screech." *Atlantic Advocate*, Vol. 71, 1981.

Dicks, Kathy. "Historical beverages unique to Newfoundland." *Newfoundland Herald*, April 16, 1994.

Furlong, Tom. "Catacombs of St. John's." *Newfoundland Lifestyles*, Vol. 12(1), 1994.

Gothe, Jurgen. "Privateer Label: Newfoundland's rare Port is in Danger." *EnRoute*, November 1996.

Glover, Sonia B. "Brewing Company reviving traditional ale." *Newfoundland Herald*, November 16, 1996.

Guy, Ray. "There's a divinity that shapes our ends...." *Newfoundland Quarterly*, Winter 1988.

Haines, Elizabeth. "Women are drinking at St. John's Corner Tavern." *Atlantic Insight*, July 1979.

Harvey, Rev. M. "Evolution of Newfoundland Port Wine." *Parson's Christmas Annual*, 1900.

Hennessey, Bryan. "Rare Bars." *Current*, December 2006.

Hiscock, Philip. "Screech and Swish." *Downhomer*, Vol. 10(10), 1998.

Hiscock, Philip. "Spruce Beer Traditions." *Downhomer*, Vol. 14(5), 2001.

Jarvis, Dale. "The Newmans and the Newman Wine Vaults." *Newfoundland Ancestor*, Vol.14 (3), 1998.

Jardine, P. F. "Evolution of Newfoundland Port wine." *Parsons' Christmas Annual*, 1900.

LeMessurier, H. W. "Tavern Yarns." *Newfoundland Quarterly*, Vol. 6(3), December 1906.

McCarthy, Edward P. "Liquor on the Rocks: A personal account of the *Monarchy* wreck." *Downhomer*, September 2003.

McGrath, Robin. "The Case of the Missing Brewery Boy, *Newfoundland Quarterly*, Spring 1997.

Mews, Marjorie. "Port in a Storm." *Atlantic Advocate*, Vol. 49(2), 1958.

Meaney, Ted. "Newman's of Newfoundland." *Atlantic Guardian*, June-July, Vol. 1(6), 1945.

Moakler, Leo. "Screech and Prohibition." *Newfoundland Ancestor*, Vol. 7(3), 1991.

Newton, Sandy. "Tales of our Tippling houses." *Enjoy!* Winter 2004.

O'Neill, Paul. "The Temperance Wars." *Canadian Collector*, Vol. 20(2) 1985.

Outerbridge, P. E. "When Newfoundland Went Dry." *Atlantic Advocate*, Vol. 62(7), 1972.

Phillip. "The Big Drought." *St. John's Woman*, November 1963.

Pinsent, Sir Robert. "St. John's, Newfoundland, A.D. 1800-4." *Christmas Review*, 1892.

Prowse, D. W. "An Old Colonial Judge's stories." *Newfoundland Quarterly*, December 1912.

Rhys, Isaac, and Rice, Kym. "Early American Taverns." *American Historical Review*, Vol. 89(4), 1984.

Robicheau, Suzanne. "The Port of St. John's." *Saltscapes*, Vol 11(1) 2010.

Shortis, H. F. "A Unique Industry Maybe Killed by recent Prohibition." *Shortis*, Vol. 2(398), 192?

Wakeham. P. J. "The Day Our Hens Got Drunk." *New-Land Magazine*, 1963.

Walsh, Patrick. "The Total Abstinence Society of St. John's." *Newfoundland Ancestor*, Vol. 13(3), 1997.

Weston, C.S.M. "To Rum." *Veteran*, December 1927.

Woodworth, Bonnie. "The rum-running revival." *Atlantic Insight*, February 1983.

OTHER

—— "Table of Approximate Prices for Provisions in Newfoundland 1845." Commissariat House papers, 2019.

WEBSITES

Clarke, Frank, *A Most Wholesome Liquor: A study of Beer and Brewing in 18th century England and Her Colonies*. (Williamsburg, Virginia: Colonial Williamsburg Foundation Library Research Report Series, 2000) https://www.colonialwilliamsburg.org/learn/research-and-education/

Dohey, Larry. "Archival Moments." http://archivalmoments.ca/category/archival-moments/

Newfoundland and Labrador Liquor Corporation financial statement for April 2017-18. https://www.assembly.nl.ca/business/electronicdocuments/NLCAnnualReport2017-18.pdf

Heritage Newfoundland and Labrador. "Newfoundland and Labrador Customs." https://www.heritage.nf.ca/articles/society/newfoundland-labrador-customs.php

Heritage Newfoundland and Labrador. "Atlantic Brewery." https://www.heritage.nf.ca/articles/society/atlanic-brewery-stephenville.php

newfoundlandbeer.org. "Atlantic Brewery." https://newfoundlandbeer.org/category/atlantic-brewery/

Manuscripts and Special Collections, University of Nottingham. "Volumes or Capacity." https://www.nottingham.ac.uk/manuscriptsandspecialcollections/researchguidance/weightsandmeasures/volumes.aspx.

Johnson's Dictionary Online. https://johnsonsdictionaryonline.com/

Twig (v. to catch the meaning) https://twignl.wordpress.com/

Godoy, Maria. *Lust, Lies And Empire: The Fishy Tale Behind Eating Fish On Friday*, April 6, 2012. National Public Radio, Washington, DC, USA, https://www.npr.org/sections/thesalt/2012/04/05/150061991/lust-lies-and-empire-the-fishy-tale-behind-eating-fish-on-friday.

Higgins, Jenny. "Lifestyle of Fishers, 1600-1900." Heritage Newfoundland and Labrador. https://www.heritage.nf.ca/

Johnson, Nicholas K. "World War I, Part 2: The British Rum Ration." https://pointsadhsblog.wordpress.com/2014/05/29/world-war-i-part-2-the-british-rum-ration/

Taylor Fladgate, "History of Port." https://www.taylor.pt/us

Implementing Order n.º 1247-A/95 of 17th October 1995—[which] Suspends Port Wine export in bulk, http://bdjur.almedina.net/sumario.php?field=sdoc_id&value=12967.

Western Star. "N.L. and St. John's both lead country in most bars per capita." August 17, 2017 https://www.saltwire.com/?location=corner-brook#

Statistics Canada. "Heavy Drinking 2018." https://www150.statcan.gc.ca/n1/pub/82-625-x/2019001/article/00007-eng.htm

Dohey, Larry. "Let me treat you to a drink." Archival Moments. http://archivalmoments.ca/category/archival-moments/

Bank of Canada. "Inflation calculator." https://www.bankofcanada.ca/rates/related/inflation-calculator/

ALMANACS AND DIRECTORIES

McAlpine's Maritime Provinces Directory for 1870-71: containing directories of the provinces of Nova Scotia, New Brunswick, Newfoundland, Prince Edward Island with indexes and contents, and an appendix for each province, containing useful information. Halifax: Pub. by David McAlpine, 1870.

McAlpine's Maritime Provinces business directory for 1880-81.

McAlpine's Newfoundland Directory 1898. Saint John: McAlpine Directory Co., 1898.

McAlpine's Newfoundland Directory 1904. Saint John: McAlpine Directory Co., 1904.

McAlpine's St. John's Directory Containing a Directory of Citizens and Business and Street Directories Halifax: McAlpine Directory Co., 1908-09.

McAlpine's St. John's Directory 1913. Halifax: Royal Print & Litho., Ltd., 1913 (??).

McAlpine's St. John's City Directory, 1915: comprising a directory of St. John's, a classified business directory, a street directory and directory of Belle Isle, Carbonear and Harbor Grace. Halifax: Royal Print & Litho, Ltd., 1915.

A Directory Containing Names and Present Addresses of Professional Men, Merchants and Shopkeepers, burnt out by the General Conflagration of July 8th, 1892; A full account of the great fire, the customs' tariff, and other matter of general information. Newfoundland: W. J. Kent, 1892.

Lovell's Gazetteer of British North America. Montreal: Dominion Directory Office, 1871. Might and Co's Directory, 1890.

Directory for the towns of St. John's, Harbor Grace, and Carbonear, Newfoundland, for 1885-86: containing much useful information relating to the colony. St. John's: John Sharp, 1885

Hutchinson's Newfoundland Directory for 1864-65. St. John's: Thomas McConnan, 1864.

Business and General Directory of Newfoundland 1877. Montreal: Lovell Print. and Pub. Co., 1877.

Polk's City Directories 1928-1993.

St. John's City Directory 1924. Compiled by George. H Andrews, E. A Smith. St. John's: St. John's Nfld. Directory Co., 1924.

Newfoundland Directory 1928. St. John's: Newfoundland Directories, George H. Andrews Proprietor, 1928.

Newfoundland Directory 1936. St. John's: Newfoundland Directories, George H. Andrews Proprietor, 1936.

Newfoundland Directory for 1871: Names of professional and business men and other inhabitants in the cities, towns, & villages throughout the province. London: Genealogical Research Library, 1984.

Newfoundland Business Directory. Moncton, N. B.: Maritime Directories, 1936.

Newfoundland Business Directory. Truro, N.S.: Maritime Directories, Box 39,1941 and 1942

St. John's Classified Business and City Directory 1932. St. John's: St. John's Publicity Co., P.O. box 381. Compiled by E. P. Button and A. R. Thomson, 1932.

St. John's City Directory, 1919: Comprising a street directory, alphabetical directory, classified business directory, and directory of Bell Island, Carbonear, Harbor Grace, and Trinity. Halifax: Royal Print & Litho., Limited, 1919.

Henderson's St. John's, Newfoundland, City Directory. Winnipeg: Henderson Directories Ltd. 1963-71.

St. John's City Telephone Directory 1935, 1926, 1942 1943,1946, 1948,1952, 1954,1956, 1957,1958, 1961,1964.

Year Book and Almanac of Newfoundland. St. John's: David R. Thistle, King's Printer, selected years from 1928-1931.

Year Book and Almanac of Newfoundland. St. John's: J. W. Withers, Queen's Printer, 1887-1932.

The Newfoundland Almanac, for the Year of Our Lord 1873. St. John's: J. Woods, 1872.

SHEILAH ROBERTS LUKINS is the author of the non-fiction books *For Maids Who Brew and Bake*, a collection of recipes, history, and anecdotes from the 17th century (nominated in the special interest category of Cuisine Canada's National Culinary Book Awards), and *Rain, Drizzle, and Fog*, a collection of stories and miscellanea about Newfoundland weather. Her children's books include *Full Speed Ahead: Errol's Bell Island Adventure* (winner of the 2018 Bruneau Family Children's/Young-Adult Award) and most recently, *Flying Ace: Errol's Gander Adventure*.